The Book of Ḥadīth

THE BOOK OF ḤADĪTH

Selected by Charles le Gai Eaton

From Robson's Translation of

MISHKĀT AL-MAṢABIḤ

Re-translated by Mahmoud Mostafa

Edited by Kabir Helminski & Jeremy Henzell-Thomas

THE BOOK FOUNDATION
WATSONVILLE, CALIFORNIA
BRISTOL, ENGLAND

The Book Foundation
www.thebook.org

Publication Design & Cover Art by Threshold Productions.

First Book Foundation edition published 2008.

British Library Cataloguing in Publication Data
A catalogue record of this book is available from the British Library

Library of Congress Cataloging-in-Publication Data

Watsonville, California; Bristol, England: The Book Foundation, 2008.

ISBN 1904510175 (9781904510178)
1. Islam. Muhammad 2. Hadith
I. Kabir Helminski II. The Book Foundation

Table of Contents

Acknowledgments

We gratefully acknowledge a number of groups that have helped us in the presenting of these Ḥadīth, especially in verifying the Arabic and in confirming sources: Prince Ghazi bin Muhammad bin Talal, Chairman of the Board Royal Aal al-Bayt Institute for Islamic Thought, Jordan, as well as his able scholars, Shaikh Hassan and Shaikh Said from that institution. We also wish to thank Aisha, Aliaa, and Ali Rafea of the Egyptian Society for Spiritual and Cultural Research.

Notes on Transliteration

In most cases we have attempted to transliterate Arabic words as they are pronounced. Throughout this book, references to the Qurʾān are in parentheses. These refer to the name of the *sūrah,* the *sūrah* number, and verses (*āyāt*). When the Prophet Muḥammad ﷺ is mentioned, his mention is followed by the calligraphic symbol for *ṣalla Allāhu ʿalayhi wa sallam,* "May the peace and blessings of Allāh be upon him." When Muḥammad's companions are mentioned, they are followed with the symbol for *raḍīallāhu ʿanhu* (رضي الله عنه "May Allāh be pleased with him"), *raḍīallāhu ʿanha* (رضي الله عنها "May Allāh be pleased with her"), or *raḍīallāhu ʿanhum* (رضي الله عنهم "May Allah be pleased with them"). We have used the symbols to replace these blessings, but have not added them if they were not present in the original text.

When quoting the Qurʾān or referring in the text to Allāh سبحانه وتعالى ("May He be glorified and exalted"), we have used the masculine pronoun. Please be aware that this is merely a limitation of language and that within the universe and understanding of the Qurʾān, God is without gender and far beyond any words or manner by which we might try to describe Him/Her. *Subḥān Allāhi Rabbil-ʿālamīn!*

THE BOOK OF ḤADĪTH

INTRODUCTION

Jeremy Henzell-Thomas

ḤADĪTH are accounts relating to the deeds and utterances of the Prophet Muḥammad ﷺ as remembered by his companions. They can be divided into two groups: *ḥadīth sharif* ("noble Ḥadīth"), the Prophet's ﷺ own utterances, and *ḥadīth qudsi* ("sacred Ḥadīth") in which God Himself speaks on the tongue of the Prophet ﷺ.

Reflecting on how best to approach the writing of an Introduction to this beautiful selection by Charles le Gai Eaton from the *Mishkāt al-Maṣābīḥ*, it struck me that what might most engage readers would be an authentic personal response to these Ḥadīth with some suggestions on how to use them in an educational context, rather than a detailed discussion of the complex and involved science of the study of Ḥadīth in which I do not claim to be an expert.

There is a vast literature on this subject which the reader may wish to consult, but it is not my purpose here to attempt to summarise in any systematic way the principles of this science. It will suffice to say here that the *Mishkāt al-Maṣābīḥ* is a collection of over 6,000 Ḥadīth revised by Walī ad-Dīn Muḥammad ibn ᶜAbdullāh al-Khaṭīb at-Tabrīzī (d. *737 AH*/1337 CE) from the *Masābīḥ as-Sunnah* by Abū Muḥammad al-Ḥusayn ibn Masᶜūd al-Baghawī (d. *510*/1116), the best known of the later large compilations which drew upon the early authoritative collections. These collections included the "Six Muṣannaf", the canon of six books (*al-kutub as-sittah*) comprising the two *Saḥīḥs (or Saḥīḥayn)* – the foremost and most revered collections of Abū ᶜAbdullāh Muḥammad Ibn Ismāᶜīl al-Bukhārī (d. *256*/870) and Abū-l-Ḥusayn Muslim ibn al-Ḥajjāj al-Qushayrī an-Nīsābūrī (d. *261*/875) (the latter is usually simply called "Muslim") – and the four collections of Abū Dāwūd as-Sijistānī (d. *261*/875), Abū ᶜĪsā ibn Muḥammad ibn ᶜĪsā at-

Tirmidhī (d. *279*/892 or *302*/915), Abū ^{c}Abdur-Raḥmān Aḥmad ibn ^{c}Alī ibn Shu^{c}ayb an-Nasāʾī (d. *303*/915), and Muḥammad ibn Yazīd ar-Rabī^{c} ibn Mājāh (d. *273*/886). Other collections drawn on in the *Mishkāt al-Maṣābīḥ* include the *Musnad* of Aḥmad ibn Muḥammad ibn Ḥanbal Abū ^{c}Abd Allāh (d. *241*/855), the *Sunan* of Aḥmad ibn al-Ḥusayn ibn ^{c}Alī al-Bayhaqī Abū Bakr (d. *458*/1066) and the *Sunan* of Abū Muḥammad ^{c}Abdullah ibn ^{c}Abdur-Raḥmān at-Tamīmī ad-Dārimī (d. *255*/869).

As interesting and important as the various scholarly and interpretive questions may be, it seemed to me that what was really important in responding to this selection was to discover how the material presented here might be practically utilized in the spirit of the Prophet's ﷺ own preference for "useful knowledge", reiterated by him in many sayings: "I seek refuge in God from a knowledge which has no use," and "The knowledge from which no benefit is derived is like a treasure from which no charity is bestowed in the way of the Lord." Or, as Haḍrat ^{c}Alī put it, "Many an intellectual has been killed by his ignorance, his knowledge failing to profit him." This "ignorance" is essentially the lower intellectualising process that overvalues the accumulation of inert facts and the fruitless spinning out of rationalizations, unsubstantiated opinions, conjectures, and speculations.

After all, the Ḥadīth have been transmitted to us not to encourage disputation but for our spiritual benefit, to guide us as we strive inwardly to conform to the divine pattern or image of God in which we were created, for, as the Qurʾān tells us, *God does not change the condition of a people until they change what is in themselves* (13.11).

When the Prophet ﷺ spoke of "knowledge which has no use", he was not of course referring to knowledge which fails to serve merely utilitarian ends. He was referring to knowledge that is neither real nor permanent, that contributes nothing to our understanding of the ultimate purpose for which we were created – that is, the knowledge and service of God. He was referring also to knowledge which remains abstract, and is not actively realised, lived, practised and embodied through the transformation of the lower self through inner work (the greater *jihād*) and thereby through right action in the world. Authentic action in the world for the wider betterment of society emerges first and foremost from the polished Heart, from the inner space of spiritual practice, deep reflection, contemplation and love.

The imperative to polish the Heart as a prerequisite for the transformation of society is powerfully expressed by Thomas Merton, the Catholic monk: "Those who attempt to act and do things for others or for the world without deepening their own self-understanding, freedom, integrity and capacity to love, will not have anything to give others. They will communicate to them nothing but the contagion of their own obsessions, their aggressiveness, their ego-centered ambitions, their delusions about ends and means, their doctrinaire prejudices and ideas."

Given the primary intention to discover how we might make personal use of these sayings to draw us closer to God, we might wish to avoid a determined attempt to delve into the many controversial issues concerning their authenticity, in the same way as we might judge this not to be the place for a scholarly treatise on the science of Ḥadīth in all its complexity. However, the fact is that that the valuation of Ḥadīth ranges from unquestioned acceptance of the reliability of the authoritative collections to the controversial contention that many of the Ḥadīth even in the revered collections can no longer be accepted as authentic.

The reader may well agree that such disparities in the valuation of Ḥadīth can hardly be ignored. How, it may reasonably be asked, can one draw out authentic guidance from sayings whose own authenticity is open to question? Is there not a danger that we may direct our lives and the lives of others on the basis of fabricated sayings which were spuriously attributed to the Prophet ﷺ but which were in fact motivated by the bigotry of those with a defective understanding of Islam?

In answer to this, Muḥammad Asad emphasises the critical scrutiny that was rigorously applied in order to sift genuine from concocted accounts:

"The fact that there were numberless spurious *aḥādīth* did not in the least escape the attention of the *Muḥaddithūn,* as European critics naively seem to suppose. On the contrary, the critical science of *ḥadīth* was initiated by the necessity of discerning between authentic and spurious, and the very Imāms Bukhārī and Muslim, not to mention the lesser Traditionists, are direct products of this critical attitude. The existence, therefore, of false *aḥādīth* does not prove anything against the system of *ḥadīth* as a whole."[1]

In the case of the chain of transmission (*isnād*), the science of *Asmāᶜ ar-Rijāl* was developed so as to scrutinise critically the lives of narrators. Meticulous and painstaking attention was paid to gathering every minute detail of their lives with impartiality, honesty, thoroughness and objectivity, and a similar rigour was applied to examining their intellectual abilities and moral standing. For example, the reliability of each narrator's memory was thoroughly investigated so as to reinforce the likelihood that he or she should have correctly heard the words of the speaker, had understood their meaning, and had reproduced them accurately at the time of the narration. Furthermore, reliable narrators should be shown to have had an unblemished character. That good character and piety alone were insufficient qualifications, but should go hand in hand with depth of understanding, was made clear in the reaction of the Prophet's beloved wife, ᶜĀᵓisha, on hearing an account reported on the authority of Ibn ᶜUmar. Rejecting this account, she is reported to have remarked: "You and your transmitters do not tell lies, but sometimes one misunderstands."

Taking this reassuring critical science as a starting-point, we can then go further by applying the formula offered by Ibn Khaldūn for

---

[1] Muhammad Asad, *Islam at the Crossroads*. Gibraltar: Dar al-Andalus, 1982, page 91.

interpreting Ḥadīth. This requires all acceptable traditions to be validated according to two criteria: the Qurʾān and Reason. The overriding importance of the Qurʾān as the touchstone for acceptability is, of course, derived from none other than the Prophet ﷺ himself: "There will be narrators reporting ḥadīth from me, so judge by the Qurʾān; if a report agrees with the Qurʾān, accept it, if otherwise, reject it."

Now, it cannot be denied that there has been an unwarranted elevation over time of the Ḥadīth as a source of guidance in competition with the Qurʾān itself, to the extent that verses of the Qurʾān which appear to conflict with favourite Ḥadīth may be declared to be abrogated by other verses which agree with the Ḥadīth in question. This idolization of Ḥadīth contradicts the incontrovertible truth that the Qurʾān alone should always be referred to as infallible guidance even if the Ḥadīth have been second only to the Qurʾān as the basis of Islamic law *(sharīʿah)*.

One striking example will suffice to show the many conflicts between the Qurʾān and the Ḥadīth: The Qurʾān clearly allows freedom of religion, but both Bukhārī and Abū Dāwūd include the bizarre Ḥadīth, "If anyone leaves his religion, then kill him" (Bukhārī 52:260). Similarly, a very early source, the Al-Muwaṭṭaʾ of Mālik ibn Anas (d.179/795), states that anyone who leaves Islam for something else and divulges it is called upon to repent, but if he does not turn in repentance, he is killed. The penalty of death for apostasy is repeated elsewhere in Bukhārī: "Whoever changes his Islamic religion, then kill him" (Bukhārī 84:57). Another Ḥadīth (Bukhārī 83:37) holds that death is required in three cases: for a murderer, for a married person committing illegal sexual intercourse, and for one who deserts Islam. In this last case, historical evidence makes it clear that the apostates referred to here can be identified with those who are waging war against the Muslim community, and I will return to this critical point in due course.

The most oft-quoted Ḥadīth in Bukhārī, "If anyone leaves his religion, then kill him," can be questioned on the grounds that its chain of transmission (isnād) goes through a source whose narrations were rejected by Imām Muslim because of the accusations of some scholars that the man concerned (ᶜIkrimah) was a liar who also accepted gifts from various political authorities. Besides, the content of this Ḥadīth would also apply to anyone changing his religion to Islam, or from Christianity to Judaism or vice versa, and this clearly contradicts the Prophet's ﷺ command that "No one is to be turned away from their Judaism or Christianity."

But the widespread assumption that Islam pronounces death for apostasy (*ridda, irtidād*) can be most persuasively challenged and definitively rejected from the evidence of the Qurʾān and the actions of the Prophet ﷺ and his Companions.[2]

The Qurʾān repeatedly and unequivocally states that faith and denial are matters of personal choice in which there can be no coercion or interference, and that, in accordance with what Muḥammad Asad describes as a fundamental principle of Islamic ethics, each human soul must take personal responsibility for the consequences of that choice:

There shall be no coercion in matters of faith (2:256).

And say: The truth has now come from your Sustainer: let, then, him who wills, believe in it, and let him who wills, reject it (18:29).

Behold, from on high have We bestowed upon thee this divine writ, setting forth the truth for the benefit of all mankind. And whoever chooses to be guided thereby, does so for his own good, and whoever chooses to go astray, goes but astray to his own hurt: and thou hast not the power to determine their fate (39:41).

The Qurʾān also makes it clear that the Messengers of God are only warners and bringers of glad tidings, without any power to coerce or enforce:

---

[2] I am indebted to Mahmoud Mostafa for many of the citations which follow.

I am nothing but a warner, and a herald of glad tidings unto people who will believe *(7:188).*

But if they turn away from thee, O Prophet, remember that thy only duty is a clear delivery of the message entrusted to thee (16:82).

Furthermore, the Qur'ān teaches that differences in belief are aspects of the diversity which God has ordained for human beings and that only God can give a final verdict on such differences:

Unto every one of you have We appointed a different law and way of life. And if God had so willed, He could surely have made you all one single community: but He willed it otherwise in order to test you by means of what He has vouchsafed unto you. Vie, then, with one another in doing good works! Unto God you all must return and then He will make you truly understand all that on which you were wont to differ (5:48).

For never would thy Sustainer destroy a community for wrong beliefs alone so long as its people behave righteously towards one another. And had thy Sustainer so willed, He could surely have made all mankind one single community: but He willed it otherwise, and so they continue to hold divergent views - all of them, save those upon whom thy Sustainer has bestowed His grace. (11:117-119).

And on whatever you may differ, O believers, the verdict thereon rests with God (42:10).

Qur'ān 5:48 above has been described as a "virtual manifesto of religious pluralism" and "a structural guarantee for the survival of more than one religion and every Muslim should know it by heart".[3] In his note to the same verse, Muḥammad Asad explains how "unity in diversity" is frequently stressed in the Qur'ān (as, for example, in the first sentence of 2:148, in 21:92-93, or in 23:52) and describes 11:118 as stressing once again "that the unceasing differentiation in men's views

---

[3] Murad W. Hofmann, "Religious Pluralism and Islam", in *Islam and Global Dialogue, Religious Pluralism and the Pursuit of Peace*, edited by Roger Boase (Aldershot: Ashgate, 2005), pp. 238-239.

and ideas is not incidental but represents a God-willed, basic factor of human existence."

Finally, the Qur'ān does not lay down any legal penalty for apostasy; rather it addresses the consequences of spiritual regression, the falling back and willful denial of the truth after having accepted it, and this would apply to the followers of any religious community, not solely the Muslims.

As for anyone who denies God after having once attained to faith – and this, to be sure, does not apply to one who does it under duress, the while his heart remains true to his faith, but only to him who willingly opens up his heart to a denial of the truth: upon all such falls God's condemnation, and tremendous suffering awaits them (16:106).

This, and other verses such as 47:25 which refer to those who turn their backs on the message after guidance has been given to them, can legitimately be regarded as referring to the willful denial of truth in its widest sense, and not to the act of leaving institutional Islam.

Those who advocate death for apostates often hold that the much-quoted verse in the Qur'ān which forbids coercion in religion (2:256) is abrogated by the later revelation of 9:29:

And fight against those who – despite having been vouchsafed revelation aforetime – do not truly believe either in God or the Last Day.

However, as Muḥammad Asad demonstrates, this verse does not justify unprovoked aggression against non-believers and this is a timely opportunity to remind ourselves of the explicit Qur'ānic rule that only defensive warfare is permissible in Islam:

"In accordance with the fundamental principle – observed throughout my interpretation of the Qur'ān – that all of its statements and ordinances are mutually complementary and cannot, therefore, be correctly understood unless they are considered as parts of one integral whole, this verse, too must be read in the context of the clear-cut Qur'anic rule that war is permitted only in self-defence. In other words, the above injunction to fight is relevant only in the event of aggression committed against the Muslim community or state, or in the presence of an unmistakable threat to its security… a view which has been shared by that great Islamic thinker, Muḥammad ʿAbduh. Commenting on this verse, he declared: 'Fighting has been made obligatory in Islam only for the sake of defending the truth and its followers.... All the campaigns of the Prophet ﷺ were defensive in character; and so were the wars undertaken by the Companions in the earliest period of Islam' (*Manār* X, 332). In the context of an ordinance enjoining war against them, this 'something' can mean only one thing – namely, *unprovoked aggression*: for it is this that has been forbidden by God through *all the apostles* who were entrusted with conveying His message to man. Thus, the above verse must be understood as a call to the believers to fight against such – and only such – of the nominal followers of earlier revelation as deny their own professed beliefs by committing aggression against the followers of the Qurʾān."[4]

This explanation points the way back to the Ḥadīth reported in Bukhārī with which I began this discussion on apostasy. One of these requires death for one who deserts Islam and who is also fighting against God and His Messenger. This is often quoted without any reference to its militant context. The apostates implicated here are those who were committing unprovoked aggression against the followers of the Qurʾān and against whom defensive warfare was therefore legitimately enjoined. In explaining the fact that the Prophet ﷺ accepted the repentance of some apostates but ordered others to be killed, even ibn Taimiyyah concluded that only apostasy that involved enmity and aggression against Muslims was unforgivable. It is clear that those apostates who were killed were those who were attacking Muslims or in alliance with their enemies and were therefore to be treated as enemy combatants intent on violent opposition to the Prophet's ﷺ mission. This punishment was necessitated by the difficult circumstances of the time.

The actions of the Prophet ﷺ himself give no credence to the belief that apostates who were not waging unprovoked war on Muslims should be killed. Several individuals and groups left Islam during the life

---

[4] Muhammad Asad, note to Qurʾān 9:29 in *The Message of the Qur'an*. Bristol: The Book Foundation, 2003, pages 294-295.

of the Prophet ﷺ, some of them several times, but he never called for their death. One of his scribes recanted and was unabashed in his apostasy, claiming that "Muḥammad only knows what I wrote for him!", but in spite of this the Prophet ﷺ left him completely free and interceded for the man on his deathbed. A group of twelve Muslims recanted and left Medina for Mecca, but the Prophet ﷺ did not spill any of their blood nor did he pronounce the death penalty on any of them. Two young men converted to Christianity and their father asked the Prophet ﷺ to curse them, but instead he recited the verse, *There shall be no coercion in matters of faith* (Qurʾān 2:256).

These cases, and others, prove that the Prophet ﷺ did not know, command or apply any penal code for apostasy.

Two final questions might be addressed in this necessarily brief study of the problem of apostasy.

Firstly, if the Qurʾān and the Prophet ﷺ give no justification for the killing of those apostates who are not waging war on Muslims, how does one explain the decision of Abū Bakr to wage war on the "apostates"? First of all, Abū Bakr did not start the war. It was the rebellious tribes who marched on Medina when they learned that the Muslim army had been sent north to Persia. The issue at stake was not apostasy, but their rejection of the payment of Zakāt and the authority of Abū Bakr, for they would only accept obedience to the Prophet ﷺ and no one after him. In fact, ʿUmar and some of the Companions did not agree with Abū Bakr that he should wage war on these tribes when they were actually Muslims who declared the oneness of God and the Prophethood of Muḥammad ﷺ. The decision to do so was a matter of upholding the authority of the state, and was not a conflict over articles of faith.

Secondly, in view of the tolerance of the Companions in the face of the deviations from normative beliefs which they saw amongst various groups, how can one explain the development of uncompromising coercive principles, such as the death penalty for apostates, by rigidly authoritarian religious scholars?

The fact is that the Companions did not accuse the Qādirīyyah nor the Jābirīyyah of apostasy nor did the Successor Generation accuse the Muʿtazilites, the Murjiʿites, or the Jahmites of apostasy, despite their deviant doctrines, which included the denial that the Qurʾān is God's Word, the rejection of the existence of any attributes of God, and the belief that whoever declares the two testimonies (no God but God and Muḥammad is His Messenger) is complete in his faith and has no need to perform a single action.

The elevation of Ḥadīth such as those pronouncing death for apostasy came about as a result of the desire of scholars to codify religious knowledge and to solidify laws towards the end of the Umayyad period and the beginning of the ʿAbbasid period, during a time of great strife between competing ideologies that gravely threatened the unity of the Ummah. In acting as protectors of the law and upholders of authority, they developed two principles to deal with anyone who rebelled against them: labelling as an apostate anyone who rejected their formulations and rulings, and coercing such people into compliance by the threat of death.

These two spurious principles are the product of historical circumstances and the need to uphold power and authority. They contradict the spirit of Islam and are not in line with the values and principles of the Qurʾān, nor with the life of the Prophet ﷺ and the Companions.

As for Ibn Khaldūn's second criterion for validating Ḥadīth, that of Reason, this is explicitly referred to as a praiseworthy means of validating truth in Qurʾān 39:17-18: *Give, then, this glad tiding to those of my servants who listen closely to all that is said, and follow the best of it: for it is they whom God has graced with His guidance, and it is they who are truly endowed with insight.* Muḥammad Asad notes that, "according to Rāzī, this describes people who examine every religious proposition (in the widest sense of this term) in the light of their own reason, accepting that which their mind finds to be valid or possible, and rejecting all that does not measure up to the test of reason. In Rāzī's words, the above verse expresses 'a praise and commendation of following the evidence supplied by one's reason (*ḥujjat al-ᶜaql*), and of reaching one's conclusions in accordance with critical examination (*naẓar*) and logical inference (*istidlāl*).'" Asad points out that "a somewhat similar view is advanced, albeit in simpler terms, by Ṭabarī."[5]

I would only add this caveat, so as not to reduce the faculty of "insight" to an exclusively rational level. The faculty of Reason or Insight to which the Qur'ān refers should not be confined to the lower rational process of intellectualization, referred to by Rumi as the intellect reduced to a "husk". What the Qur'ān is referring to is the faculty of Intellection, the higher Intellect with a capital "I", in the same way as the spiritual Heart can be distinguished from the heart, its physical or emotional counterpart. The faculty of ᶜ*aql* encompasses both the analytical capacities of the logical mind and the higher faculty of spiritual intelligence, or discerning insight (*albāb*) which is also denoted in the Qur'ān by other terms, such as *baṣīrah* and *a*ᶜ*rāf*. To this should also be added a quality of moral valuation, for the Qur'ānic vision never separates cognitive from moral faculties. To exercise Reason, or to be "endowed with insight", is also to hold to a standard or touchstone (*furqān*) which enables us to discern what is true from what is false and to distinguish what is right from what is wrong.

This faculty of discernment is an integral part of the essential nature or primordial disposition (*fiṭrah*) with which the human being has been imprinted by God and which gives him or her the potential to become His representative (*khalīfah*) on earth. It is a part of human character, for the word 'character' originally meant a stamp. Discernment is stamped, impressed or engraved on the soul as part of the authentic character of the human being who was created by God *fī 'aḥsani taqwīm*, '*in the best of moulds*' (Qur'ān 95:4), although it is the responsibility of each of us to live according to that divine pattern and to fulfill the sublime purpose

[5] Muhammad Asad, *The Message of the Qur'an*, op. cit., page 798.

for which we were created. At a largely unconscious level, it is simply 'common sense', a faculty possessed by all, "original" in its true sense.

To Ādam was imparted the gift of the Names (Qurʾān 2:31), and this knowledge also conferred on us the linguistic faculty of verbal definition and conceptualisation which enables us to make rational choices.

This is not to imply, of course, that we can disregard the whole apparatus of Ḥadīth scholarship and resort to selecting only those Ḥadīth that appeal subjectively to our personal taste, or our prejudices and predilections. The faculty of discernment is a critical faculty that searches out the truth; it is not something that takes us into the comfort zone or panders to a mentality which wishes only to have its inclinations and biases confirmed or its ideological perspective reinforced.

Above all, it is a faculty dedicated to balance and equilibrium. As part of our *fiṭrah*, it is fashioned by God, like everything in Creation, *in due measure and proportion* (Qurʾān 54:49) as a fitting reflection of divine order and harmony. The word *taqwīm* in the phrase *fī ʾaḥsani taqwīm* quoted above also has the sense of 'symmetry' as well as 'mould'.

There are many Ḥadīth on this central Islamic virtue of steering between extremes. On one occasion, the Prophet ﷺ said to Abū Bakr: "I passed you when you were praying in a low voice." Abū Bakr said, "The One with whom I was holding intimate conversation heard me, O Messenger of God!" He then turned to ʿUmar and said, "I passed you when you were raising your voice while praying." He replied, "Messenger of God, I was waking the drowsy and driving away the devil." The Prophet ﷺ said, "Raise your voice a little, Abū Bakr," and to ʿUmar he said, "Lower your voice a little."

This is a beautiful commentary on the statement in the Qurʾān that Muslims are *a community of the middle way* (2:143), which suggests, according to Muḥammad Asad, "a call to moderation in every aspect of life".

But what is meant by moderation? A dull compromise? A state of mediocrity or half-heartedness? A mere avoidance of difficult choices?

Certainly not. Returning again to those verses in the Qurʾān in *Sūrah* 39 which urge us to use our reason in validating the truth, we are urged to *listen closely to all that is said, and follow the best of it.* Certainly, the best of it may often be the position which is most balanced and moderate, but it is not arrived at by a kind of quantitative calculation which finds a mathematical average or apparently equitable compromise irrespective of what is actually just, right and fair. The word 'fair' in English originally meant what is 'fitting' and 'proportionate' and its two modern meanings – 'just' and 'beautiful' – have preserved that connection to its original sense. Moderation and balance are qualitative states which honour what is appropriate and proportionate. The English word comes from Latin *modus*, 'keeping within due measure', which is related to another word which is also the source of English 'modest'. Etymologically, moderation has the same inherent meaning in English as modesty, a connection which is also truly Islamic. The Prophet ﷺ himself said that "True modesty is the source of all virtues." He said too that "Every religion has a distinctive feature and the distinctive feature of Islam is modesty."

Charles le Gai Eaton has, himself, written beautifully on the topic of balance and equilibrium:

"But, in talking of beauty and praise, the healing powers of nature and the meaning hidden in sticks and stones, have I left out something important? What about the "Do's" and "Don'ts" of religion? They have, ultimately, one purpose, and that is to establish harmony, balance, order within the individual personality as also in society; the same harmony, balance and order visible in creation as a whole, maintaining the birds in their flight, turning the growing plant towards the life-giving sun, and bringing the fruit to ripeness on the tree. In the disordered personality and in the disordered society, the "Do's" and "Don'ts" may have to be imposed, but those are conditions under which the equilibrium inherent in creation has already been disturbed, as happens when people forget who they are and where they are going."

And again,

"Let me, in conclusion, emphasise one of the most basic principles of Islam. Balance, both in spiritual life and in our human existence as creatures plunged into the light and shade of this world. As the Muslim sees it, there is another word for balance, and that is peace. The very word Islam is derived from the Arabic word for peace. Where balance is lacking there is conflict and disorder, both outward and inward. While it is maintained, men and women are free to turn to God as plants turn to the sun.[6]"

This is a strikingly beautiful affirmation of the harmony and equilibrium inherent in the created order. If we can remember "who we are and where we are going" and by so doing restore in ourselves that balance, we will have access to that inner discernment which will enable us to be true to the Qurʾānic injunction to *listen closely to all that is said, and follow the best of it.*

In offering this selection of Ḥadīth by one whose clear, balanced and loving approach to Islam has opened so many hearts and eyes to what it means to be conscious of God, I could not be more confident that in making his selection he has been truly discerning in *following the best of it.* As I read these Ḥadīth over and over again, and reflected on them, I was repeatedly reminded of those verses of the Qurʾān which challenge us to wake up to a full sense of the moral and spiritual stature with which we have been endowed, and which was so perfectly embodied in the Prophet ﷺ.

And every human being will come forward with his erstwhile inner urges and his conscious mind, and will be told: "indeed, unmindful hast thou been of

---

[6] These quotations are from the precious series of short talks on Islam, ninety in all, which Gai Eaton gave for the *Reflections* and *Words of Faith* series of broadcasts by the BBC World service between 1978 and 1996. These are as yet unpublished, although they are currently being serialised on the Book Foundation website (www.TheBook.org).

this Day of Judgement; but now We have lifted from thee thy veil, and sharp is thy sight today!" (Qur'ān 50:21-22)

To paraphrase Muḥammad Asad's detailed note on these verses,[7] they refer to the contending nature of the two fundamental motive forces within man: on one side, that which drives (*sā'iq*), his primal, instinctive urges, inordinate appetites and unrestrained desires (often symbolized as *shayṭān*), and on the other side, his conscious reason (*shahīd*), both intuitive and reflective, or the awakening of the deeper layers of his consciousness, the "lifting of the veil" that leads to a sudden perception or witnessing of his own moral reality.

If we can move beyond a conception of Ḥadīth which selectively seeks to make them conform to a personal and self-righteous liking for rigid moralising; if we can lovingly discern the universal *principles* beneath the historically determined *forms*; if we can, above all, reflect on them not as a means of pontificating to others, or controlling, harassing and oppressing them, but as a means, in Asad's terms, of awakening the deeper layers of our own consciousness, we would make progress in abiding by the Prophet's ﷺ own advice that "He who knows himself knows his Lord", a saying so completely in harmony with the Qur'ānic statement that *God does not change the condition of a people until they change what is in themselves* (13.11).

And that leads me to the practical purpose of this Introduction, for I began it not with the intention of writing a scholarly or explanatory treatise but with the more pressing experiential intention of exploring how these Ḥadīth can be a transformational influence in a living educational process which seeks to make us more fully human. For it can hardly be denied that if the sayings of the Prophet ﷺ, *al-insān al-kāmil*, the Perfect, Universal Man, play no part in helping us to improve our own character in emulation of his, then they fail to realise his own vision of a knowledge that is truly useful. To emulate the character of the Prophet ﷺ is also to approach closer to understanding the Qur'ān,

---

[7] Muhammad Asad, *The Message of the Qur'ān*, op. cit., page 909.

for, as Haḍrat ʿĀʾisha is reported to have said in response to a man who asked her about the character of God's Messenger: "The Prophet's character was that of the Qurʾān."

In the process of discovering and exploring the profound utility of these Prophetic sayings, we discover many levels. They show the deep humanity, kindness, and beneficence of the Prophet ﷺ at a time when there is a pressing need to correct not only the many distortions about him, whether motivated by ignorance or malice, but also the widespread misconceptions about the intrinsically beautiful Islam which he revealed to us. We also find that the Ḥadīth enunciate and clarify doctrine and offer commentary upon it. They offer guidance for the deepening of knowledge, the improvement of conduct and character, and the strengthening of faith. Finally, and above all, they remain a luminous spiritual source of inspirational material for the transformation of Hearts, for without the Heart no injunction can ever be fully internalised, lived and embodied.

In considering how to exemplify a living educational approach to this selection of Ḥadīth, it finally dawned on me after much reflection that the most authentic illustration could only come from a description of how I had applied such an approach so as to expand my own understanding of the character of the Prophet ﷺ. And it also became clear that the best way to do this was to focus on just one example and describe in depth the learning processes which illuminated it.

In searching for a Ḥadīth to exemplify this learning process, I was guided by these opening words of a talk entitled *The Mercifulness of the Messenger of God* by the late Martin Lings, "The mercifulness of Sayyidunā Muḥammad ﷺ is affirmed by the Qurʾānic verse *We sent thee not save as a mercy to the worlds.*"[8]

There seemed to me to be no greater need at this time than to bring to light the merciful nature of the Prophet ﷺ. To repeat Haḍrat ʿĀʾisha's affirmation, "the Prophet's character was that of the Qurʾān",

---

[8] International Seerat Conference in Islamabad, 1985.

and every chapter of the Qurʾān, with only one single exception, begins with the *Basmalah* which contains the two names of Divine Mercy, *ar-Raḥmān* and *ar-Raḥīm*.

One does not have to look very far in this selection to find many Ḥadīth which testify eloquently to the Prophet's kindness, benevolence and mercy.

Two examples immediately come to mind:

Jābir and Ḥudhaifah related that the Messenger of God said, "Every act of kindness is charity" (Bukhārī & Muslim).

Abū Hurayrah reported that the Messenger of God said, "Forgiveness was granted to a prostitute who came upon a dog panting and almost dead from thirst at the mouth of a well. She took off her shoe, tied it with her head-covering, and drew some water for it. On that account she was forgiven." He was asked if people received a reward for what they did for animals, and he replied, "A reward is given in connection with every living creature." (Bukhārī)

But the one which led to the most exhaustive reflection and ultimately helped me to move closer to an understanding of the depth of the Prophet's ﷺ humanity was this one:

Ibn ʿAbbās reported that a man came to the Prophet ﷺ complaining, "My wife rejects no one who lays a hand on her!" The Prophet ﷺ told him, "Divorce her." But the man told him, "I really love her." So the Prophet ﷺ said to him, "Then, hold on to her" (Abū Dāwūd).

Much reflection and discussion ensued over this Ḥadīth during the editing process. Reservations were felt about the potential difficulty in interpreting it in these times. It could be regarded as distinctly elliptical in that it does not state what surely must have been implicitly understood by the hearer – that some action, including discussion, advice and admonition, should also be taken to resolve this problem. Otherwise, we would have to believe that the Prophet ﷺ, recognising the strength of the man's love for his errant wife, is compassionately advising the man to turn a blind eye to her immorality. Could this be so, given our understanding of the totality of the Prophet's ﷺ character and given our knowledge of the Qurʾān?

In the absence of knowledge about the kind of moral norms which would have been understood by the hearer, was there not a danger that this Ḥadīth could be misinterpreted to sanction promiscuity and adultery? In answer to this reservation, it was pointed out that without explanatory commentary which also takes account of the context of the utterance, many Ḥadīth are open to broad and possibly skewed interpretation in the same way as the Qurʾān is commonly misinterpreted by those who fail to take a holistic view of the text. The Qurʾān itself warns us against this piecemeal approach: *Those who are deeply rooted in knowledge say: "We believe in it, the whole of the divine writ is from our Sustainer..."* (3:7).

Thus, the Ḥadīth under discussion presented interpretive challenges which were not essentially different from those presented by many other Ḥadīth compiled into collections offered without commentary.

A deep discussion then ensued which finally converged on what seemed to be the essential message of this Ḥadīth. We wanted to discover the core of that message in the same way as we understood how vital it was to try to absorb the message of the Qurʾān into our hearts instead of trying to fit it into an existing perspective or ideology, whether patriarchal, liberal, or anything else.

The Prophet ﷺ here deals in a most compassionate way with a situation that might be expected to lead to inevitable divorce. Furthermore, in terms of the rigid social traditions associated with a dogmatic legalistic approach to enforcing puritanical moral codes in dealing with women whose sexual behaviour was judged to be unacceptable, such a woman might have been subject to violence, or at the very least might have been ostracized. And we need to acknowledge fully that such attitudes are still prevalent today and cause much suffering amongst women.

But the Prophet ﷺ does not adopt a legalistic or punitive approach to resolving this matter; he leaves a private relationship to be worked out between the two parties. He guides his companion to be patient and to let his love for his wife work its transforming power upon her. The Ḥadīth also shows how the Prophet ﷺ treated women with equity, because if the roles were reversed, a wife would not have been able to apply force or act with violence to restrain her husband from immoral conduct; she would have had the option of either exercising patience in working on the relationship or separating from him. He gave his companion the same choices that his wife would have had. Such equity is fully in keeping with the fact that a very significant part of his mission to humanity was the emancipation of the weak and oppressed, and this applied especially to women. Regrettably, this still applies to the treatment of women in many Islamic (and other) societies today, not only in obvious examples of inequality and subjugation sanctioned by oppressive laws and social traditions but also in the widespread ill-treatment of women even in those supposedly liberal societies where equality is enshrined in law.

If the Qurʾān lays down principles of equity and if many of the Prophet's ﷺ own statements broke the conventional mould of a rigidly patriarchal, tribal order, then when determining the authenticity of a Prophetic saying, are we to give more credence to statements that seem to defend and justify an unjust patriarchal order or those that establish respect and fairness towards women?

As my understanding of the full humanity of the Prophet ﷺ continued to grow from further meditation on this Ḥadīth, I recalled his love for women, and his luminous statement, much beloved in the deepest spiritual circles of Islam, "Three things have been made beloved to me in this world: women, fragrance, and prayer, in which is the delight of my eyes." And, affirming too his deep respect for ʿĀʾisha, he said of her, "Take half of your religion from this red-haired one."

Guided by the Qurʾānic vision of the precedence of the Divine Mercy, I recalled, too, the famous incident reported in the Gospels in which the Pharisees, in an attempt to discredit Jesus, brought a woman charged with adultery before him. Being the epitome of a rigidly legalistic mentality, they reminded Jesus that adultery was punishable by stoning under Mosaic Law and challenged him to judge the woman so that they might then accuse him of disobeying the law. Jesus thought for a moment and then replied, "He that is without sin among you, let him cast the first stone at her." The people crowded around him were so touched by their own consciences that they departed. When Jesus found himself alone with the woman, he asked her who were her accusers. She replied, "No man, lord." Jesus then said, "Neither do I condemn thee: go and sin no more." (Gospel of St. John 8:7)

My understanding was strengthened too by reflecting on other Ḥadīth in the collection which gave further evidence of the humanity, kindness and sheer common sense of the Prophet ﷺ. Two of them, for example, amongst many others, showed very clearly his compassionate awareness of human limitations and his loving concern that we should not oppress ourselves with unsustainable spiritual burdens and disproportionate self-criticism:

Ibn ʿAbbās related that a man came to the Prophet ﷺ and said, "I have thoughts of such a nature that I would rather be burned to a crisp than speak about them!" Muḥammad ﷺ said, *Praise be to God who has limited the matter to promptings of the mind.* (Abū Dāwūd)

ʿĀʾishah also reported that the Messenger of God said: "Take on those practices which you have the capacity to sustain, for God does not grow weary unless you do" (Bukhārī & Muslim).

And finally: ʿĀʾishah narrated that the Messenger of God ﷺ said, "Avoid the infliction of prescribed penalties on Muslims as much as you can and, if there is any way out, let a man go; for it is better for a leader to make a mistake in forgiving than to make a mistake in punishing." (Tirmidhī)

The picture we can form from such sayings of the balanced and practical wisdom of the Prophet ﷺ gives all the more credence to the conciliatory marital advice he gives to his companion. More and more, a vista opened upon the all-encompassing "mercifulness of the Messenger of God".

I have necessarily simplified here a dialectical learning process which in fact negotiated many complex issues and encountered some challenging paradoxes which will continue to provoke much further discussion and reflection. That is surely as it should be, for just as the Prophet ﷺ himself prayed to God to increase his knowledge and improve his character, so it is incumbent upon those men and women of faith who seek to emulate him to be open to the same possibility of advancement at all times, for, with the Grace of God, there is no end to the knowledge which is being continually revealed to us.

That said, here are eleven principles that have emerged for me in exploring the Ḥadīth in question:

1. Follow the touchstone given by the Prophet ﷺ himself: "There will be narrators reporting ḥadīth from me, so judge by the Qurʾān; if a report agrees with the Qurʾān, accept it, if otherwise, reject it."
2. When judging by the Qurʾān, follow the over-arching principles enshrined in the Holy Book as a whole.
3. Follow the Qurʾānic advice to *listen to all that is said and follow the best of it.* In other words, adopt the additional criterion (after the Qurʾān) of Reason proposed by Ibn Khaldūn, realising that this is not just a cerebral rational process (important as this is for the development of critical thinking) but the activation of the higher faculty of discernment or insight arising from deep reflection and contemplation.
4. Immerse yourself in the character of the Prophet ﷺ through extensive reading, so that you form as faithful and complete a picture of him as you can and are therefore more able to interpret a particular saying in the light of the totality of his character. Identify the recurring aspects of his character which can act as leitmotifs or orienting points of reference for interpreting his sayings: thus, his flexibility, kindness, humanity, mercifulness, moderation. This holistic awareness of the major

themes in the Prophet's ﷺ character is an exact parallel to the process of identifying the over-arching principles in the text of the Qurʾān as a whole.

5. Engage in dialogue and discussion with people of knowledge, insight and character so as to refine your own understanding through the dialectical process.
6. Through honest self-examination, identify the false certainties provided by your own fixed ideas, inherited dogmas, conditioned belief systems, cultural preconceptions, sectarian affiliations, limiting perspectives, and ideologies. You cannot swim in the Ocean of the Prophet's ﷺ character while you remain rooted to one small island within it.
7. Seek parallels in the revealed scriptures of other religious traditions in order to strengthen your grasp of the universal principles governing the *dīn al-fiṭra*.
8. Reflect upon how the reforming mission of the Prophet ﷺ (to bring social justice, for example) still applies in the contemporary world and work peacefully in your own way to make that justice a reality in your own society.
9. Having done the work of acquiring knowledge through all the processes described above, open your heart to the promptings of the Spirit which can guide you to a clear and uncluttered vision of the Truth. At this stage, there is the possibility that a deeper illumination can emerge which distils the essence of what one needs to know and which discards much complex detail in the process.
10. Strive to embody the virtues of The Prophet ﷺ in your own life. He is reported to have said, "Who are the learned? Those who practise what they know." An example: practise daily acts of kindness towards people and animals. Scan the Ḥadīth for ways in which the Prophet ﷺ taught that charity could be shown, remembering that even a smile is Charity.

11. Above all, remember that the Prophet ﷺ guides us to a spiritual reality which transcends our life on this earth. This spiritual reality is ultimately the Only Reality, for if the character of the Prophet ﷺ is the Qurʾān, and if the Qurʾān is a book for those who acknowledge the Unseen, *al-ghayb*, that which is beyond the reach of human perception (Qurʾān 2:3), then the Prophet's ﷺ example guides us to that ultimate reality beyond anything which can, in the words of Muḥammad Asad, "be proved or disproved by scientific observation or even adequately comprised within the accepted categories of speculative thought."

In conclusion, and as a commentary on this eleventh and most important principle, I can think of nothing more beautiful or appropriate than to quote some words of Martin Lings from the *The Mercifulness of the Messenger of God*, the source with which I began this exploration of a single Ḥadīth of the Prophet ﷺ from the collection offered to you here:

"To be the Key of Mercy means being of a paradisal nature, and many things in the Prophet's ﷺ life suggest that once the *Miʿrāj* had taken place Heaven refused to relinquish him altogether, and that it still clung to him after he returned to earth. His sayings confirm this: we read for example in Saḥīḥ al-Bukhārī that on one occasion he was seen to stretch out his hand as if to take something, and then he drew it back. When his companions questioned him about it he said: 'I saw paradise, and I reached out for a cluster of its grapes. If I had taken it, ye would have eaten of it as long as this world endureth.' To take another example, he said from his pulpit in the Mosque on the day when his last illness began: 'I go before you and I am your witness. Your meeting with me is at the pool, which I see from here, where now I stand.'

"The very essence of the Prophet's ﷺ mercifulness is that, returning from his direct experience of Paradise, the Prophet ﷺ lived with his people to guide them to that place of the '99 mercies of God.'

"God has rooted deeply, in every human soul, the imperative desire for perfect happiness that will never end; and the existence of this desire is a proof – not logical, but intellectual and metaphysical – that man was originally made for Paradise, as all religions teach. Any meditation by man upon his own mysteriously transcendent appetite can be immeasurably helped by recalling that aspect of the Holy Prophet ﷺ which we have dwelt on here, his fidelity to Paradise as man's one and only homeland…'"

May God guide the readers of these Prophetic sayings to the realisation that the Holy Prophet ﷺ, the Key of Mercy, is also the Key of Paradise.

Jeremy Henzell-Thomas
Saint Michel de Montjoie
France

On Islām, Īmān (Faith), and Iḥsān (Righteousness)

عن أبي هريرة رضي الله عنه : قال رسول الله – صلى الله عليه وسلم – :
"الإيمان بضع و سبعون شعبة، فأفضلها قول لا إله إلا الله، و أدناها إماطة الأذى
عن الطريق، و الحياء شعبة من الإيمان." متفق عليه

The Messenger of God ﷺ said, "Faith has more than seventy branches, the best of which is to declare *Lā ilāha illā Allāh*, and the least of which is the removal of harm from the path; and modesty is one of the branches of faith." (Universally Agreed)

عن عبد الله بن عمرو رضي الله عنهما : قال رسول الله – صلى الله عليه
وسلم – : "المسلم من سَلِمَ المسلمون من لسانه و يده، و المهاجر من هجر ما نهى
الله عنه." أخرجه البخاري

The Messenger of God ﷺ said, "The Muslim is one from whose tongue and hand the Muslims are safe, and the emigrant is he who abandons what God has prohibited." (Bukhārī)

عن سفيان بن عبد الله الثقفي قال: قلت يا رسول الله، قل لي في الإسلام قولا،
لا أسأل عنه أحدا بعدك، قال رسول الله – صلى الله عليه وسلم – : " قل آمنت
بالله، فأستقم." أخرجه مسلم

Sufyān ibn ʿAbdullāh Atthaqafi asked the Messenger of God to "Tell me about Islām that which will suffice me from asking anyone else after you about it." The Prophet ﷺ replied, "Say, 'I have faith in Allāh,' then become upright." (Muslim)

عن معاذ بن جبل رضي الله عنه قال : كنت ردف النبي صلى الله عليه وآله وسلم على حمار يقال له عُفَيرٌ فقال : " يا معاذ، هل تدري ما حق الله على عباده؟ و ما حق العباد على الله ؟." قلت: الله و رسوله أعلم. قال: " فإن حق الله على العباد أن يعبدوه ولا يشركوا به شيئا، و حق العباد على الله أن لا يعذب من لا يشرك به شيئا." فقلت: يا رسول الله، أفلا أبشر به الناس؟ قال:"لا تبشرهم فيتَّكِلوا." أخرجه البخاري

The Messenger ﷺ asked one of his Companions, "O Muᶜādh! Do you know Allāh's right over His servants and their right over Him? Allāh's right over His servants is that they serve Him alone and associate nothing with Him. And their right is that He should not punish anyone who does not associate with Him anything." Muᶜādh said, "Shall I give this good news to the people?" The Prophet replied, "Do not tell them, or they will depend on it and stop exerting themselves." (Bukhārī & Muslim)

وعن عبادة بن الصامت قال: قال رسول الله – صلى الله عليه وسلم – : "من شهد أن لا إله إلا الله وحده لا شريك له، و أن محمدا عبده و رسوله، و أن عيسى عبد الله و رسوله، و ابن أمته، و كلمته ألقاها إلى مريم، و روح منه، والجنة حق، والنار حق، أدخله الله الجنة على ما كان من العمل." أخرجه البخاري

ᶜIbadah Ibn Assamet related that the Messenger of God ﷺ said, "If anyone bears witness that there is no deity save God alone, who has no partner, that Muḥammad is His Servant and His Messenger, that Jesus is God's Servant and Messenger, the son of His Handmaid, and His Word which He cast into Mary and a Spirit from Him, and that Paradise and Hell are real, God will cause him to enter Paradise, no matter what he has done." (Bukhārī & Muslim)

عن عمرو بن العاص رضي الله عنه : قال رسول الله صلى الله عليه :" أما عَلِمتَ أن الإسلام يهدم ما كان قبله، و أن الهجرة تهدم ما كان قبلها، و أن الحج يهدم ما كان قبله؟." أخرجه مسلم

The Prophet ﷺ said, "O ᶜAmrū! Do you not know that Islām, emigration, and *Ḥajj* all efface what was before them?" (Muslim)

عن عثمان رضي الله عنه قال : قال رسول الله – صلى الله عليه وسلم – :"من مات و هو يعلم أنه لا إله إلا الله دخل الجنة." أخرجه مسلم

The Messenger of God ﷺ said, "Whoever dies knowing that there is no deity but God will enter Paradise." (Muslim)

عن عبد الله بن مسعود رضي الله عنه : قال رجل: يا رسول الله، أي الذنب أكبر عند الله؟ قال: " أن تدعو لله نِدّا و هو خلقك." أخرجه البخاري ومسلم

A man asked, "O Messenger of God, what is the greatest sin in the sight of God?" He said, "That you would call upon anything as if it is equal to God who created you." (Bukhārī & Muslim)

عن أنس رضي الله عنه : قال رسول الله – صلى الله عليه وسلم – :"إن الشيطان يجري من الإنسان مجرى الدم." أخرجه البخاري ومسلم

The Messenger of God ﷺ said, "The devil flows in mankind as blood flows." (Bukhārī & Muslim)

عن أبي هريرة رضي الله عنه : أن رسول الله – صلى الله عليه وسلم – قال :"ما من مولود يولد إلا نَخَسَهُ الشيطان ، فيستهل صارخا من نخسة الشيطان، إلا إبن مريم وأمّه. ثم قال أبو هريرة إقرأوا إن شئتم " وإني اعيذها بك وذريتها من الشيطان الرجيم" أخرجه البخاري ومسلم

The Prophet ﷺ said, "Every person is touched by Satan as soon as they are born and this is why the newborn cries, except for Mary and her son." Then Abū Huraira said, "Recite if you will: *And I seek refuge through you for her and her progeny from Satan the outcast.*" (3:36) (Bukhārī & Muslim)

عن جابر رضي الله عنه : قال سمعت النبي – صلى الله عليه وسلم – يقول :"إن الشيطان قد أيسَ من أن يعبده المُصَلّون في جزيرة العرب، و لكن في التحريش بينهم."(كلمة تحريش معناها إثارة الفتن). أخرجه مسلم

The Messenger of God ﷺ said, "Verily, Satan has despaired of being worshipped by those who pray in the Arabian Peninsula, but he has hopes of setting them against one another." (Muslim)

عن ابن عباس – رضي الله عنهما– جاء رجل إلى النبي صلى الله عليه وسلم فقال: يارسول الله إن أحدنا يجد في نفسه يعرضُ بالشيء لأن يكون حُممةً أحبُّ إليه من أن يتكلم به فقال : "الله أكبر الله أكبر الله أكبر الحمد لله الذي رد كيده إلى الوَسوَسة." أخرجه أبوداود

Ibn ᶜAbbās ﷺ related that a man came to the Prophet ﷺ and said, "I have thoughts of such a nature that I would rather be burned to a crisp than speak about them!" Muḥammad said, "God is Great, God is great, God is great! Praise be to God who has limited the matter to promptings of the mind." (Abū Dāᵓūd)

عن علي رضي الله عنه : قال كنا في جنازة في بقيع الغرقد فأتانا رسول الله صلى الله عليه وسلم فقعد وقعدنا حوله ومعه مخصرةٌ ، فنكّس فجعل ينكتُ بمخصرته ، ثم قال : ما منكم من أحد ، ما من نفس منفوسة إلا وقد كتبَ الله مكانها من الجنة والنار، وإلا وقد كتبت شقية أو سعيدة قال : فقال رجل يا رسول الله أفلا نتكل على كتابنا وندعُ العمل ؟ فقال " من كان من أهل السعادة فسيصير الى عمل اهل السعادة ومن كان من أهل الشقاوة فسيصير الى عمل أهل الشقاوة . فقال : اعملوا فكلٌ ميسر ، اما أهل السعادة فييسرون لعمل أهل السعادة ، وأما أهل الشقاوة فييسرون لعمل أهل الشقاوة . ثم قرأ " فأما من اعطى واتقى (5) وصدق بالحسنى (6) فسنيسره لليسرى (7) وأما من بخل واستغنى (8) وكذب بالحسنى (9) فسنيسره للعسرى (10) ." أخرجه البخاري ومسلم

Ali relates that, "We were at a funeral in Baqīᶜ when the Messenger of God ﷺ came and sat down and we sat down around him. He had a walking staff with him and he started to turn it and strike the ground with it. Then he said, "Every one of you, without exception, has their place in the fire or the garden prescribed and is decreed to suffering or happiness." They replied, "Then should we depend on our destiny and abandon action?" He answered, "Whoever is among the people of happiness is compelled to to the actions of the people of happiness and whoever is among the people of suffering is compelled to the actions of the people of suffering. Act, for everyone is aided, those who are among the people of happiness are aided to do the work of happiness and those who are among the people of suffering are aided to do the work of suffering." Then he recited: *As to the one who gives and is conscious of God, and is true to what is good, We shall aid him towards ease. And as for one who is stingy and withholds and denies goodness, We shall aid him towards difficulty."* (Bukhārī & Muslim)

عن أبي هريرة رضي الله عنه : قال رسول الله – صلى الله عليه وسلم – :"ما من مولود إلا يولد على الفطرة، فأبواه يهودانه، و ينصرانه، و يمجسانه كما تنتج البهيمة بهيمة جمعاء هل تحسون فيها من جدعاء ، ثم يقول أبو هريرة وأقرأوا إن شئتم " فطرت الله التي فطر الناس عليها لاتبديل لخلق الله ." أخرجه البخاري ومسلم

The Messenger of God ﷺ said, "Everyone is born with an innately pure nature, just as cattle produce whole offspring without any branding. Then their parents condition them into following organized religion, be it Judaism, Christianity, or Zoroastrianism," Then Abū Huraira recited: *In accordance with the natural disposition which God has instilled into the human being. There is no changing God's creation.* (30:30) (Bukhārī & Muslim)

عن أبي موسى رضي الله عنه قال : قام فينا رسول الله – صلى الله عليه وسلم بخمس كلمات فقال – :"إن الله عز وجل لا ينام، ولا ينبغي له أن ينام،يخفظ القسط و يرفعه، و يُرفَعُ إليه عملِ الليل قبل عمل النهار وعمل النهار قبل عمل الليل حجابه النور، لو كشفهة لأحرق سَبَحات وجهه ما إنتهى إليه بصره من خلقه" اخرجه مسلم .

The Prophet ﷺ said, "Allāh does not sleep, nor does sleep befit Him. He sends down and raises up in just measure; and all actions by night or day ascend to Him. His veil is Light. If He were to remove it, the majesty of His Countenance would burn up all of His creation." (Muslim)

عن أبي هريرة رضي الله عنه : أن رسول الله –صلى الله عليه وسلم قال – :"يد الله ملأى، لا يغيضها نفقة سحاء الليل والنهار وقال أرأيتهم ما أنفق منذ خلق السماوات والأرض فإنه لم يغض ما في يده وقال : عرشه على الماء وبيده الأخرى الميزان يخفض ويرفع ." أخرجه البخاري

The Prophet ﷺ said, "God's hand is full, undiminished by any expenditure throughout night and day. Do you see what He has given since the creation of the heavens and earth? It has not diminished what is in His hand. His throne is upon the water and in His other hand is the Scale constantly in balance." (Bukhārī & Muslim)

عن أبي هريرة – رضي الله عنه– قال: خرج علينا رسول الله – صلى الله عليه وسلم – و نحن نتنازع في القدر، فغضب حتى احمَرَّ وجهه حتى كأنما فُقِئَ في وَجنتيه الرُّمانُ، فقال: "أبهذا أُمرتُم ؟، أما بهذا أُرسلتُ إليكم ؟، إنما هلك من كان قبلكم حين تنازعوا في هذا الأمر، عَزَمتُ عليكم ألا تتنازعوا فيه." رواه الترمذي

Abū Hurayrah رضي الله عنه related that the Prophet ﷺ came upon us as we were arguing about destiny. He became angry to the point that his face was as red as a pomegranate seed and he said, "Is this what you have been commanded to do? Or is this what I have been sent to you with? Nothing but contention over this matter has caused those who came before you to perish. I urge you not to argue about this." (Tirmidhī)

عن أبي موسى الأشعري رضي الله عنه : عن النبي – صلى الله عليه وسلم قال – :"إن هذا القلب كريشة بفلاة من الأرض يقيمها الريح ظهر لبطن." مسند أحمد

The Messenger of God ﷺ said, "The heart is like a feather in desert country, which the winds keep turning over and over." (Aḥmad)

عن أبي الدرداء – رضي الله عنه – قال: بينما نحن عند رسول الله – صلى الله عليه وسلم – نتذاكر ما يكون، إذ قال رسول الله صلى الله عليه وسلم – : "إذا سمعتم بجبل زال عن مكانه فصدقوا، و إذا سمعتم برجل تغير عن خُلقه فلا تصدقوا به، وإنه يصير إلى ما جُبِلَ عليه." رواه أحمد

Abū Dardā' ﵁ related that while they were learning with the Messenger of God ﷺ he said, "When you hear that a mountain has moved from its place, believe it; but when you hear that a man's nature has changed, do not believe it, for he will remain true to his inborn disposition." (Aḥmad)

عن أم سلمة – رضي الله عنها – قالت: يا رسول الله، لايزال يصيبك كل عام وجع من الشاة المسمومة التي أكلت. قال: "ما أصابني شئ منها إلا و هو مكتوب عليَّ و آدم في طينته." رواه ابن ماجه

Umm Salamah ﵂ said, "O Messenger of God, you are still afflicted each year with pain from that poisoned sheep you ate." He replied, "I am afflicted by nothing which was not decreed for me while Adam was still a lump of clay." (Ibn Mājah)

عن جابر رضي الله عنه قال : جاءت ملائكة إلى النبي صلى الله عليه وسلم وهو نائم فقال بعضهم إنه نائم ، وقال بعضهم إن العين نائمة والقلب يقظان فقالوا : إن لصاحبكم هذا مثلاً فأضربوا له مثلاً ، فقال بعضهم : إنه نائم ، وقال بعضهم : إن العين نائمة والقلب يقظان ، فقالوا : مثله كمثل رجل بنى داراً وجعل فيها مأدبة وبعث داعياً فمن أجاب الداعي دخل الدار وأكل من المأدبة ، ومن لم يجب الداعي لم يدخل الدار ولم يأكل من المأدبة فقالوا :أولوها له بفقهها فقال بعضهم : إنه نائم وقال بعضهم إن العين نائمة والقب يقظان ، فقالوا : فالدار الجنة والداعي محمد صلى الله عليه وسلم فمن أطاع محمداً صلى الله عليه وسلم فقد أطاع الله ومن عصى محمداً صلى الله عليه وسلم فقد عصى الله ، ومحمدٌ صلى الله عليه وسلم فَرْق بين الناس . رواه البخاري

Jābir ؓ reported that angels came to the Prophet ﷺ as he slept and they said, "Verily, there is a similitude for this companion of ours, so strike it for him." Some said he is asleep and others said the eye sleeps but the heart is awake. Then they said, "His similitude is of one who builds a house and sets a great feast therein and then he sends a caller to invite people to this feast. Whoever responds to the invitation enters the house and partakes of the feast with him and whoever does not respond will not enter or partake of the feast." Then they said, "Interpret it for him so that he may understand." Then they said, "The house is Paradise, the caller is Muḥammad. So whoever responds to the caller obeys Allāh and whoever does not respond disobeys Allāh. Muḥammad is the one who distinguishes between people." (Bukhārī)

عن أنس – رضي الله عنه– قال: جاء ثلاثة رهط إلى أزواج النبي – صلى الله عليه وسلم – يسألون عن عبادة النبي – صلى الله عليه وسلم – فلما أخبِروا كأنهم تقالوها، فقالوا أين نحن من النبي – صلى الله عليه و سلم – و قد غفر الله له ما تقدم من ذنبه و ما تأخر! فقال أحدهم: أما أنا فأصلي الليل أبدا، و قال الآخر: أنا أصوم النهار أبدا ولا أفطر، و قال الآخر: أنا أعتزل النساء فلا أتزوج أبدا. فجاء النبي – صلى الله عليه وسلم – إليهم فقال: "أنتم الذين قلتم كذا و كذا ؟، أما و الله إني لأخشاكم لله و أتقاكم له، لكني أصوم و أفطر، و أصلي و أرقد، و أتزوج النساء، فمن رَغِبَ عن سنتي فليس مني ." أخرجه البخاري ومسلم

Anas ؓ related that three people came to the wives of the Prophet ﷺ to ask about his acts of worship. When they were informed of his practices they said to each other, "Where are we in comparison to the Prophet whose sins have been forgiven?" Then each one stated their intent to undertake extreme practices. One said, "I will pray throughout the night forever." And the other said, "As for me I will fast every day forever." And the third said, "I will abstain from women and never marry." Later the Prophet came to them after hearing what they were intent upon and told them, "By God, I am more in awe of Allāh than any of you, and I am more conscious of Him than any of you, yet I fast and I break my fast, and I pray the night and I sleep, and I marry and keep the company of women. Whoever desires other than my way is not of me!" (Bukhārī & Muslim)

وعن رافع بن خديج – رضي الله عنه – قال: قدم نبي الله – صلى الله عليه وسلم المدينة – وهم يُؤَبِّرونَ النخل، يقولون يلقحون النخل فقال:"ما تصنعون؟." قالوا: كنا نصنعه. قال: " لعلَّكم لو لم تفعلوا كان خيرا." فتركوه؛ فنفضت أو فنقصتْ؛ قال فذكروا ذلك له فقال: "إنما أنا بشر إذا أمرتكم بشيء من أمر دينكم فخذوا به، و إذا أمرتكم بشيء من رأي فإنما أنا بشر." رواه مسلم

Rafea Ibn Khadeej ﷺ said that one day the Prophet ﷺ passed by while people were fertilizing palm trees and asked them what they were doing. When they told him, he said, "Maybe it would be better if you did not do this." So they stopped and as a result the fruits were reduced. When they mentioned this to him, he said to them, "I am only a human being. When I command you regarding your religion, accept it; but when I command you based on my own opinion, I am merely a human being." (Muslim)

عن أبي هريرة رضي الله عنه قال : قال رسول الله – صلى الله عليه وسلم – : "بدأ الإسلام غريبا، و سيعود كما بدأ، فطُوبَى للغرباء." أخرجه مسلم

The Messenger of God ﷺ said, "Islām began as something strange and it will return to the way it started, so blessed are the strange ones." (Muslim)

عن أبي هريرة – رضي الله عنه – قال: قال رسول الله – صلى الله عليه وسلم – :"إنكم في زمان من تَرَكَ منكم عُشرَ ما أمِرَ به هلك، ثم يأتي زمان من عمل منهم بعُشرِ ما أمِرَ به نجا." رواه الترمذي

Abū Hurayrah ﷺ related that the Messenger of God ﷺ is reported to have said, "In the times in which you are living, anyone who abandons a tenth of what he is commanded will perish; but a time is coming when anyone who does a tenth of what he is commanded will be saved." (Tirmidhī)

عن معاذ بن جبل – رضي الله عنه – قال: قال رسول الله – صلى الله عليه وسلم – :"إن الشيطان ذئب الإنسان كذئب الغنم، يأخذ الشاة القاصية والناحية، فإيَّاكم والشعاب، وعليكم بالجماعة والعامة والمسجد " رواه أحمد .

Muᶜādh ibn Jabal ﵁ related that the Messenger of God ﷺ said, "The devil is to man as the wolf is to sheep; he stalks them, catching the one which is solitary, the one which strays far from the flock, and the one which wanders off. So avoid the branching paths and keep to the general community, and to the places of worship." (Aḥmad)

عن حُميد بن عبد الرحمن بن عوف قال : سمعت معاوية بن أبي سفيان وهو يخطب يقول : إني سمعت رسول – صلى الله عليه وسلم – يقول : "من يرد الله به خيرا يُفقّهه في الدين، وإنما أنا قاسم ويعطي الله." أخرجه البخاري ومسلم

The Messenger of God ﷺ said, "When God wishes good for anyone, he causes him to understand religion. I am only one who makes clear, while Allāh is the one who gives." (Bukhārī & Muslim)

عن أبي هريرة رضي الله عنه قال : قال رسول الله – صلى الله عليه وسلم – :" من نَفّس عن مؤمن كُربَة من كُرَبِ الدنيا نَفّس الله عنه كُربَة من كُرَبِ يوم القيامة، و من يَسَّر على مُعسِرٍ يَسَّر الله عليه في الدنيا و الآخرة، و من ستر مسلما ستره الله في الدنيا والآخرة، والله في عون العبد ما كان العبد في عون أخيه، و من سلك طريقا يلتمس فيه علما سَهَّل الله له به طريقا إلى الجنة، و ما اجتمع قوم في بيت من بيوت الله يَتلون كتاب الله و يتدارسونه بينهم إلا نزلت عليهم السكينة، و غشيتهم الرحمة ، و حَفّتهم الملائكة ، وذكَرَهم الله فيمن عنده، و من بَطَّأَ به عمله لم يُسرع به نَسَبُه." رواه مسلم

The Messenger of God ﷺ said, "Whoever relieves one of the faithful ones of a worldly worry, God will relieve him of one of the worries of the Day of Resurrection. And whoever eases the way for one who is destitute, God will ease the way for him in this world and the next. And whoever protects a Muslim, God will protect him in this world and the next. God helps a man as long as he helps his brother. If anyone pursues a path in search of knowledge, God will thereby make easy for him a path to Paradise. Any group that gathers in one of the houses of God to recite God's Book and study it together will have stillness descend upon them, and mercy engulf them, and the angels surround them, and God will mention them among those near to Him. And whoever procrastinates in his practices will not move forward by his lineage." (Muslim)

عن أبي الدرداء رضي الله عنه قال : سمعت رسول الله – صلى الله عليه وسلم يقول – :"من سلك طريقا يطلب فيه علما سلك الله به طريقا من طرق الجنة، و إن الملائكة لتضع أجنحتها رضا لطالب العلم، و إن العالم ليستغفر له من في السموات ومن في الأرض، والحيتان في جوف الماء، و إن فضل العالم على العابد كفضل القمر ليلة البدر على سائر الكواكب، وإن العلماء ورثة الأنبياء، وإن الأنبياء لم يُوَرِّثوا دينارا ولا درهما، وَرَّثوا العلم فمن أخذه أخذ بحظ وافر." رواه أحمد و الترمذي وأبن ماجه

The Messenger of God ﷺ said, "If anyone travels a path in search of knowledge, God will conduct him through one of the paths of Paradise; the angels will lower their wings from good pleasure with the one who seeks knowledge, and the inhabitants of the heavens and the earth, and the fish in the depths of the water will seek forgiveness for him. The superior position of the Gnostic over the worshipper is as the position of the full moon over the stars. The Gnostics are the heirs of the prophets. The prophets did not inherit any money, they have only inherited knowledge and whoever attains to it is one who has Abundant fortune." (Aḥmad, Tirmidhī, Abū Dā'ūd)

عن أبي أمامة الباهلي رضي الله عنه قال : قال رسول الله – صلى الله عليه وسلم – :"إن الله و ملائكته، وأهل السماوات والأرض، حتى النملة في جحرها، وحتى الحوت، ليصلون على مُعَلِّم الناس الخير." رواه الترمذي

The Messenger of God ﷺ said, "Verily God, His angels, and all the inhabitants of the heavens and the earth, even the ant in its hole and even the fish, invoke blessings upon the one who teaches people what is good." (Tirmidhī)

عن أبي الأحوص عن عبد الله : عن النبي – صلى الله عليه وسلم قال – :"أنزلَ القرآن على سبعة أحرف، لكل حرف منها ظهر وبطن، ولكل حد مطلع." رواه الطبري و البزار وأبو يعلي والهيثمي

The Messenger of God ﷺ said, "The Qur'ān was sent down in seven modes. Every verse in it has an external and an internal meaning and at each boundary there is a vista." (Ṭabarī)

عن أبي هريرة رضي الله عنه : قال رسول الله – صلى الله عليه وسلم – :"إن الله يبعث لهذه الأمة على رأس كل مائة سنة من يجدد لها دينها." رواه أبو داود

The Messenger of God ﷺ said, "At the beginning of every century God will send to this community one who will renew its religion." (Abū Dā'ūd)

عن عكرمة – رضي الله عنه – عن ابن عباس قال: "حَدِّثْ الناس كل جمعة مرة، فإن أبيت فمرتين، فإن أكثرت فثلاث مرات، ولا تمل الناس هذا القرآن، ولا ألفيَنّكَ تأتي القوم و هم في حديث من حديثهم فتقص عليهم، فتقطع عليهم حديثهم فتملهم، و لكن أنصت، فإذا أمروك فحدثهم و هم يشتهونه، فانظر السجع من الدعاء فاجتنبه، فإني عهدت رسول الله – صلى الله عليه وسلم – و أصحابه لا يفعلون إلا ذلك ." رواه البخاري

[This is not a Hadith, but a saying of Ibn ᶜAbbās on preaching:] "Speak to people once a week and, if you must, twice, but do not exceed three times. Do not make them weary of this Qur'ān. Do not let me see you going to people when they are in the middle of their conversation and interrupting them and thereby repelling them. Listen silently and if they ask you, then speak to them when they long for it. Beware of flowery prose in supplication; avoid it for I did not see the Prophet ﷺ and his companions doing so." (Bukhārī)

عن أبي هريرة رضي الله عنه قال : قال رسول الله – صلى الله عليه وسلم – :"إن مما يلحق المؤمن من عمله و حسناته بعد موته: علما علمه و نشره، و ولدا صالحا تركه، و مصحفا وَرَّثَـه، أو مسجدا بناه، أو بيتا لابن السبيل بناه، أو نهرا أجراه، أو صدقة أخرجها من ماله في صحته و حياته، يلحقه من بعد موته." رواه ابن ماجه

The Messenger of God ﷺ said, "Among the actions and good deeds for which the faithful will continue to receive reward after his death are knowledge which he taught and spread, a good offspring whom he left behind, or a copy of the Qur'ān which he left as a legacy, or a mosque which he built, or a house which he built for the traveler, or a stream which he caused to flow, or a charity which he gave from his property when he was alive and well which continues after he is dead." (Ibn Mājah)

عن عبد الله بن مسعود رضي الله عنه قال : قال رسول الله – صلى الله عليه وسلم – :" من جعل الهموم هَمّاً واحدا– هم آخرته– كفاه الله هَمَّ دنياه، ومن تشعبت به الهموم في أحوال الدنيا لم يُبال الله في أي أوديتها هلك." رواه ابن ماجه

The Messenger of God ﷺ said, "If anyone makes the care of his eternal welfare the sum total of his cares, God will protect him from worldly care; but if he has a variety of cares relating to the matters of this world, God will not be concerned in which of its valleys he perishes." (Ibn Mājah)

عن الأحوص بن حكيم عن أبيه : سأل رجل النبي – صلى الله عليه وسلم – عن الشر فقال:"لا تسألوني عن الشر، وسَلوني عن الخير." يقولها ثلاثا ، ثم قال : " ألا إن شرّ الشّرِ شرار العلماءِ ، وإن خير الخير خِيَار العلماءِ ". رواه الدارمي

A man asked the Prophet ﷺ about evil and he said, "Do not ask me about evil, but ask me about good." And he repeated it three times. Then he added, "Truly the most evil of all evil are evil scholars and the best of the good are the good scholars." (Dārimī)

و عن أبي هريرة – رضي الله عنه – قال: "حفظت من رسول الله – صلى الله عليه وسلم – دعاءين فأما أحدهما فبثثته ، و أما الآخر فلو بثثته قُطِعَ هذا البلعوم - يعني مجرى الطعام." رواه البخاري

Abū Hurayrah ﵁ said, "I have by heart two supplications from God's Messenger ﷺ, one of which I have transmitted to you; but were I to disclose the other, my throat would be cut." (Bukhārī)

Purification

عن أبي مالك الأشعري رضي الله عنه قال : قال رسول الله – صلى الله عليه وسلم – : "الطهور شطر الإيمان، و الحمد لله تملأ الميزان، و سبحان الله و الحمد لله تملآن أو تملأ ما بين السماوات والأرض، و الصلاة نور، والصدقة برهان، والصبر ضياء، والقرآن حُجَّة لك أو عليك، كل الناس يغدو، فبايعٌ نفسه: فمُعتِقها أو مُوبِقها." رواه مسلم

The Messenger of God ﷺ said, "Purity completes faith. Praise fills the scale. Glorification and praise fill what is between the heavens and earth. Prayer is light. Charity is evidence. Patience enlightens. And the Qur᾽ān is an argument for you or against you. Everyone sets out each day and trades his soul, either emancipating it or oppressing it." (Muslim)

عن أبي هريرة رضي الله عنه قال : قال رسول الله – صلى الله عليه وسلم – :" ألا أدُلُّكم على ما يمحو الله به الخطايا و يرفع به الدرجات ؟." قالوا: بلى، يا رسول الله. قال: "إسباغ الوضوء على المَكاره، و كثرة الخُطا إلى المساجد، وانتظار الصلاة بعد الصلاة، فذلكم الرباط." رواه مسلم

The Messenger of God ﷺ said, "Shall I guide you to that by which Allāh effaces your mistakes and elevates your stations? It is when you make your ablutions complete, even when you find it difficult, frequenting mosques, and patiently waiting from one prayer to the next. This is true perseverance." (Muslim)

عن عثمان بن عفان رضي الله عنه قال : قال رسول الله – صلى الله عليه وسلم – :" من توضأ فأحسن الوضوء، خرجت خطاياه من جسده حتى تخرج من تحت أظفاره." أخرجه البخاري ومسلم

The Messenger of God ﷺ said, "If anyone performs their ablution well, his sins will come out from his body, even coming out from under his nails." (Bukhārī & Muslim)

عن أبي هريرة رضي الله عنه قال : قال رسول الله – صلى الله عليه وسلم – :"إذا توضأ العبد المسلم– أو المؤمن – فغسل وجهه خرج من وجهه كل خطيئة نظر إليها بعينيه مع الماء أو مع آخر قطر الماء، فإذا غسل يديه خرج من يديه كل خطيئةٍ كان بطشتها يداه مع الماء أو مع آخر قطر الماء فإذا غسل رجليه خرجت كل خطيئةٍ مشتها رجلاه مع الماء أو مع آخر قطرِ الماء حتى يخرج نقياً من الذنوب." رواه مسلم

The Messenger of God ﷺ said, "When the faithful one does his ablutions, as he washes his face every sin he contemplated with his eyes will come out from his face along with the water or with the last drop of it. And when he washes his hands, every sin committed by his hands will come out with the water or with the last drop of it. And when he washes his feet, every sin towards which his feet have walked will come out with the water or with the last drop of it, so that he will come forth pure from all sins." (Muslim)

عن ثوبان رضي الله عنه قال : قال رسول الله – صلى الله عليه وسلم – :"استقيموا ولن تحصوا، واعلموا أن أفضل أعمالكم الصلاة، ولا يحافظ على الوضوء إلا مؤمن." رواه مالك وأحمد و ابن ماجه

The Messenger of God ﷺ said, "Keep to the straight path and you will not be denied. And know that your best action is prayer, and that only the faithful observe ablution carefully." (Mālik, Aḥmad, Ibn Mājah)

عن جابر بن عبد الله رضي الله عنه قال : قال رسول الله – صلى الله عليه وسلم – : "مفتاح الجنة الصلاة، ومفتاح الصلاة الطهور." رواه أحمد

The Messenger of God ﷺ said, "The key to Paradise is prayer, and the key to prayer is purification." (Aḥmad)

عن عائشة – رضي الله عنها – قالت: "كان النبي – صلى الله عليه وسلم – يحب التَّيَمُّنَ في شأنه كله، في طهوره، و تَرَجُّلِه، و تَنَعُّلِه." رواه البخاري ومسلم

ᶜĀʾishah ﷺ said, "The Prophet ﷺ liked to begin with the right as much as possible in all his affairs; in his purification, combing his hair, and putting on his sandals." (Bukhārī & Muslim)

عن عائشة – رضي الله عنها – قالت: "كان رسول الله – صلى الله عليه وسلم – إذا اغتسل من الجنابة يبدأ فيغسل يديه ثم يُفرغُ بيمينه على شماله فيغسل فرجه ثم يتوضأ وضوءهُ للصلاة ثم يأخذ الماء ، فيدخلُ أصابعه في أصول الشعر حتى إذا رأى أن قد استبرأ حفن على رأسه ثلاث حفنات ثم أفاض على سائر جسده ثم غسل رجليه." أخرجه البخاري ومسلم

ᶜĀʾishah ﷺ said, "When God's Messenger ﷺ washed following intercourse, he first poured water over his hands, then he performed ablution, then he soaked his fingers in water and rubbed his scalp, then he filled his hands with water and poured it over his head three times, then he let the water flow over his entire skin." (Muslim)

قالت عائشة: " كان رسول الله – صلى الله عليه وسلم – يغتسل من الجنابة ثم يستدفئ بي قبل أن أغتسل." رواه ابن ماجه والترمذي

ᶜĀʾishah said, "God's Messenger ﷺ used to wash after intercourse, then he would warm himself against me before I washed." (Tirmidhī)

عن كبشة بنت كعب بن مالك – رضي الله عنهما – أن أبا قتادة دخل عليها فسكبت له وضوءا، فجاءت هِرَّة لتشرب منه، فأصغَى لها الإناء حتى شَرِبَتْ. قالت كبشة: فرآني أنظر إليه . فقال: أتعجبين يا ابنة أخي ؟. قالت: فقلت: نعم . فقال: إن رسول الله – صلى الله عليه وسلم – قال: "إنها ليست بنَجَس، إنما هي من الطَّوافين عليكم أو الطَّوافات." رواه مالك والترمذي وآخرين

Kabsha رضي الله عنها, daughter of Kaᶜb, said that Abū Qatada visited her and she poured out water for him for ablution. A cat came and drank some of it, and he tilted the vessel for it until it had drunk. Kabsha said that when he saw her looking at him, he said, "Are you suprised, my niece?" When she replied that she was, he said that God's Messenger ﷺ had said, "It is not unclean; it is one of those who go around among you." (Mālik, Tirmidhī, & others)

عن أبي هريرة – رضي الله عنه – قال: قام أعرابي فبال في المسجد، فتناوله الناس . فقال لهم النبي – صلى الله عليه وسلم : " دعوه، و هَريقوا على بوله سَجْلاً من ماء أو ذنوبا من ماء ، فإنما بُعثتم مُيسرين و لم تبعثوا مُعسرين." رواه البخاري ومسلم

Abū Huraira related that when a Bedouin Arab got up and urinated in the mosque, the people seized him, but the Prophet ﷺ said to them: "Leave him alone, and pour a bucket of water over what he has passed; for you have been sent only to make things easy, and not to make things difficult." (Bukhārī)

عن شقيق قال : كنت جالساً مع عبد الله وأبي موسى الأشعري فقال له أبو موسى : لو أن رجلاً أجنب فلم يجد الماء شهراً أما كان يتيمم ويصلي ، فكيف تصنعون بهذه الآية في سورة المائدة " فلم تجدوا ماءً فتيمموا صعيداً طيباً " فقال عبد الله لو رُخص لهم في هذا لأوشكوا إذا يرد عليهم الماء أن يتيمموا الصعيد قلت : وإنما كرهتم هذا لذا قال نعم : فقال أبو موسى ألم تسمع قول عمار لعمر بعثني رسول الله صلى الله عليه وسلم في حاجة فاجنبت فلم أجد الماء فتمرغت في الصعيد كما تمرَّغُ الدابة فذكرت ذلك للنبي صلى الله عليه وسلم فقال : إنما كان يكفيك ان تصنع هكذا فضربَ بكفِّه ضربةً على الأرض ثم نفضها ثم مسح بهما ظهر كفه بشماله أو ظهر شماله بكفه ثم مسح بها وجهه . " رواه البخاري

Shaqiq related that he was sitting with Abdullah and Abū Musa Al Ashᶜarī who said, "If a man had intercourse and found no water for a month would he not use dust for ablution and pray? What do you do about this verse: *if you find no water then wipe from a goodly earth?*" Abdullah said, "If they were given license in this they would keep using dust even after they find water. So you only made using dust undesirable for this reason?" And he said, "Yes." Abū Musa then said, "Did you not hear what ʿAmmār said to ʿUmar ibn al-Khaṭṭāb ﵁?, "I was sent on a certain matter by the Messenger of God. I had intercourse and could not find water, so I rolled myself on the ground in the dust like an animal and then prayed. I mentioned that afterwards to the Prophet ﷺ, and he said, 'It would have been enough for you to do this,' and he struck the ground with the palm of his hand, shook the dust off, then wiped the back of his other hand with it, then wiped his face." (Bukhārī)

قالت عائشة – رضي الله عنها – كان النبي – صلى الله عليه وسلم – يتـَّكِئ في حجري وأنا حائض ثم يقرأ القرآن. رواه البخاري .وعن عائشة أيضا قالت: قال لي النبي – صلى الله عليه وسلم– : "ناوليني الخُمْرَة من المسجد (و هي سجادة من سعف النخل)." قالت فقلت : إني حائض. فقال:"إن حيضتك ليست في يدك." رواه مسلم

ʿĀʾishah ﵂ said, "The Prophet ﷺ would recline in my lap, although I was menstruating, then recite the Qurʾān." She also related that he had once said to her: "Fetch me the prayer mat from the mosque." When I replied that I was menstruating, he said, "Your menstruation is not in your hand!" (Muslim)

Prayer

عن أنس – رضي الله عنه – قال: جاء رجل الى النبي صلى الله عليه وسلم فقال: يا رسول الله، أصَبتُ حَدّا فأقِمه عليَّ قال . و حضرت الصلاة، فصلى مع رسول الله – صلى الله عليه وسلم– فلما قضَى الصلاة قال: يا رسول الله، إني أصبت حدا فأقم فيَّ كتاب الله. قال: " هل حضرت الصلاة معنا ؟." قال: نعم.. قال:" قد غفر لك." أخرجه البخاري ومسلم

Anas ﵁ told of a man who came and said, "Messenger of God ﷺ, I have broken the law, so give me my punishment!" The Prophet did not question him about what he did, and when the time for prayer came the man prayed along with him. Then, when the Prophet had finished the prayer, the man got up and said, "Messenger of God, I have done something which merits punishment, so carry out what God has decreed!" He finally asked, "Did you not pray along with us?" And when the man replied that he had, he said, "Well, God has forgiven you your offense!" (Bukhārī & Muslim)

عن أبي هريرة رضي الله عنه : قال سمعت رسول الله – صلى الله عليه وسلم يقول – :"أرأيتم لو أن نهراً بباب أحدكم يغتسل فيه كل يوم خمس مرات، هل يبقى من درنه شئ؟." قالوا: لا يبقى من درنه شئ . قال: "فذلك مثل الصلوات الخمس، يمحو الله بهن الخطايا." رواه البخاري ومسلم

The Messenger of God ﷺ said, "Tell me, if one of you had a river at the door of his house in which he washed five times daily, would any filth remain?" When he received the reply that none would remain, he said, "That is like the five times of prayer, by which God effaces sins." (Bukhārī & Muslim)

عن ابن مسعود – رضي الله عنه– قال: سألت النبي – صلى الله عليه وسلم – أي الأعمال أحب إلى الله ؟. قال: "الصلاة على وقتها." قال: ثم أي ؟. قال: "ثم بر الوالدين." قال : ثم أي؟. قال: "الجهاد في سبيل الله." قال: حدثني بهن، و لو استزدته لزادني. أخرجه البخاري ومسلم

Ibn Masʿūd ؓ asked the Prophet ﷺ what action was dearest to God, and he replied. "Prayer, at its proper time." I asked what came next, and he replied that it was kindness to parents. I asked what came next and he replied that it was struggle on God's path." (Bukhārī & Muslim)

عن عبدالله– رضي الله عنه – قال: جاء رجل إلى النبي – صلى الله عليه وسلم – فقال: يا رسول الله، إني عالجت امرأة في أقصى المدينة، و إني أصبت منها ما دون أن أمسها، فأنا هذا، فاقض فيَّ ما شئت. فقال له عمر : لقد سترك الله لو سترت نفسك. قال: و لم يَرُدَّ النبي – صلى الله عليه وسلم – شيئا، فقام الرجل فانطلق، فأتبعه النبي – صلى الله عليه وسلم – رجلا، دعاه و تلا عليه هذه الآية " و أقم الصلاة طرفي النهار و زلفا من الليل إن الحسنات يذهبن السيئات ذلك ذكرى للذاكرين" فقال رجل من القوم: يا نبي الله، هذا له خاصة ؟. فقال: "بل للناس كافة." رواه مسلم

ʿAbdullāh ibn Masʿūd ؓ related that a man came to the Prophet ﷺ saying, "Messenger of God, I sported with a girl on the outskirts of Medina, and got what I wanted from her short of having intercourse with her. Now here I am, so decide what you wish about me!" ʿUmar said to him, "God would have concealed this about you if you had kept it to yourself." The Prophet gave no reply, so the man got up and went away. Then the Prophet sent a man after him to summon him back, and he recited this verse: *And observe the prayer at the two ends of the day and in the nearness of the night, for good deeds remove evil deeds: this is a reminder to those who remember* (*Sūrah Hūd* 11:114). Someone asked, "Prophet of God, is this meant for him in particular?" "No," he said, "it is for all people." (Muslim)

عن أبي ذر – رضي الله عنه– أن النبي – صلى الله عليه وسلم – خرج زمن الشتاء و الورق يتهافت، فأخذ بغصنين من شجرة، قال: فجعل ذلك الورق

يتهافت. قال: فقال: "يا أبا ذر." قلت: لبيك، يا رسول الله . قال: "إن العبد المسلم لَيُصلِّ الصلاة يريد بها وجه الله، فتهافت عنه ذنوبه، كما يتهافت هذا الورق عن هذه الشجرة." رواه أحمد

Abi Dhar related that the Prophet ﷺ went out in winter when the leaves were falling, and took two branches of a tree whose leaves began to fall. He called out, "O Abū Dhar!" to which I responded, "Here I am at your service, O Messenger of God!" He said, "A Muslim observes prayer for God's sake, and his sins fall from him as these leaves fall from this tree." (Aḥmad)

عن سيار بن سلامة أبي المنهال قال سمعت أبا الأسلمي يقول كان رسول الله – صلى الله عليه وسلم – يؤخر العشاء إلى ثلث الليل، ويكره النوم قبلها و الحديث بعدها وكان يقرأ في صلاة الفجر من المائة الى الستين وكان ينصرف حين يعرف بعضنا وجه بعض . رواه البخاري ومسلم

It is reported that the Prophet ﷺ did not mind postponing the night prayer until a third of the night had passed; and he did not like sleeping before it, or talking after it. He used to recite between sixty and a hundred verses during Fajr prayer and would leave when our faces became evident from the daylight." (Bukhārī & Muslim)

عن أنس بن مالك رضي الله عنه قال : قال نبي الله – صلى الله عليه وسلم –: "من نسي صلاة أو نام عنها، فكفارته أن يصليها إذا ذكرها." أخرجه البخاري ومسلم

The Messenger of God ﷺ said, "If anyone forgets a prescribed prayer or sleeps without performing it, expiation is made by observing it when he remembers it." (Bukhārī & Muslim)

عن أبي هريرة رضي الله عنه قال : قال رسول الله – صلى الله عليه وسلم – : " ولو يعلمون ما في التهجير لاستبقوا إليه، و لو يعلمون ما في العتمة و الصبح لأتوهما و لو حَبوا." أخرجه البخاري ومسلم

The Messenger of God ﷺ said, "If people knew what lies in abandonment (of desires) they would race toward it, and if they knew what blessing lies in the prayers of the night and early morning they would come to them, even if they had to crawl to do so." (Bukhārī & Muslim)

عن أبي هريرة رضي الله عنه قال : قال رسول الله – صلى الله عليه وسلم – : " المُؤذن يُغفر له مَدَى صوته، و يشهد له كل رطب و يابس." رواه أحمد و أبوداود و ابن ماجه

The Messenger of God ﷺ said, "The one who makes the call to prayer will receive forgiveness to the extent to which his voice reaches, and every moist and dry place will bear witness to him." (Aḥmad, Abū Dāʾūd)

عن أم سلمة – رضي الله عنها – قالت: علمني رسول الله – صلى الله عليه وسلم – أن أقول عند أذان المغرب: "اللهم هذا إقبال ليلك، و إدبار نهارك، و أصوات دعاتك، فاغفر لي." أخرجه أبوداود

Umm Salamah رضي الله عنها said, "God's Messenger ﷺ taught me to say, when the Call for the sunset prayer was made, 'O God, this is the time when Your night approaches and Your day recedes, and the voices of Your supplicants are heard, so forgive me.'" (Abū Dāʾūd)

عن أبي هريرة وأبي سعيد رضي الله عنهما : قال رسول الله– صلى الله عليه وسلم – :"سبعة يُظلُّهم الله في ظله، يوم لا ظل إلا ظله: إمام عادل، و شاب نشأ في عبادة الله، و رجل قلبه مُعلَّق بالمسجد إذا خرج منه حتى يعود إليه، و رجلان تَحابَّا في الله فأجتمعا على ذلك وافترقا عليه، و رجل ذكر الله خاليا ففاضت عيناه، و رجل دعته امرأة ذات منصب وجمال فقال: إني أخاف الله، و

رجل تصدق بصدقة فأخفاها حتى لا تعلم شماله ما تنفق يمينه." رواه البخاري ومسلم

The Messenger of God ﷺ said, "There are seven whom God will cover with His shade on the Day when there will be no shade but His: a just imām; a young man who grows up worshipping God; a man whose heart is attached to the mosque from the time he leaves it until he returns to it; two people who love one another for God's sake, meeting thus and separating thus; a man who remembers God in solitude and his eyes flow with tears; a man who, when tempted by a woman of rank and beauty, says 'I fear God!'; and a man who gives alms secretly so that his left hand does not know what his right hand bestows." (Bukhārī & Muslim)

عن ابن عمر عن النبي – صلى الله عليه وسلم قال – :"اجعلوا من صلاتكم في بيوتكم، ولا تتخذوها قبورا." أخرجه البخاري ومسلم

The Messenger of God ﷺ said, "Do not make your homes into graveyards! Perform some of your prayers in them." (Bukhārī & Muslim)

قال أبو ذر رضي الله عنه : سألت رسول الله صلى الله عليه وسلم عن أول مسجد وُضع في الأرض قال : المسجد الحرام قلت : ثم أيٌّ قال : المسجد الأقصى قلت كم بينهما قال : أربعون عاماً ثم الأرض لك مسجد فحيثما أدركتك الصلاة فصلِّ ." أخرجه البخاري ومسلم

Abū Dharr asked the Messenger of God ﷺ about the first place of worship to be established on earth. He said, "The Sacred Mosque." Abū Dharr asked, "Then which one?" He said, "The Farthest Mosque." He asked him, "How long between them?" and he said, "Forty years. The earth is a place of prostration for you, so whenever the time for prayer arrives, pray wherever you are." (Bukhārī & Muslim)

و عن عائشة – رضي الله عنها – قالت: كان النبي – صلى الله عليه وسلم – يصلي من الليل و أنا مُعترضة بينه و بين القبلة كاعتراض الجنازة. رواه البخاري ومسلم

ʿĀʾishah ﷺ said, "The Prophet ﷺ used to pray at night while I lay between him and the *qiblah* like a corpse on a bier." (Bukhārī)

عن علي رضي الله عنه قال : كان رسول الله – صلى الله عليه وسلم – إذا ركع قال: "اللهم لك ركعت، و بك آمنت، و لك أسلمت، خشع لك سمعي، و بصري، و مخي، و عظمي، وعصبي." أخرجه مسلم

When the Messenger of God ﷺ bowed in prayer he used to say, "O God, to You I bow down, in You I put my faith, and to You I submit myself. My hearing, my sight, my brain, my bones, and my sinews humble themselves in awe before You!" (Muslim)

عن علي رضي الله عنه قال : كان رسول الله – صلى الله عليه وسلم – إذا سجد قال: "اللهم لك سجدت، و بك آمنت، و لك أسلمت، سجد وجهي للذي خلقه و صوره، و شقّ سمعه و بصره، تبارك الله أحسن الخالقين." . رواه مسلم

When the Messenger of God ﷺ prostrated in prayer he used to say, "O My God! To You I prostrate myself, in You I put my faith, and to You I submit. My face is prostrated before the One who created it, fashioned it, and brought forth its hearing and sight. Blessed is Allāh who is the best of creators!" (Muslim)

عن عائشة – رضي الله عنها – قالت: فقدتُ رسول الله – صلى الله عليه وسلم – ليلةً من الفراش، فالتمسته فوقعتْ يدي على بطن قدميه و هو في المسجد و هما منصوبتان، و هو يقول: "اللهم أعوذ برضاك من سخطك، و بمعافاتك من عقوبتك، و أعوذ بك منك، لا أحصِي ثناء عليك، أنت كما أثنيت على نفسك." . رواه مسلم

ʿĀʾishah ﷺ said, "One night I woke up to find God's Messenger ﷺ not in bed, and when I felt for him in the dark my hand fell upon the soles of his feet while he was in the act of prostration. And he was saying, 'O My God, I seek refuge in Your contentment from Your displeasure, and in Your forgiveness from Your punishment, and I seek refuge in You from You. I cannot reckon Your praise. You are as You have praised Yourself.'" (Muslim)

عن أبي هريرة رضي الله عنه : أن رسول الله – صلى الله عليه وسلم قال – :"أقرب ما يكون العبد من ربه و هو ساجد، فأكثروا الدعاء." . رواه مسلم

The Messenger of God ﷺ said, "The nearest a servant comes to his Lord is when he is prostrate in prayer, so increase your supplications when you are in prostration." (Muslim)

عن عمر بن الخطاب – رضي الله عنه – قال: "إن الدعاء مَوقوف بين السماء و الأرض، لا يصعد منه شئ حتى تصلي على نبيك صلى الله عليه وسلم ." رواه الترمذي

ʿUmar ﷺ said, "Supplications are stopped between heaven and earth, none of them ascending, until you invoke blessing on your Prophet." (Tirmidhī)

عن معاذ بن جبل – رضي الله عنه– أن رسول الله صلى الله عليه وسلم : أخذ بيده وقال يا معاذ والله إنّي لأحبك والله إني لأحبك ." فقلت: و أنا أحبك يا رسول الله . قال: " فلا تَدَعْ أن تقول في دُبُرِ كل صلاة: رب أعِنـّي على ذكرك، و شكرك، و حسن عبادتك." رواه أحمد وأبو داود

Muʿādh ibn Jabal ﷺ said that God's Messenger took him by the hand and said, "By God I love you, Muʿādh, I love you!" to which he replied, "And I love you, Messenger of God!" He then told him not to omit to say at the end of every prayer, "My Lord, help me to remember You, and to thank You, and to serve You in the best of ways." (Aḥmad, Abū Dā'ūd)

عن أبي قتادة الأنصاري – رضي الله عنه– قال: رأيت النبي – صلى الله عليه وسلم – يَؤمُّ الناس و أمامةُ بنت أبي العاص وهي ابنة زينب بنت النبي صلى الله عليه وسلم على عاتقه، فإذا ركع وضعها، و إذا رفع من السجود أعادها. أخرجه البخاري ومسلم

Abū Qatādah ﷺ said, "I saw the Prophet ﷺ leading the people in prayer with Umāmah, daughter of Abū'l-ʿĀṣ, daughter of Zeinab the daughter of the Prophet, on his shoulder. When he bowed, he put her down, and when he rose up after the prostration he put her back on his back." (Bukhārī & Muslim)

عن إبن عباس – رضي الله عنهما قال: بِتُّ ذات ليلة عند خالتي ميمونة، فقام النبي – صلى الله عليه وسلم – يصلي متطوعاً من الليل فقام النبي صلى الله عليه وسلم إلى القربة فتوضأ فقام فصلى فقمت لما رأيته صنع ذلك فتوضأت من القربة ثم قمت إلى شقه الأيسر ، فأخذ بيدي من وراء ظهره، يعدلني كذلك من وراء ظهره إلى الشِّقِّ الأيمن قلت أفي التطوع كان ذلك قال : نعم ". أخرجه البخاري ومسلم

Ibn ʿAbbās ﷺ said, "When I was spending a night in the house of my maternal aunt, Maymūnah, God's Messenger ﷺ stood up to pray the night vigil. He got up and did his ablutions and stood in prayer. I stood at his left side, and he took my hand behind his back and directed me to stand at his right side. I asked him if it should be this way even in suprarogatory prayers, and he said, 'Yes.'" (Bukhārī & Muslim)

عن أنس – رضي الله عنه – قال: ما صليت وراء إمام قط أخفَّ صلاة ولا أتمَّ من النبي – صلى الله عليه وسلم– ، و إنْ كان ليَسمع بكاء الصبي، فيخفف مَخافة أن تُفتن أمه. رواه البخاري ومسلم

Anas ﵁ said, "I never prayed behind an Imām whose prayer was lighter or more complete than that of the Prophet ﷺ. When he was leading the prayer he would shorten it if he heard a child crying, for fear its mother might be distressed." (Bukhārī & Muslim)

عن أبي سعيد – رضي الله عنه– قال: جاءت امرأة إلى رسول الله – صلى الله عليه وسلم – و نحن عنده، فقالت: يا رسول الله إن زوجي صفوان بن المعطل يضربني إذا صليت، و يُفطرني إذا صُمت، ولا يصلي الفجر حتى تطلع الشمس، قال – و صفوان عنده – قال: فسأله عما قالت، فقال: يا رسول الله، أما قولها: يضربني إذا صليت، فإنها تقرأ بسورتين و قد نهيتها، قال: فقال له رسول الله – صلى الله عليه وسلم– : " لو كانت سورة واحدة لكَفَتْ الناس." قال: و أما قولها : يُفطرني ، فإنها تنطلق فتصوم و أنا رجل شاب فلا أصبر ، فقال رسول الله – صلى الله عليه وسلم– يومئذ: " لا تصوم امرأة إلا بإذن زوجها." و أما قولها: إني لا أصلي حتى تطلع الشمس، فإنا أهل بيت قد عُرِفَ لنا ذاك، لا نكاد نستيقظ حتى تطلع الشمس قال:" فإذا استيقظت فصَلِّ." رواه أبوداود و ابن ماجه

Abū Saʿīd reported that the wife of Ṣafwān ibn Al-Muʿṭil complained to the Messenger of God ﷺ that her husband beat her when she prayed, and would force her to break her fast, and did not pray the dawn prayer until after the sun had risen. The Prophet asked Ṣafwān about this and he replied, "As for her claim that I beat her when she prays, it is because she keeps reciting only two *sūrahs* and I told her not to." The Prophet ﷺ told him, "Even if it were only one *sūrah* it would suffice all of humanity." Then Ṣafwān said, "As for my forcing her to break her fast it is because she keeps fasting and I am a young man and don't have the patience to be without her." To this the Messenger ﷺ said, "A wife should not fast without her husband's agreement." Finally Ṣafwān said, "As for not performing the *fajr* prayer until the sun rises, we are known to be a household that is unable to awake before sunrise!" The Prophet said, "Then pray as soon as you wake up, Ṣafwān." (Abū Dāʾūd & Ibn Mājah)

عن أبي قتادة – رضي الله عنه – : أن النبي – صلى الله عليه وسلم – خرج ليلة فإذا هو بأبي بكر رضي الله عنه يصلي يخفض من صوته، قال و مر بعمر بن الخطاب و هو يصلي رافعا صوته، قال: فلما اجتمعا عند النبي – صلى الله

عليه وسلم – قال: "يا أبا بكر، مررت بك و أنت تصلي تخفض صوتك." قال: قد أسمعت من ناجيت يا رسول الله. قال و قال لعمر: "مررت بك و أنت تصلي رافعا صوتك." قال فقال: يا رسول الله، أوقظ الوسنان، وأطرد الشيطان. زاد الحسن في حديثه فقال النبي – صلى الله عليه وسلم – : "يا أبا بكر، ارفع من صوتك شيئا." وقال لعمر: "اخفض من صوتك شيئا." . رواه أبوداود .

Abū Qatādah ﵁ related that one night the Messenger of God ﷺ passed by Abū Bakr who was praying in a low voice and then he passed by ʿUmar who was praying in a loud voice. Later when Abū Bakr and ʿUmar were both with him, he said to the former, "I passed you when you were praying in a low voice." Abū Bakr said, "The One with whom I was holding intimate conversation heard me, O Messenger of God!" He then turned to ʿUmar and said, "I passed you when you were raising your voice while praying." He replied, "Messenger of God, I was waking the drowsy and driving away the devil." The Prophet said, "Raise your voice a little, Abū Bakr," and to ʿUmar he said, "Lower your voice a little." (Abū Dāʾūd)

عن أبي هريرة – رضي الله عنه – قال: قال رسول الله – صلى الله عليه وسلم – : "يعقد الشيطان على قافية رأس أحدكم إذا هو نام ثلاث عقد، يضرب كلَّ عقدة: عليك ليل طويل فارقد، فإن استيقظ فذكر الله انحلـَّت عقدة، فإن توضأ انحلت عقدة، فإن صلى انحلت عقدة. فأصبح نشيطا طيب النفس، و إلا أصبح خبيث النفس كسلان." رواه البخاري ومسلم

Abū Hurayrah ﵁ reported that the Messenger of God ﷺ said, "When one of you goes to sleep, the devil ties three knots at the back of his neck, sealing each knot with, 'You have a long night, so sleep!' So, if one awakens and remembers God, the first knot will be loosened, and if he performs ablution the second knot will be loosened, and if he prays the last knot will be loosened. And in the morning he will be active and in good spirits. And if he doesn't awaken, he gets up lazy and in bad spirits." (Bukhārī & Muslim)

عن أبي هريرة – رضي الله عنه – قال: قال رسول الله – صلى الله عليه
وسلم – " ينزل ربنا تبارك و تعالى كل ليلة إلى السماء الدنيا حين يبقى ثلث الليل
الآخر، يقول: من يدعوني فأستجيب له؟، من يسألني فأعطيه؟، من يستغفرني
فأغفر له؟." رواه البخاري ومسلم

Abū Hurayrah reported that the Messenger of God ﷺ said, "Our Lord, most blessed and exalted, descends each night to the lowest heaven when the last third of the night remains and says, "Who is supplicating Me that I may respond to him? Who asks of Me that I may give to him? Who asks for My forgiveness that I may forgive him?" (Bukhārī & Muslim)

عن عائشة – رضي الله عنها – قالت: كان رسول الله صلى الله عليه وسلم
ينام أول الليل، و يحيي آخره، ثم إن كانت له حاجة إلى أهله قضى حاجته ثم ينام،
فإذا كان عند النداء الأول وثب فأفاض عليه الماء، و إن لم يكن جُنُبا توضأ
للصلاة ثم صلى ركعتين. رواه البخاري ومسلم

ʿĀʾishah said that the Messenger of God ﷺ would sleep in the early part of the night and keep awake in the latter part. If he then wished for intercourse with his wife, he satisfied his desire and then slept. Then if upon the first call to prayer he was in a state of impurity, he would pour water upon himself; and if he was not, then he would perform ablution, and pray two cycles. (Bukhārī & Muslim)

عن عمرو بن عبسة أنه سمع النبي – صلى الله عليه وسلم – يقول:" أقرب
ما يكون الرب من العبد في جوف الليل الآخر، فإن استطعت أن تكون ممن يذكر
الله في تلك الساعة فكُنْ." رواه الترمذي

The Messenger of God ﷺ said, "The Lord is nearest to the servant in the course of the last part of the night. So if you are able to be among those who remember God at that hour, do so." (Tirmidhī)

عن عائشة – رضي الله عنها – قالت: قال رسول الله – صلى الله عليه وسلم – : "أَحَبُّ الأعمال إلى الله أدومها و إنْ قلَّ." رواه البخاري ومسلم

ᶜĀᵓishah ﷺ reported that the Messenger of God ﷺ said, "The practices most pleasing to God are those which are sustained, even if they are small." (Bukhārī & Muslim)

عن عائشة – رضي الله عنها – قالت: قال – صلى الله عليه وسلم– : " خذوا من الأعمال ما تطيقون، فإن الله لا يَمَلُّ حتى تَمَلُّوا وإن أحبَّ الأعمال إلى الله ما دام وإن قلَّ ." رواه البخاري ومسلم

ᶜĀᵓishah ﷺ also reported that the Messenger of God ﷺ said, "Take on those practices which you have the capacity to sustain, for God does not grow weary unless you do. The practices most pleasing to God are those that endure, even if they are small." (Bukhārī & Muslim)

عن أنس بن مالك – رضي الله عنه – قال: دخل النبي – صلى الله عليه وسلم – : " فإذا حبلٍ ممدود بين الساريتين فقال : ما هذا الحبل قالوا: هذا حبل لزينب فإذا فَتَرَت تعلّقت فقال النبي صلى الله عليه وسلم : لا حُلُّوهُ لِيُصَلِّ أحدكم نشاطه، فإذا فتـر فليقعد." رواه البخاري ومسلم

And Anas ﷺ reported the Messenger of God ﷺ saw a rope hanging between two posts and he asked, "What is this rope?" They told him, "It is rope for Zeinab that she used to hang on to when she gets tired from prayer." The Prophet said, "No, untie it. One should pray as long as one has the energy for it, and if one wanes, then one should rest." (Bukhārī & Muslim)

عن عبد الله بن مسعود رضي الله عنه قال : قال رسول الله – صلى الله عليه وسلم – :"عجب ربنا من رجلين، رجل ثار عن وطائه و لحافه من بين حبه و أهله إلى صلاته، فيقول الله لملائكته: انظروا إلى عبدي، ثار عن فراشه و وطائه

من بين حبه و أهله إلى صلاته رغبة فيما عندي، و شفقة مما عندي." رواه الإمام البغوي في كتاب شرح السنة

The Messenger of God ﷺ said, "Our Sustainer wonders at the man who quits his bed and leaves his beloved and his family for his prayers. God says to His angels: 'Look at my servant and what he does for the sake of what is with Me, and out of concern for what is with Me.'" (Baghawī)

ورد في حديث قتادة عن زرارة أن حكيم بن أفلح وسعد بن هشام بن عامر استأذنا على عائشة رضي الله عنها فأذنت لهما فدخلا عليها فقالت : أحكيمٌ فَعَرَفتهُ فقال : نعم فقالت : من معك ؟ قال سعد بن هشام قالت : من هشام؟ قال : ابن عامر فتَرَحمتْ عليه وقالت خيراً قال قتادة وكان أصيب يوم أحد فقلت : يا أم المؤمنين أنبئيني عن خلق رسول الله – صلى الله عليه وسلم – . قالت: ألست تقرأ القرآن؟. قلت: بلى. قالت: فإن خلق نبي الله – صلى الله عليه وسلم – كان القرآن. أخرجه مسلم

Ḥakīm ibn Aflaḥ and Saʿd ibn Hishām went to ʿĀʾishah and Ḥakīm said; "Mother of the faithful, tell me about the character of God's Messenger ﷺ." She replied, "Do you not recite the Qurʾān?" When he said he did, she said, "The Prophet's character was the Qurʾān." (Muslim)

عن أبي هريرة رضي الله عنه قال : سمعت رسول الله صلى الله عليه وسلم يقول : " لن يُدخل الجنة أحداً عمله قالوا : ولا أنت يا رسول الله قال : ولا أنا إلا أن يتغمدني الله منه بفضل ورحمة فسددوا وقاربوا ولا يتمنى أحدكم الموت إما محسناً فلعله أن يزداد، وأما مسيئاً فلعله أن يستعتب " . رواه البخاري

The Messenger of God said, "No one's acts can lead to Paradise." They asked, "Not even you, Messenger of God?" He said, "Not even me, unless God enfolds me with His favor and mercy. So fulfill your commitments and draw near. Let no one wish for death. If you are one of the righteous, it may be that your blessings will increase, and if you are one of the wrong-doers, it may be that you will repent." (Bukhari)

عن أبي ذر – رضي الله عنه – قال: قال رسول الله – صلى الله عليه وسلم– : "يصبح على كل سُلامَى من أحدكم صدقة، فكل تسبيحة صدقة، و كل تحميدة صدقة، و كل تهليلة صدقة، و كل تكبيرة صدقة، و أمر بالمعروف صدقة، و نـهي عن المنكر صدقة ويجزئ من ذلك ركعتان يركعهما من الضحى ." رواه مسلم

Abū Dharr ﷺ recounted that the Messenger of God ﷺ said, "Each morning, charity is due from every bone in your fingers and toes. Each glorification is charity, and each praise is charity, and each remembrance of God is charity, and each exaltation of God is charity, and each enjoining of good and forbidding of evil is charity. The two cycles of morning prayer are part of this charity." (Muslim)

عن جابر بن عبد الله رضي الله عنهما : قال كان رسول الله – صلى الله عليه وسلم – يعلمنا الاستخارة في الأمور كلها كما يعلمنا السورة من القرآن يقول:" إذا هَمَّ أحدكم بالأمر، فليركع ركعتين من غير الفريضة، ثم ليقل: اللهم إني أستخيرك بعلمك، و أستقدرك بقدرتك، و أسألك من فضلك العظيم، فإنك تقدر ولا أقدر، و تعلم ولا أعلم، و أنت علام الغيوب، اللهم إن كنت تعلم أن هذا الأمر خير لي في ديني و معاشي و عاقبة أمري – أو قال: عاجل أمري و آجله – فأقدره لي، و يسره لي ثم بارك لي فيه، و إن كنت تعلم أن هذا الأمر شر لي في ديني، و معاشي، و عاقبة أمري – أو قال في عاجل أمري و آجله– فاصرفه عني، و اصرفني عنه، و أقدر لي الخير حيث كان، ثم أرضني ." قال:"و يسمي حاجته." رواه البخاري

The Messenger of God ﷺ said, "When one of you is about to undertake an action, he should pray two extra cycles, then say, 'O God, I seek Your guidance by Your knowledge, I ask Your power by Your ability, and I ask You of Your great Abundance; for You have power and I am powerless, You know and I do not know, and You are the One who is aware of the unseen. O God, if You know this matter to be good for my religion, my livelihood, and my future well-being, ordain it for me, make it easy for me, and then bless me in it. But if You know this matter to be bad for me, turn it away from me and turn me away from it. Ordain good for me, wherever it is, then make me content with it.'" (Bukhārī)

عن أبي هريرة – رضي الله عنه – قال: قال رسول الله – صلى الله عليه وسلم –: "إن أول ما يحاسب الناس به يوم القيامة من أعمالهم الصلاة قال : يقول ربنا جل وعز لملائكته وهو أعلم انظروا في صلاة عبدي أتمها أم نقصها فإن كانت تامة كتبت له تامة وإن كان انتقص منها شيئاً قال انظروا هل لعبدي من تطوع فإن كان له تطوع قال أتموا لعبدي فريضته من تطوعه ثم تؤخذ الأعمال على ذاكم فإن صَلُحَت فقد أفلح وأنجح." رواه أبوداود

Abū Hurayrah ﷺ told of hearing God's Messenger ﷺ say, "Prayer is the first deed for which a man will be taken into account on the Day of Resurrection. Our Sustainer the Majestic and Great says to His angels, even though He knows: Look at the prayers of My servant. Did he complete it or diminish it? If it is complete, it is written for him as complete and if he diminished it God says: Look, does My servant have voluntary acts? If he does, God says: Make complete My servant's obligation from his voluntary acts. Then all other deeds follow, so if they are sound, he is made successful and saved." (Abū Dāʾūd)

عن عمار بن ياسر رضي الله عنه : قال إني سمعت رسول الله – صلى الله عليه وسلم – يقول : " إن طول صلاة الرجل و قِصَر خطبته مَئِنَّة من فقهه، فأطيلوا الصلاة، و أقصروا الخطبة، و إن من البيان سِحرا ." رواه مسلم

The Messenger of God ﷺ said, "The length of a man's prayer and the shortness of his sermon are a sign of his understanding. So prolong prayers and shorten sermons. " (Muslim)

عن عبدالله بن عباس – رضي الله عنهما – قالوا: يا رسول الله، رأيناك تناولت شيئا في مقامك هذا ثم رأيناك تكعكعتَ، فقال: "إني رأيت الجنة أو أريت الجنة فتناولت منها عنقودا، و لو أخذته لأكلتم منه ما بقيت الدنيا ." أخرجه البخاري ومسلم

ʿAbd Allāh ibn ʿAbbās ﷺ said that the people said, "Messenger of God, we saw you reach out to something when you were standing here, then we saw you draw back." He replied, "I saw Paradise and reached out for a cluster from it and, had I taken it, you would have eaten of it as long as the world endures." (Bukhārī & Muslim)

عن أنس – رضي الله عنه– قال: أصابنا و نحن مع رسول الله – صلى الله عليه وسلم – مطر، قال: فحسر رسول الله – صلى الله عليه وسلم – ثوبه حتى أصابه من المطر، فقلنا: يارسول الله، لم صنعت هذا ؟، قال " لأنه حديث عهد بربه تعالى ." رواه مسلم

Anas ؓ said, "A shower of rain fell when we were with God's Messenger ﷺ, and he removed his garment until some of the rain fell on him. We asked him why he did this, and he replied, 'Because it has recently come from its Lord.'" (Muslim)

عن أبي هريرة – رضي الله عنه– قال: سمعت رسول الله – صلى الله عليه وسلم – يقول: "خرج نبي من الأنبياء بالناس يستسقي، فإذا هو بنملة رافعة بعض قوائمها إلى السماء، فقال: ارجعوا فقد استجيب لكم من أجل شأن هذه النملة ." رواه الدارقطني

Abū Hurayrah ؓ said, "I heard God's Messenger ﷺ say that a prophet took the people out to pray for rain, and when he saw an ant raising its legs to the sky he said, 'Return! Your prayers have been answered because of this ant.'" (Dārquṭnī)

عن أبي هريرة – رضي الله عنه– قال: قال رسول الله – صلى الله عليه وسلم – :" حق المسلم على المسلم ست." قيل: ما هن يا رسول الله ؟. قال: " إذا لقيته فسلم عليه، و إذا دعاك فأجبه، و إذا استنصحك فانصح له، و إذا عطس فحمد الله فشمته، و إذا مرض فَعُدْهُ، و إذا مات فاتَّبعه ." رواه مسلم

Abū Hurayrah رضي الله عنه reported that the Messenger of God ﷺ said, "A Muslim has six rights over you." He was asked what these were and he said, "When you meet him salute him; when he calls upon you, respond to him; when he asks your advice, advise him; when he sneezes and praises God, say 'God have mercy on you!'; when he is ill, visit him; and when he dies, accompany him to his grave." (Muslim)

عن أبي هريرة – رضي الله عنه– قال: قال رسول الله – صلى الله عليه وسلم – :" إن الله عز وجل يقول يوم القيامة: يا ابن آدم، مرضت فلم تعدني . قال: يا رب كيف أعودك و أنت رب العالمين ؟. قال: أما علمت أن عبدي فلانا مرض فلم تعده، أما علمت أنك لو عُدته لوجدتني عنده ؟، يا ابن آدم ، استطعمتك فلم تطعمني . قال: يا رب كيف أطعمك و أنت رب العالمين؟ .قال: أما علمت أنه استطعمك عبدي فلان فلم تطعمه، أما علمت أنك لو أطعمته لوجدت ذلك عندي ؟ يا ابن آدم، استسقيتك فلم تسقني . قال: يارب كيف أسقيك و أنت رب العالمين ؟. قال:استسقاك عبدي فلان فلم تسقه,أما علمت أنك لو سقيته لوجدت ذلك عندي ؟." رواه مسلم

Abū Hurayrah رضي الله عنه said that the Messenger of God ﷺ said, "On the Day of Resurrection, God most high will say, 'O Son of Adam, I was sick and you did not visit me.' He will reply, 'My Lord, how could I visit You when You are the Lord of the worlds?' He will say, 'Did you not know that my servant so-and-so was ill, and yet you did not visit him? Did you not know that if you had visited him you would have found Me with him? O Son of Adam, I asked you for food but you gave me none.' He will reply, 'My Lord, how could I feed You when You are the Lord of the worlds?' He will say, 'Did you not know that my servant so-and-so asked you for food and yet you gave him none? Did you not know that, if you had fed him, you would have found the same with Me? O Son of Adam, I asked you for drink but you gave me none.' He will reply, 'My Lord, how could I give you to drink when You are the Lord of the worlds?' He will say, 'Did you not know that my servant so-and-so asked you for drink and yet you gave him none? Did you not know that, if you had given him water, you would have found the same with Me?'" (Muslim)

عن أبي سعيد وأبي هريرة رضي الله عنهما : قال رسول الله – صلى الله عليه وسلم – :" ما يصيب المسلم من نَصَبٍ، ولا وَصَبٍ، ولا هَمٍّ، ولا حَزَنٍ، ولا أذى، ولا غَمٍّ حتى الشوكة يُشاكها إلا كفَّر الله بها من خطاياه ." أخرجه البخاري ومسلم

The Messenger of God ﷺ said, "No Muslim is afflicted by difficulty, continuous pain, anxiety, grief, injury, or depression, or even by a thorn with which he is pierced, without God making it an atonement for his sins." (Bukhārī & Muslim)

عن كعب بن مالك عن أبيه – رضي الله عنهما – قال: قال رسول الله – صلى الله عليه وسلم – :" مَثل المؤمن كمثل الخامة من الزرع تفيئها الرياح، تصرعها مرة و تعدلها أخرى، حتى تهيج يأتيه أجله، و مَثل المنافق مَثَلُ الأرزة المجذية التي لايصيبها شيء حتى يكون انجعافها مرة واحدة ." أخرجه البخاري ومسلم

Kaᶜb ibn Mālik ؓ related that the Messenger of God ﷺ said, "The faithful one is like a tender plant, swayed back and forth by the winds, sometimes being bent down and sometimes made to stand up straight, until his appointed time comes; but the hypocrite is like a cedar tree standing firmly, which is unaffected by anything until it is uprooted at once from the ground." (Bukhārī & Muslim)

عن جابر بن عبد الله أن رسول الله – صلى الله عليه وسلم – دخل على أم السائب أو أم المسيب فقال: " مالك يا أم السائب أو يا أم المسيب تـُزفزفين ؟." قالت: الحُمَّى. لا بارك الله فيها، فقال: "لا تسبي الحُمَّى، فإنها تـُذهِبُ خطايا بني آدم، كما يُذهِبُ الكِيرُ خَبَثَ الحديد ." رواه مسلم .

The Messenger of God ﷺ visited Umm Aṣ-Ṣāʾib, who was sick, and asked her, "Why are you fluttering like this?" She replied, "Fever, may God curse it." He said, "Do not revile fever, for it removes the sins of the children of Adam, just as the bellows remove the impurities from iron." (Muslim)

عن أمية أنها سألت عائشة – رضي الله عنها – عن قول الله تعالى " إن تبدوا ما في أنفسكم أو تخفوه يحاسبكم به الله " وعن قوله " من يعمل سوءا يُجزَ به " فقالت: ما سألني عنها أحد منذ سألت رسول الله – صلى الله عليه وسلم – فقال: "هذه معاتبة الله العبد فيما يصيبه من الحُمَّى و النكبة، حتى البضاعةُ يضعُها في كمِّ قميصه فيفقدها فيفزع لها، حتى إن العبد ليخرج من ذنوبه كما يخرج التبر الأحمر من الكير." رواه الترمذي .

Umayyah asked ʿĀʾishah ﵂ about the verses *Whether you reveal what is in your selves or coneal it, God takes you to account for it (Sūrah al-Baqarah* 2:284) and *whoever does evil will be requited for it* (*Sūrah al-Nisāʾ* 4:123). She said, "No one has asked me about this since I myself asked the Messenger of God ﷺ about it, and he said, 'It is the admonishment of the servant by God through affliction of fever or misfortune, or even loss of goods over which he is in distress. This continues until the servant comes out from his sins as the pure gold comes out of the crucible.'" (Tirmidhī)

عن عبد الله بن مغفل رضي الله عنه قال : قال رسول الله – صلى الله عليه وسلم – : " إن عِظَمَ الجزاء مع عِظَمَ البلاء، و إن الله عز وجل إذا أحب قوما ابتلاهم فمن رضي فله الرضا، و من سخط فله السخط ." رواه الترمذي و ابن ماجه .

The Messenger of God ﷺ said, "The greater the trial, the greater the reward. When God, who is great and glorious, loves people, he afflicts them. And those who accept it will receive contentment, but those who are discontent will receive displeasure." (Tirmidhī & Ibn Mājah)

عن عامر الرام رضي الله عنه قال : ذَكَرَ رسول الله – صلى الله عليه وسلم – الأسقام فقال:" إن المؤمن إذا أصابه السقم، ثم أعفاهُ الله منه، كان كفَّارة لما مضى من ذنوبه، و موعظة له فيما يستقبل، وإنَّ المنافق إذا مرض ثم أعفي كان كالبعير عَقله أهله ثم أرسلوه، فلم يَدرِلِمَ عقلوه ولَمْ يدرِ لِمَ أرسلوه ." فقال رجل ممن حوله : يا رسول الله و ما الأسقام ؟، و الله ما مرضت قط . فقال رسول الله صلى الله عليه وسلم : " قم عنا، فلست منا ." رواه أبوداود.

The Messenger of God ﷺ recalled afflictions and said, "When a believer is afflicted by illness and then Allāh causes him to recover from it, the illness is absolution for his past sins and admonishment for his future. But when a hypocrite becomes ill and then is cured, he is like a camel that has been tethered and then let loose by its owners, but does not know why they tethered it and why they let it loose." When a man asked God's Messenger what illnesses were, swearing he had never been ill, he said, "Get up and leave us; you are not one of us!" (Abū Dā'ūd)

عن أبي سعيد الخدري قال : قال رسول الله – صلى الله عليه وسلم– : " إذا دخلتم على المريض فنفِّسوا له في أجَله، فإن ذلك لا يرد شيئا و يطيب نفسهُ ." رواه الترمذي و ابن ماجه .

The Messenger of God ﷺ said, "When you go in to visit the ill, show how much you value his life. That will not avert anything, but it will comfort him." (Tirmidhī & Ibn Mājah)

عن جابر بن عبد الله – رضي الله عنه قال – قال رسول الله – صلى الله عليه وسلم – :" من عاد مريضا، لم يزل يخوض في الرحمة حتى يجلس فإذا جلس اغتمس فيها ." رواه مالك و أحمد .

Jābir ﷺ reported that the Messenger of God ﷺ said, "Whoever goes to visit a person who is ill, it is as if he plunges into mercy until he sits with the person; and when he sits down, he is immersed in this mercy." (Mālik & Aḥmad)

عن أنس رضي الله عنه قال : قال رسول الله – صلى الله عليه وسلم – : " لايتمنين أحدكم الموت من ضُرٍّ أصابه، فإذا كان لابد فاعلا فليقل: اللهم أحيني ما كانت الحياة خيرا لي و توفني إذا كانت الوفاة خيرا لي ." رواه البخاري ومسلم .

The Messenger of God ﷺ said, "Let none of you wish for death because of an affliction that may strike you. If you must wish for something, then say, 'O my God, give me life as long as life is good for me, and take me back to You if returning to You is better for me.'" (Bukhārī & Muslim)

تابع: عن أبي قتادة بن ربعي الأنصاري– رضي الله عنه– أنه كان يحدث أن رسول الله – صلى الله عليه وسلم – مُرَّ عليه بجنازة قال: " مستريح و مستراح منه." قالوا: يا رسول الله، ما المستريح و المستراح منه ؟. قال: " العبد المؤمن يستريح من نَصَب الدنيا وأذاها إلى رحمة الله، و العبد الفاجر يستريح منه العباد، والبلاد، والشجر، والدواب." رواه البخاري ومسلم

Abū Qatādah ﷺ reported that when a funeral passed, God's Messenger ﷺ said, "He has either been relieved or others have been relieved of him!" They asked him about this and he replied, "The faithful servant is relieved, by God's Mercy, from the hardship and hurt of this world. As for the tyrannical servant, the rest of us are relieved of his harm, including the land, trees, and animals." (Bukhārī & Muslim)

عن عبد الله بن عمر – رضي الله عنهما– قال: أخذ رسول الله – صلى الله عليه وسلم – بمنكبي فقال: "كُنْ في الدنيا كأنك غريب أو عابر سبيل." و كان ابن عمر يقول: إذا أمسيت فلا تنتظر الصباح، و إذا أصبحت فلا تنتظر المساء، و خُذ من صحتك لمرضك، و من حياتك لموتك . رواه البخاري .

ᶜAbdullāh ibn ᶜUmar ﷺ said that God's Messenger ﷺ took him by the shoulders and said, "Be in the world as though you were a stranger or a passing traveler." And Ibn ᶜUmar, who told this, used to say, "If you reach the evening, do not expect to see the morning; and if you reach the morning, do not expect to see the evening. Take something, when in health, to serve you in time of sickness; and something in your life to serve you in your death." (Bukhārī)

عن عبد الله بن عمرو – رضي الله عنهما– قال: قال رسول الله – صلى الله عليه وسلم – :" تحفة المؤمن الموت." رواه البيهقي .

ᶜAbdullāh ibn ᶜUmar ﷺ also said that the Messenger of God ﷺ said, "Death is a gift for the faithful." (Bayhaqī)

تابع – عن أنس – رضي الله عنه– أن النبي – صلى الله عليه وسلم – دخل على شاب و هو في الموت، فقال: " كيف تَجِدُك ؟." قال: والله يا رسول الله إني أرجو الله ، و إني أخاف ذنوبي. فقال رسول الله – صلى الله عليه وسلم – : " لايجتمعان في قلب عبد في مثل هذا الموطن، إلا أعطاه الله مايرجو و أمَّنَه مما يخاف." رواه الترمذي و ابن ماجه .

Anas ﷺ said that the Messenger of God ﷺ visited a young man who was dying and asked him how he was. "I wish for God, O Messenger of God, and I am fearful regarding my sins." He said, "The two cannot come together in a man's heart at a time like this without God giving him what he hopes for and granting him security from what he fears." (Tirmidhī & Ibn Mājah)

عن عائشة – رضي الله عنها – أن النبي – صلى الله عليه وسلم – قبَّل عثمان بن مظعون و هو ميت، و هو يبكي أو قال عيناه تذرفان . رواه الترمذي و أبوداود

ᶜĀʾishah ﷺ said that God's Messenger ﷺ kissed ᶜUthmān ibn Mazᶜūn when he was dead, and that he wept so much that his tears flowed over ʿUthmān's face. (Tirmidhī, Abū Dāʾūd)

عن البراء بن عازب – رضي الله عنه – قال: خرجنا مع النبي – صلى الله عليه وسلم – في جنازة رجل من الأنصار فانتهينا إلى القبر، و لما يلحد، فجلس رسول الله – صلى الله عليه وسلم – و جلسنا حوله، وكأن على رؤوسنا الطير، و في يده عود ينكت في الأرض، فرفع رأسه فقال: " استعيذوا بالله من عذاب القبر ." مرتين أو ثلاثا، ثم قال:" إن العبد المؤمن إذا كان في انقطاع من الدنيا، و إقبال من الآخرة، نزل إليه ملائكة من السماء بيض الوجوه، كأن وجوههم الشمس، معهم كفن من أكفان الجنة ، وحنوط من حنوط الجنة حتى يجلسوا منه مَدَّ البصر، ثم يجئ ملك الموت عليه السلام، حتى يجلس عند رأسه، فيقول: أيتها النفس الطيبة، اخرجي إلى مغفرة من الله و رضوان، قال: فتخرج تسيل كما تسيل القطرة من فيِّ السِّقاء، فيأخذها، فإذا أخذها لم يدعوها في يده طرفة عين حتى يأخذوها، فيجعلوها في ذلك الكفن و في ذلك الحنوط ، و يخرج منها كأطيب نفحة مسك وُجِدَتْ على وجه الأرض ."، قال:" فيصعدون بها، فلا يمرون – يعني بها– على ملأ من الملائكة إلا قالوا: ما هذا الروح الطيب ؟. فيقولون فلان بن فلان، بأحسن أسمائه التي كانوا يسمونه بها في الدنيا، حتى ينتهوا بها إلى السماء الدنيا، فيستفتحون له، فيفتح لهم، فيشيعه من كل سماء مقربوها إلى السماء التي تليها، حتى يُنْتَهى به الى السماء السابعة، فيقول الله عز وجل: اكتبوا كتاب عبدي في عليين و أعيدوه إلى الأرض فإني منها خلقتهم، و فيها أعيدهم، و منها أخرجهم تارة أخرى ." قال: " فتعاد روحه في جسده، فيأتيه ملكان، فيجلسانه، فيقولان له: مَنْ ربك ؟. فيقول: ربي الله فيقولان له: ما دينك ؟. فيقول: ديني الإسلام . فيقولان له: ما هذا الرجل الذي بُعِث فيكم ؟ . فيقول: هو رسول الله – صلى الله عليه وسلم – فيقولان له: و ما علمك؟ فيقول: قرأت كتاب الله فآمنت به و صدقت .فينادي مناد في السماء: أن صدق عبدي، فأفرشوه من الجنة، و ألبسوه من الجنة، و افتحوا له بابا إلى الجنة ". قال: " فيأتيه من روحها و طيبها، فيفسح له في قبره مد بصره." قال: " و يأتيه رجل حسن الوجه، حسن الثياب، طيب الريح، فيقول: أبشر بالذي يسرك، هذا يومك الذي كنت توعد . فيقول له: من أنت ؟ فوجهك الوجه يجئ بالخير. فيقول: أنا عملك الصالح. فيقول: رب أقم الساعة، حتى أرجع إلى أهلي و مالي ." قال: " و إن العبد الكافر إذا كان في انقطاع من الدنيا، و إقبال من الآخرة، نزل إليه من السماء ملائكة سود الوجوه، معهم المسوح، فيجلسون منه مَدَّ البصر ، ثم يجئ ملك الموت، حتى يجلس عند رأسه، فيقول: أيتها النفس الخبيثة، اخرجي إلى سخط من الله وغضبه ." قال: فتفرق في جسده فينتزعها كما ينتزع السفود من الصوف المبلول، فيأخذها فإذا أخذها لم يَدعوها في يده طرفة عين، حتى يجعلوها في تلك المسوح، و يخرج منها كأنتن ريح جيفة وجدت على وجه الأرض، فيصعدون بها، فلا يمرون بها على ملأ من الملائكة إلا قالوا: ما هذا الروح الخبيث ؟ فيقولون: فلان بن فلان، بأقبح أسمائه التي كان يُسمَّى بها في الدنيا، حتى يُنتهى به إلى السماء الدنيا، فيستفتح له، فلا يفتح له. ثم قرأ رسول الله – صلى الله عليه وسلم – : { لا تفتح لهم أبواب السماء

ولا يدخلون الجنة حتى يلج الجمل في سم الخياط } فيقول الله عز وجل: اكتبوا كتابه في سجين، في الأرض السفلى، فتطرح روحه طرحا."، ثم قرأ {و من يشرك بالله فكأنما خر من السماء فتخطفه الطير أو تهوي به الريح في مكان سحيق}." فتعاد روحه في جسده، و يأتيه ملكان فيجلسانه، فيقولان له: من ربك ؟. فيقول: هاه، لا أدري . فيقولان له: ما دينك ؟. فيقول: هاه هاه، لا أدري . فيقولان له: ما هذا الرجل الذي بعث فيكم ؟. فيقول: هاه، لا أدري . فينادي مناد من السماء: أن كذب فافرشوا له من النار، و افتحوا له بابا إلى النار، فيأتيه من حرها و سمومها، و يضيق عليه قبره حتى تختلف فيه أضلاعه، و يأتيه رجل قبيح الوجه، قبيح الثياب، منتن الريح، فيقول: أبشر بالذي يسوءك، هذا يومك الذي كنت توعد. فيقول من أنت؟، فوجهك الوجه يجئ بالشر. فيقول: أنا عملك الخبيث . فيقول: رب، لا تقم الساعة ." رواه أحمد

We accompanied the Prophet ﷺ to the funeral of one of the Companions. At the grave we sat quietly around the Prophet who was drawing on the ground with a stick. Then he raised his head and said, "Seek refuge with Allāh from the torment of the grave.

"When the faithful servant's time ends, angels with sunlit faces will descend upon him as far as the eye can see with a heavenly shroud and heavenly burial ointments. Then the Angel of Death will sit at his head and will say, 'O good soul, come forth to forgiveness and contentment from Allāh.' And the soul will flow as easily as a drop of water. And it is swiftly placed into the shroud and covered with the burial ointments, and the sweetest scent of musk will come from it. Then the angels will ascend with it, and as they pass by other angels, they will ask them, 'What is this sweet scent?' And they will tell them who the person was, referring to him by his best qualities. They will continue to ascend with the good soul until they reach the seventh heaven, and God will say, 'Record the book of My Servant in the Highest of the High. Then return him to the earth, for I created them from it and to it I return them, and from it shall I bring them forth anew.' So the spirit is returned to his body. And two angels come to him and ask him, 'Who is your Lord?' He will reply, 'Allāh is my Lord.' They will ask him, 'And what is your religion?' He will reply, 'My religion is submission (Islām).' And they will ask, 'Who is this man who was sent to you?' He will reply, 'He is Allāh's Messenger ﷺ.' They will ask him, 'What is your knowledge?' He will reply, 'I read Allāh's Book and had faith in it and believed in it.' Then a sound from Heaven will announce, 'My Servant is truthful. Spread things out for him from Heaven, clothe him from Heaven, and open for him a door to Heaven.' And he will then smell its scent and sense its breath and his grave will be widened as far as the sight can see. And a man with a beautiful face, beautiful garments, and sweet scent will come to him and say, 'Be glad, for this is your promised day!' He will ask, 'Who are you?' The man will reply, 'I am your good deeds!' Then the deceased will cry out, 'My Lord, bring about the Hour!'

"As for the one who is in denial, when his time ends and he is facing the end, angels from Heaven with dark faces will descend upon him as far as the eye can see, and they will have a burial cloth of coarse hair. Then the Angel of Death will sit at his head and will say, 'O wicked soul! Come forth to Allāh's displeasure.' And the soul will scatter within his body but the Angel of Death will rip it out and he will not keep it in his hands for even a blink of an eye before they place it in the coarse burial cloth, and the worst smell of a stinking corpse will rise from it. Then the angels will ascend with it, and as they pass by other angels they will ask them what is this wicked soul, and they will tell them who the person was, referring to him by his worst qualities until they reach the lowest heaven. They will ask for it to be opened on his behalf, but it will not be opened for him. *The gates of Heaven will not be opened for them and they shall not enter Paradise until the camel passes through the eye of the needle* (*Sūrah al-Aᶜrāf* 7:40). And Allāh will say, 'Record his book in *Sijjīn* in the lowest earth. And so his soul will be flung down, *For whoever associates others with Allāh is like one who falls from the sky and is snatched by birds or is thrown by the wind into a desolate place* (*Sūrah al-Ḥajj* 22:31). Thus his soul will be returned to his body and two angels will come to him and ask him, 'Who is your Lord?' He will reply, 'Oh, oh, I don't know!' They will ask him, 'And what is your religion?' He will reply, 'Oh, oh, I don't know!' And they will ask, 'Who is this man who was sent to you?' He will reply, 'Oh, oh, I don't know!' Then a caller from Heaven will announce, 'He lies! Spread things out for him from the Fire, and open for him a door to the Fire.' And he will receive its heat and poison, and his grave will become constricted until his limbs are twisted upon one another. And a man with an ugly face, ugly garments, and awful smell will come to him and say, 'Be warned, for this is the day of your harm!' He will ask, 'Who are you?' The man will reply, 'I am your wicked deeds!' Then the deceased will cry out, 'My Lord, do not bring about the Hour!'" (Aḥmad)

عن أبي هريرة – رضي الله عنه– أن امرأة سوداء كانت تَقُمُّ المسجد أو شابا ففقدها رسول الله – صلى الله عليه وسلم – فسأل عنها، أو عنه، فقالوا: مات. قال: " أفلا كنتم آذنتموني؟ " قال: فكأنهم صغروا أمرها أو أمره فقال: "دلوني على قبره." فدلّوه فصلى عليها، ثم قال: إن هذه القبور مملوءة ظلمة على أهلها، و إن الله عز وجل ينورها لهم بصلاتي عليهم ." رواه البخاري ومسلم

Abū Hurayrah ﷺ said a negress used to sweep the mosque. God's Messenger ﷺ missed her, and when he asked about her, the people told him she had died. He asked why they had not informed him, for it appeared as if they had treated her as of little account. He asked the people to lead him to the grave, and when they did so he prayed over her and then told them, "These graves are filled with darkness for its occupants and Allāh lights it up for them through my prayers." (Bukhārī & Muslim)

عن عبد الرحمن بن أبي ليلى قال كان سهل بن حنيف، و قيس بن سعد قاعدين بالقادسية، فمروا عليهما بجنازة فقاما، فقيل لهما: إنها من أهل الأرض، أي من أهل الذمة، فقالا: إن النبي – صلى الله عليه وسلم – مرت به جنازة فقام، فقيل له: إنها جنازة يهودي فقال:" أليست نفسا ؟." رواه البخاري ومسلم

Sahl ibn Ḥanīf and Qays ibn Saᶜd were sitting in Qadissiyah when a funeral procession passed by them and they stood up in respect for the dead. They were told that the deceased was not a Muslim. So they replied, "A bier came past God's Messenger ﷺ and he stood up. He was then told it contained a Jew. He said, 'Is it not a soul?'" (Bukhārī & Muslim)

عن أنس بن مالك – رضي الله عنه– قال: دخلنا مع رسول الله – صلى الله عليه وسلم – على أبي سيف القين، و كان ظئرا لإبراهيم عليه السلام فأخذ رسول الله – صلى الله عليه وسلم – إبراهيم فقبّله و شمّه، ثم دخلنا عليه بعد ذلك و إبراهيم يجود بنفسه، فجعلت عينا رسول الله – صلى الله عليه وسلم – تذرفان فقال له عبدالرحمن بن عوف رضي الله عنه : و أنت يا رسول الله ؟. فقال " يا ابن عوف ، إنها رحمة ." ثم أتبعها بأخرى، فقال صلى الله عليه وسلم : " إن

العين تدمع، والقلب يحزن، ولا نقول إلا ما يَرضَى ربنا، و إنَّا بفراقك يا إبراهيم لمحزونون." رواه البخاري ومسلم

Anas ﷺ said, We went in with God's Messenger ﷺ to visit Abū Sayf, the smith, who was foster-father to Ibrāhīm (the Prophet's son, who died in infancy). And God's Messenger picked up Ibrāhīm, kissed him, and smelled him. We went to visit him later, when Ibrāhīm was giving up his soul, and tears began to fall from God's Messenger's eyes; whereupon Ibn ʿAwf said to him: "You, too, Messenger of God?" He replied, "Ibn ʿAwf, it is compassion!" Then he shed more tears, and said, "The eye weeps and the heart grieves, but we say only that with which our Lord is pleased; and we are grieved over being separated from you, Ibrāhīm." (Bukhārī & Muslim)

عن أسامة بن زيد – رضي الله عنهما – قال: أرسلت ابنة النبي – صلى الله عليه وسلم إليه – : أن ابنا لي قبض فائتنا. فأرسل يُقرِئ السلام و يقول: "إن لله ما أخذ، و له ما أعطى، و كل عنده بأجل مسمى، فلتصبر ولتحتسب." فأرسلتْ إليه تقسم عليه ليأتينها، فقام و معه سعد بن عباده، و معاذ بن جبل، و أبي بن كعب، و زيد بن ثابت و رجال، فرفع إلى رسول الله – صلى الله عليه وسلم الصبي – و نفسه تتقعقع، قال حسبته أنه قال كأنها شَنٌّ ففاضت عيناه . فقال سعد: يا رسول الله، ما هذا ؟. فقال: "هذه رحمة، جعلها الله في قلوب عباده، وإنما يرحم الله من عباده الرحماء." رواه البخاري ومسلم

Usāmah bin Zayd ﷺ related that the Prophet's daughter sent a message to him saying that a son of hers was dying and asking him to come to them. He sent her a greeting, saying at the same time, "What God has taken belongs to Him, what He has given belongs to Him, and He has an appointed time for everyone, so let her show endurance and seek her reward from God." She then sent a message, imploring him to come to her. So he came with several of his Companions. The boy, who was on the point of death, was lifted up to God's Messenger ﷺ, whose eyes overflowed with tears. Saʿd said, "What is this, Messenger of God?" He replied, "This is compassion, which God has placed in the heart of His servants. God shows compassion to those of His servants who are compassionate." (Bukhārī & Muslim)

عن معاوية بن قرة عن أبيه : أن رجلا كان يأتي النبي – صلى الله عليه وسلم – و معه ابن له. فقال له النبي – صلى الله عليه وسلم:"أتحبه؟" فقال: "يا رسول الله، أحبك الله كما أحبه." ففقده النبي – صلى الله عليه وسلم – فقال لي :"ما فعل ابن فلان ؟." قالوا: يا رسول الله، مات. فقال النبي – صلى الله عليه وسلم – :" لأبيه أما تحب أن لا تأتي بابا من أبواب الجنة إلا وجدته ينتظرك؟." فقال الرجل : يا رسول الله، أله خاصة أم لكلنا ؟ . قال: "بل لكلكم ." رواه أحمد

The Prophet ﷺ asked a man who used to come to him along with his son whether he loved his son, and the man replied, "O Messenger of God, may God love you as I love him!" The Prophet missed him, and on inquiring what had happened to the man's son was told that he had died. Thereupon he said, "Would you not like to find him waiting for you, no matter to which gate of Paradise you came?" Upon hearing this one of the people asked, "Is this for him in particular, or for all of us?" whereupon the Prophet replied, "It is for all of you." (Aḥmad)

Generosity, Kindness and Zakāt

عن الزبير بن العوام – رضي الله عنه– قال: قال رسول الله – صلى الله عليه وسلم – :" لأن يأخذ أحدكم حبلا فيأتي فيأخذ حزمة من حطب فيبيع ، فيكف الله به وجهه، خير من أن يسأل الناس أعطي أو منع ." رواه البخاري

The Messenger of God ﷺ said, "It is better for one of you to take his rope, bring a load of firewood on his back and sell it, God thereby preserving his self-respect, than that he should beg from people, whether they give to him or not." (Bukhārī)

عن حكيم بن حزام – رضي الله عنه– قال: سألت رسول الله – صلى الله عليه وسلم – فأعطاني، ثم سألته فأعطاني، ثم قال لي: " يا حكيم، إن هذا المال خضر حُلْو، فمن أخذه بسخاوة نفس بورك له فيه، و من أخذه بإ شراف نفس لم يُبارك له فيه، و كان كالذي يأكل ولا يشبع، و اليد العليا خير من اليد السفلى ." قال حكيم: فقلت: يا رسول الله، و الذي بعثك بالحق لا أرزأ أحدا بعدك شيئا حتى أفارق الدنيا فكان أبو بكر يدعو حكيماً ليعطيه العطاء فيأبى أن يقبل منه شيئاً ثم إن عمر دعاه ليعطيه فيأبى أن يقبله فقال : يا معشر المسلمين إني أعرض عليه حقه الذي قسم الله له من هذا الفيء فيأبى أن يأخذه فلم يرزأ حكيم أحداً من الناس بعد النبي صلى الله عليه وسلم حتى توفي رحمه الله . رواه البخاري ومسلم

Ḥakīm ibn Ḥizām ؓ said he asked for something from God's Messenger ﷺ, and he gave to him; and he asked again and he gave to him. And then he said to him, "Ḥakīm, this wealth is green and sweet, and he who receives it with a generous soul will be blessed in it; but he who receives it with an avaricious soul will not be blessed in it, being like one who eats without being satisfied. And the hand that gives is better than the hand that takes." Hearing this Ḥakīm said to him, "O Messenger of Allāh, by the One who sent you with the truth, I will never take anything from anyone after you until I leave this life." Later Abū Bakr would summon Ḥakīm to give money to him but he would decline and afterwards ʿUmar summoned him to give him money and still he declined whereupon

ʿUmar declared, "O Muslims, I offer him his right which God has apportioned to him from this treasury but he refuses it!" And so did Ḥakīm not accept anything from anyone after the Prophet until he died. (Bukhārī & Muslim)

عن أنس بن مالك – رضي الله عنه– أن رجلا من الأنصار أتى النبي – صلى الله عليه وسلم – يسأله، فقال: " أما في بيتك شئ ؟ ." قال: بلى، حِلسٌ نلبس بعضه و نبسط بعضه، و قعب نشرب فيه من الماء . قال: " ائتني بهما قال ." فأتاه بهما، فأخذهما رسول الله – صلى الله عليه وسلم – بيده، و قال: "من يشتري هذين ؟." قال رجل: أنا آخذهما بدرهم . قال: " من يزيد على درهم ." مرتين أو ثلاثا، قال رجل: أنا آخذهما بدرهمين، فأعطاهما إياه وأخذ الدرهمين، وأعطاهما الأنصاري وقال:" اشتر بأحدهما طعاما، فانبذه إلى أهلك، و اشتر بالآخر قدوما، فائتني به." فأتاه به، فشد فيه رسول الله – صلى الله عليه وسلم – عودا بيده ثم قال له : " اذهب فاحتطب و بع، ولا أرينك خمسة عشر يوما ." فذهب الرجل يحتطب و يبيع، فجاء و قد أصاب عشرة دراهم، فاشترى ببعضها ثوبا، و ببعضها طعاما، فقال رسول الله – صلى الله عليه وسلم – : " هذا خير لك من أن تجيء المسألةُ نكتة في وجهك يوم القيامة، إن المسألة لا تصلح إلا لثلاثة: لذي فقر مدقع، أو لذي غرم مفظع، أو لذي دم مُوجع ." رواه أبوداود و روى ابن ماجه إلى قوله "يوم القيامة."

Anas ﵁ said that a man of the Anṣār came to the Prophet ﷺ and begged from him. He asked him whether he had anything in his house. When he replied that he had a cloth, part of which he wore and part of which he spread on the ground, and a wooden bowl from which he drank water, God's Messenger told him to bring them to him. When he did so, he took them in his hand and said, "Who will buy these?" When a man offered a dirham, he asked twice or thrice, "Who will offer more than a dirham?" and he gave them to a man who offered two. He then gave the two dirham to the Anṣārī and said to him, "Buy food with one of them and give it to your family, and buy an axe with the other and bring it to me." When he brought the axe, God's Messenger fixed a handle on it with his own hand, and said, "Go gather firewood and sell it, and don't let me see you for a fortnight." So the man went to work cutting wood and selling it. He returned to the Prophet after fifteen days, having earned ten dirham with which he bought food and clothes. The Prophet told him, "This is better for you than to have your begging strike your face on the Day of Resurrection. Begging is acceptable in only three cases: to one who is in abject poverty, or one who is under a distressing debt, or one who is suffering from painful disease." (Abū Dāʾūd)

عن أسماء – رضي الله عنها – قالت: قال رسول الله – صلى الله عليه وسلم – : "أنفقي ولا تُحصي فيحصي الله عليك، ولا توعي فيوعي الله عليك، ." رواه البخاري ومسلم

The Messenger of God ﷺ said to ʿAṣmāʾ ؓ, daughter of Abū Bakr, "Give without calculating lest God calculate concerning you; and don't hold back, lest God hold back from you. Give as much as you are able." (Bukhārī & Muslim)

عن أبي ذر – رضي الله عنه – قال: انتهيت إلى النبي – صلى الله عليه وسلم – و هو في ظل الكعبة، يقول:" هم الأخسرون و رب الكعبة." هم الآخرون قلت ما شأني أيرى فيَّ شيء ما شأني فجلست إليه وهو يقول فما استطعت أن أسكت وتغشاني ما شاء الله فقلت من هم بأبي أنت وأمي يا رسول الله ؟. قال:" الأكثرون أموالا، إلا من قال: هكذا وهكذا و هكذا، من بين يديه، و من خلفه، و عن يمينه، و عن شماله، و قليل ما هم." رواه البخاري

Abū Dharr ؓ said, "I came to the Prophet ﷺ when he was sitting in the shade of the Kaʿbah, and heard him say, 'By the Lord of the Kaʿbah, they are the ones who suffer the greatest loss!' I wondered if something was wrong with me, and if he meant me. So I sat next to him and could not remain silent, and so I said to him, 'I would sacrifice my mother and father for you! Who are "they?"' He replied, '"They" are those who have the most wealth; except those who give in every way they can, but how very few those are!'" (Bukhārī & Muslim)

عن أبي هريرة – رضي الله عنه – قال: قال رسول الله – صلى الله عليه وسلم – : "السَّخِيُّ قريب من الله قريب من الجنة، قريب من الناس بعيد من النار،

و البخيل بعيد من الله، بعيد من الجنة، بعيد من الناس قريب من النار، و لجاهل سَخِيٌّ أحب إلى الله عز وجل من عالم بخيل." رواه الترمذي

Abū Hurayrah ﷺ reported that the Messenger of God ﷺ said, "The generous man is close to God, close to Paradise, close to people, and far from Hell; while the stingy man is far from God, far from Paradise, far from people, and close to Hell. Verily, a generous ignorant man is more beloved to Allāh than a stingy scholar." (Tirmidhī)

عن أبي بكر الصديق – رضي الله عنه – قال: قال رسول الله – صلى الله عليه وسلم – : " لا يدخل الجنة خِبٌّ ولا منان، ولا بخيل." رواه الترمذي

Abū Bakr Aṣ-Ṣādiq ﷺ reported that the Messenger of God ﷺ said, "Those who are crooked, and those who are stingy, and those who like to recount their favors upon others cannot enter Paradise." (Tirmidhī)

عن عائشة – رضي الله عنها– أن بعض أزواج النبي – صلى الله عليه وسلم – قلن للنبي – صلى الله عليه وسلم – : أيُّنا أسرع بك لحوقا؟ قال: "أطولكن يدا." فأخذوا قصبة يذرعونها، و كانت سَودَة أطولهن يدا، فعلِمنا بعد أنَّما كان طول يدها الصدقة، و كانت أسرعنا لحوقا به زينب، و كانت تحب الصدقة." رواه البخاري

ʿĀʾishah ﷺ said that when some of the wives of the Prophet asked him which of them would join him soonest, he replied that it would be the one with the longest reach. So they took a rod and measured their arms and found that Sawdah had the longest reach. Later they came to understand that charity was what he meant by "the longest reach," for Zaynab was the one who joined him soonest, and she loved giving charity. (Bukhārī)

عن أبي هريرة رضي الله عنه : قال رسول الله – صلى الله عليه وسلم– : " من أنفق زوجين من شئ من الأشياء في سبيل الله، دُعِيَ من أبواب يعني الجنة ،

يا عبد الله هذا خير فمن كان من أهل الصلاة دُعِـيَ من باب الصـلاة، و من كـان من أهل الجهاد دُعِـيَ من باب الجهاد، و من كان من أهل الصـدقة دُعِـيَ من بـاب الصدقة، و من كان من أهل الصيام دُعِـيَ من بـاب الصيام و بـاب الريـان." فقـال أبو بكر: ما على هذا الذي يدعى من تلك الأبواب من ضرورة ، وقال هل ، يدعى منها كلها أحد يا رسول الله ؟ قال: "نعم، و أرجو أن تكون منهم يا أبا بكر ." رواه البخاري

The Messenger of God ﷺ said, "Whoever gives just a pair of anything for the sake of God will be called to one of the gates of Paradise. Paradise has its gates. Those who are the people of prayer will be invited to enter by the gate of prayer; those who are the people of struggle *(jihad)* will be invited to enter by the gate of struggle; those who are the people of charity will be invited to enter by the gate of charity; and those who are the people of fasting will be invited to enter by the well-watered gate." Abū Bakr said, "No distress will rest upon someone who is invited to enter by one of those gates, but will anyone be invited to enter by all those gates?" He replied, "Yes, and I hope you may be one of those who are." (Bukhārī & Muslim)

عن جابر بن عبد الله – رضي الله عنهما – قال: قال رسول الله – صلى الله عليه وسلم – :" كل معروف صدقة." رواه البخاري ومسلم

Jābir and Ḥadhīfah ﷺ related that the Messenger of God ﷺ said, "Every act of kindness is charity." (Bukhārī & Muslim)

عن أبي ذر – رضي الله عنه – قال: قال لي رسول الله – صلى الله عليه وسلم– : " لا تَحْقِرَنَّ من المعروف شيئا، و لو أنْ تلْقى أخاك بوَجه طَلَقٍ ." رواه مسلم

Abū Dharr ﷺ reported that the Messenger of God ﷺ said, "Do not consider any act of kindness insignificant, even meeting your brother with a cheerful face." (Muslim)

عن أبي هريرة – رضي الله عنه – قال: قال رسول الله – صلى الله عليه وسلم– : " كل سُلامَى من الناس عليه صدقة كل يوم تطلع فيه الشمس: قال تعدل بين اثنين صدقة، و تُعينُ الرجل في دابته فتحمله عليها أو ترفع له عليها متاعه صدقة، قال: والكلمة الطيبة صدقة، و كل خطوة تمشيها إلى الصلاة صدقة، وتميط الأذى عن الطريق صدقة". رواه البخاري ومسلم

Abū Hurayrah recounted the Messenger of God saying, "Charity is incumbent upon every member of the body each day the sun rises. Every greeting to people is charity. Every day in which justice is dealt between two people is charity. If one helps a man with his beast, lifting his goods onto it, it is charity. A good word is charity. And if anyone removes any hazards from the road, it is charity." (Bukhārī & Muslim)

عن أبي ذر – رضي الله عنه أن ناساً من أصحاب النبي صلى الله عليه وسلم قالوا للنبي صلى الله عليه وسلم : يارسول الله ذهب أهل الدثور بالأجور يصلون كما نصلي ويصومون كما نصوم ، ويتصدقون بفضول أموالهم قال : أوليس قد جعل الله لكم ما تصدقون إن بكل تسبيحة صدقة، و كل تكبيرة صدقة، و كل تحميده صدقة، و كل تهليلة صدقة، و أمر بالمعروف صدقة، و نهي عن المنكر صدقة، و في بضع أحدكم صدقة قالوا : يارسول الله أيأتي أحدنا شهوته ويكون له فيها أجر ؟ قال : أفرأيتم لو وضعها في حرام أكان عليه فيها وزر ؟ فكذلك إذا وضعها في الحلال كان له أجر." رواه مسلم

Abū Dharr reported that some of the Companions came to the Prophet complaining that the people of wealth have surpassed them in reward, "They pray as we do, they fast as we do, and they give away of their excess wealth." The Messenger of God said, "God has given you what you can give in charity. Verily, every glorification is charity, every exaltation is charity, every praise is charity, every remembrance is charity, enjoining what is good is charity, forbidding what is bad is charity, even in your sex organs is charity." They asked, "Messenger of God! Are we rewarded even for satisfying our desire?" He replied, "If you seek your pleasure unlawfully would it not be a burden against you? Likewise if you seek your pleasure in what is lawful you will be rewarded." (Muslim)

عن أبي هريرة – رضي الله عنه – قال: قال رسول الله – صلى الله عليه
وسلم– : " غُفِرَ لامرأة مومسة، مرت بكلب على رأس ركي، يلهث، قال كاد
يقتله العطش، فنزعت خفها فأوثقته بخمارها، فنزعت له من الماء فغُفِرَ لها
بذلك " قال: قيل: إنَّ لنا في البهائم أجرا؟. قال:" في كل كبد رطبة أجر." رواه
البخاري ومسلم

Abū Hurayrah reported that the Messenger of God ﷺ said, "Forgiveness was granted to a prostitute who came upon a dog panting and almost dead from thirst at the mouth of a well. She took off her shoe, tied it with her head-covering, and drew some water for it. On that account she was forgiven." He was asked if people received a reward for what they did for animals, and he replied, "A reward is given in connection with every living creature." (Bukhārī)

عن ابن عمر رضي الله عنهما : قال رسول الله – صلى الله عليه وسلم– :
"عُذبَتْ امرأة في هرة، حبستها حتى ماتت جوعاً، فلم تكن تطعمها، ولا تُرسلها
فتأكل من خِشاش الأرض." رواه البخاري ومسلم

The Messenger of God ﷺ said, "A woman was tormented on account of a cat which she kept shut up until it died of hunger. She neither fed it nor let it out to eat from the creatures of the earth." (Bukhārī & Muslim)

عن أبي سعيد الخدري – رضي الله عنه – قال: قال رسول الله – صلى الله
عليه وسلم– : " أيَّما مسلم كسا مسلما ثوبا على عُري، كساه الله من خُضْر الجنة،
و أيَّما مسلم أطعم مسلما على جوع، أطعمه الله من ثمار الجنة، و أيَّما مسلم سقى
مسلما على ظمأ، سقاه الله من الرحيق المختوم." رواه أبوداود والترمذي

Abū Saʿīd ؓ reported that the Messenger of God ﷺ said, "If any Muslim clothes a Muslim when he is naked, God will clothe him with the green garments of Paradise. If any Muslim feeds a Muslim when he is hungry, God will feed him with the fruits of Paradise. And if any Muslim gives a Muslim to drink when he is thirsty, God will give him of the pure, sealed wine to drink." (Abū Dāʾūd & Tirmidhī)

عن جابر بن عبد الله – رضي الله عنه – قال: قال رسول الله – صلى الله عليه وسلم– : " من أحيا أرضا ميتة فله فيها أجر، و ما أكلت العافية منها له فله فيها صدقة." رواه النسائي والدارمي

Jābir ﷺ said that the Messenger of God ﷺ said, "If anyone brings to life a dead land, he will have a reward for it, and what any creature eats of it will count as charity from him." (Nasā'ī & Dārimī)

عن مرثد بن عبدالله اليزني قال: حدثني بعض أصحاب رسول الله – صلى الله عليه وسلم– : أنه سمع رسول الله – صلى الله عليه وسلم – يقول: " إن ظِلَّ المؤمن يوم القيامة صدقته." رواه أحمد

The Messenger of God ﷺ said, "The believer's shade on the Day of Resurrection will be his charity." (Aḥmad)

عن سلمان بن عامر – رضي الله عنه – قال: سمعت رسول الله – صلى الله عليه وسلم يقول : " الصدقة على المسكين صدقة، و الصدقة على ذي الرحم اثنتان: صدقة و صِلَة." رواه أحمد والترمذي

The Messenger of God ﷺ said, "Charity given to a poor person is charity, and when it is given to a relative it serves a double purpose being both charity and a bond of relationship." (Aḥmad, Tirmidhī)

عن أبي هريرة – رضي الله عنه– قال: بينما نحن جلوس عند النبي – صلى الله عليه وسلم – إذ جاءه رجل فقال: يا رسول الله، هلكت. قال: "ما لكَ؟." قال: وقعت على امرأتي وأنا صائم . فقال رسول الله – صلى الله عليه وسلم– : " هل تجد رقبة تعتقها ؟." قال: لا . قال: " فهل تستطيع أن تصوم شهرين متتابعين ؟." قال: لا. قال: " هل تجد إطعام ستين مسكينا ؟." قال: لا. قال " ." فمكث النبي – صلى الله عليه وسلم– فبينما نحن على ذلك أتى النبي – صلى الله عليه وسلم – بِعَرَقٍ فيه تمر، والعرق المكتل قال: " أين السائل ؟." قال: أنا. قال: " خذها، فتصدقْ به." فقال الرجل: أعلى أفقر مني يا رسول الله ؟ فوالله ما بين

لابـتيها – يريد الحرتين – أهل بيت أفقر من أهل بيتـي، فضـحك النبـي – صـلى الله عليه وسلم – حتى بدت أنيابه، ثم قال: " أطعمه أهلك ." رواه البخاري ومسلم

Abū Hurayrah ﷺ said that the Companions were sitting with the Prophet ﷺ when a man came to him and said, "Messenger of God, I am ruined!" He asked him what had happened to him and he replied that he had had intercourse with his wife while he was fasting (during the daylight hours of Ramaḍān). God's Messenger then asked him if he could set a slave free, but he replied that he could not. He asked if he could fast for two consecutive months, but he replied that he could not. He asked if he could provide food for sixty poor people, and when he replied that he could not, the Prophet told him to sit down. The Prophet then waited for a time, and meanwhile a basket containing dates was brought to him. He asked where the man who had questioned him was, and he said to him, "Take this and give it as charity." The man asked, "Am I to give it to one who is poorer than I am, Messenger of God? I swear by God there is no poorer family than mine between the two lava plains of Medina!" Hearing this, the Prophet laughed so that his eye-teeth were visible and said, "Give it to your family to eat!" (Bukhārī & Muslim)

عن عبد الله بن عمرو بن العاص – رضـي الله عنهما– قال: قـال لـي رسـول الله – صـلـى الله عليـه وسلم– : " يـا عبـد الله، ألـم أخبـر أنـك تصـوم النـهـار و تقـوم الليل ؟." فقلت: بلى، يا رسول الله. قال:" فلا تفعل. صم و أفطر، و قم و نـم، فـإن لجسدك عليك حقا، و إن لعينك عليك حقا، و إن لزوجك عليك حقـا، و إن لـزورك عليك حقـا، و إن بحسبك أن تصـوم كل شـهر ثلاثـة أيـام فـإن لك بكل حسـنة عشـر أمثالها فإن ذلك صيام الدهر كله فشددت فشدد عليَّ قلت يا رسول الله إني أجد قوة قال فصم صيام نبي الله داود عليه السلام ولا تزد عليه قلت وما كان صيام نبي الله داود عليه السلام قال : نصف الدهر فكان عبد الله يقول بعدما كبر يـا ليتنـي قبلـت رخصـة النبي صلى الله عليه وسلم ." رواه البخاري ومسلم

The Prophet ﷺ told ᶜAbdullāh ibn ᶜAmrū ibn Al-ᶜĀṣ ﷺ, "O ᶜAbdullāh, I've been informed that you fast every day and keep night vigils every night." ᶜAmrū said, "Yes, this is true, Messenger of God!" The Prophet then told him, "Don't do it. Fast and eat; stay up at night and sleep. For truly your body has a right over you, and your eyes have a right over you, and your wife has a right over you, and your visitors have a right over you. If you fast three days a month, that is as good as fasting all month long, so fast three days a month." ᶜAmrū replied, "But I have the capacity for more than this!" So he told him, "Then fast the best of fasts, the fast of David; fast one day and eat one day." later in his old age, ᶜAbdullāh would lament, "I wish I had accepted the license given to me by the Messenger of God!" (Bukhārī & Muslim)

The Station of the Qurʿān

عن أبي موسى الأشعري – رضي الله عنه – قال: قال رسول الله – صلى الله عليه وسلم– : " مثل المؤمن الذي يقرأ القرآن مثل الأترُجَّة ريحها طيب، و طعمها طيب ومثل المؤمن الذي لا يقرأ القرآن كمثل التمرة لا ريح لها وطعمها حلو ومثل المنافق الذي يقرأ القرآن مثل الريحانة ريحها طيب وطعمها مُر ومثل المنافق الذي لا يقرأ القرآن كمثل الحنظلة ليس لها ريح وطعمها مُر ." رواه البخاري ومسلم

Abū Mūsā said that the Messenger of God ﷺ said, "A believer who recites the Qurʾān is like a citron whose fragrance is sweet and whose taste is sweet. A believer who does not recite the Qurʾān is like a date fruit with no fragrance but a sweet taste. A hypocrite who recites the Qurʾān is like basil whose fragrance is sweet but tastes bitter. A hypocrite who does not recite the Qurʾān is like a colocynth with no fragrance and a bitter taste." (Bukhārī & Muslim)

عن أبي أمامة – رضي الله عنه– قال: سمعت رسول الله – صلى الله عليه وسلم – يقول: " اقرأوا القرآن، فإنه يأتي يوم القيامة شفيعا لأصحابه، اقرأوا الزهراوين:سورة البقرة و سورة آل عمران، فإنهما تأتيان يوم القيامة كأنهما غمامتان، أو غيايتان، أو كأنهما فرقان من طير صواف، تحاجان عن أصحابهما، اقرأوا سورة البقرة فإن أخذها بركة و تركها حسرة، ولا يستطيعها البطلة." رواه الطبراني

Abū Umāmah related that the Messenger of God ﷺ said, "Recite the Qurʾān, for on the Day of Resurrection it will come as an intercessor for its companions. Recite the two shining ones, *Al-Baqarah* and *Āl ʿImrān,* for they will both become like rain clouds on the Day of Resurrection. Recite *Al-Baqarah* for having it is a blessing and leaving it is bitter regret, and no falsehood can reach it." (Ṭabarānī)

عن أبي الدرداء رضي الله عنه : قال رسول الله – صلى الله عليه وسلم– :
" أيعجز أحدكم أن يقرأ في ليلة ثلث القرآن ؟." قالوا: و كيف يقرأ ثلث القرآن.
قال: " قل هو الله أحد، تعدل ثلث القرآن ." رواه مسلم

The Messenger of God ﷺ said, "Can any of you fail to recite one third of the Qur'ān in a single night?" They replied, "How can we do this?" He told them, "*Say, He is Allāh, the One* (*Sūrah al-Ikhlāṣ*) is equivalent to a third of the Qur'ān." (Muslim)

عن أنس – رضي الله عنه– قال: أن رجلا قال: يا رسول الله، إني أحب هذه
السورة " قل هو الله أحد ". قال:" إن حبك إياها أدخلك الجنة ." رواه الترمذي

Anas ﵁ said that a man told God's Messenger that he particularly liked the *Sūrah* with '*Say, "He is God, the One…"*' (*Sūrah al-Ikhlāṣ* 112:1); to which he replied, "Your love of it has brought you into Paradise." (Muslim)

عن عقبة بن عامر – رضي الله عنه– قال: قال رسول الله – صلى الله عليه
وسلم – : " ألم تر آيات أنزلت الليلة لم يُرَ مثلهن قط،" قل أعوذ برب الفلق، و قل
أعوذ برب الناس ." رواه مسلم

ᶜUqbah ibn ᶜĀmir ﵁ said that the Messenger of God ﷺ said, "What wonderful verses have been sent down tonight! The like of them has never been seen. They are *Say, I seek refuge in the Lord of the Dawn* (*Sūrah al-Falaq* 113:1) and *Say, I seek refuge in the Lord of Men* (*Sūrah an-Nās* 114:1)." (Muslim)

عن أبي سعيد – رضي الله عنه– قال: قال رسول الله – صلى الله عليه
وسلم– : " يقول الرب تبارك عز وجل : من شغله القرآن وذكري عن مسألتي،
أعطيته أفضل ما أعطي السائلين، و فضل كلام الله عن سائر الكلام، كفضل الله
على خلقه." رواه الترمذي

Abū Saᶜīd ﵁ reported that the Messenger of God ﷺ said, "The Lord, most blessed and exalted, says, 'Whoever is preoccupied by the Qurᵓān and My remembrance from asking Me about their needs, I will give them better than what I give those who ask Me.' The superiority of God's words over all other words is like God's superiority over his creatures." (Tirmidhī)

عن أبي هريرة رضي الله عنه قال : قال رسول الله – صلى الله عليه وسلم– : " تعلموا القرآن، و اقرأوه، فإن مثل القرآن لمن تعلمه ، فقرأه، و قام به، كمثل جراب محشو مسكا، يفوح ريحه في كل مكان، و مثل من تعلمه فيرقد و هو في جوفه كمثل جراب وُكئ على مسك." رواه الترمذي

The Messenger of God ﷺ said, "Learn the Qurᵓān and recite it, for one who does so is like a bag that is filled with musk whose scent flows everywhere. And he who learns it (the Qurᵓān) and goes to sleep having it within him is like a bag with musk tied up in it." (Tirmidhī)

عن ابن عمر – رضي الله عنهما– قال: قال رسول الله – صلى الله عليه وسلم– : " إن هذه القلوب تصدأ، كما يصدأ الحديد إذا أصابه الماء" قيل: يا رسول الله، و ما جلاؤها ؟. قال: " كثرة ذكر الموت، و تلاوة القرآن." رواه البيهقي

Ibn ᶜUmar ﵄ reported that the Messenger of God ﷺ said, "These hearts become rusty, just as iron does when water gets to it." On being asked what could polish them he replied, "Frequent remembrance of death and recitation of the Qurᵓān." (Bayhaqī)

عن مقعل بن يسار المزني أن النبي– صلى الله عليه وسلم قال– : " من قرأ يس، ابتغاء وجه الله عز وجل، غفر له ما تقدم من ذنبه، فاقرأوها عند موتاكم." رواه البيهقي

The Messenger of God ﷺ said, "If anyone recites *Sūrah Yā Sīn* out of a desire for God's favor, his past sins will be forgiven him; so recite it upon those of you who are dying." (Bayhaqī)

عن ابن مسعود – رضي الله عنه– قال: سمعت رجلا قرأ، و سمعت النبي – صلى الله عليه وسلم – يقرأ خلافها، فجئت به النبي – صلى الله عليه وسلم – فأخبرته، فعرفت في وجهه الكراهية، وقال: " كلاكما محسن" ولا تختلفوا فإن من كان قبلكم اختلفوا، فهلكوا." رواه البخاري

Ibn Mas'ūd ﷺ said, "I heard a man who recited the Qur'ān, and as I had heard the Prophet ﷺ reciting differently I took him to the Prophet and told him, and I noticed that he gave a disapproving look. He then said, 'Both of you are doing it well, so do not disagree; for your predecessors disagreed and perished.'" (Bukhārī)

Supplications

عن أبي هريرة – رضي الله عنه– قال رسول الله – صلى الله عليه وسلم– :" إذا دعا أحدكم، فلا يقل اللهم اغفر لي إن شئت، و لكن ليعزم المسألة، و ليعظم الرغبة، فإن الله لا يتعاظمه شئ أعطاه." رواه مسلم

Abū Hurayrah ﷺ reported that the Messenger of God ﷺ said, "When you make supplication do not say, 'O God, forgive me if You will (*insh'Allah*)' but rather be filled with determination in your asking and let your desire be great, for nothing is too great for God to give." (Muslim)

عن النعمان بن بشير – رضي الله عنه– قال: قال رسول الله – صلى الله عليه وسلم– : " الدعاء هو العبادة " ثم قرأ "و قال ربكم ادعوني أستجب لكم." رواه أحمد والترمذي

An-Nuᶜmān ibn Bashīr ﷺ related that the Messenger of God ﷺ said, "Supplication is worship," and he then recited, "*and your Lord said, 'Call upon Me, I will respond to you*'" (*Sūrah Ghāfir* 40:60). (Aḥmad & Tirmidhī)

عن عبد الله ابن مسعود – رضي الله عنه– قال: قال رسول الله – صلى الله عليه وسلم– : " سلوا الله من فضله، فإن الله عز وجل يحب أن يُسأل، وأفضل العبادة انتظار الفرج." رواه الترمذي

Ibn Masᶜūd ﷺ reported that the Messenger of God ﷺ said, "Ask God of His bounty, for God likes to be asked, and the most excellent worship is to wait patiently for relief." (Tirmidhī)

عن أبي هريرة – رضي الله عنه– قال: قال رسول الله – صلى الله عليه وسلم– : " ادعوا الله، و أنتم موقنون بالإجابة، و اعلموا أن الله لا يستجيب دعاءً من قلب غافل، لاهٍ." رواه الترمذي

Abū Hurayrah reported that the Messenger of God ﷺ said, "Call unto God with certainty that your call will be answered. And know that God does not answer a supplication which comes from a heedless and distracted heart." (Tirmidhī)

عن سلمان الفارسي – رضي الله عنه– قال: قال رسول الله – صلى الله عليه وسلم– : " إن الله حيي كريم، يستحيي إذا رفع الرجل إليه يديه أن يردهما صفرا خائبتين ." رواه الترمذي

Salmān ؓ reported that the Messenger of God ﷺ said, "Your Lord is alive and generous, and would be embarrassed to turn away empty the hands of a servant when he raises them to Him in supplication." (Tirmidhī)

عن عمر بن الخطاب – رضي الله عنه– قال: استأذنت النبي – صلى الله عليه وسلم – في العمرة، فأذن لي و قال: " لا تنسنا يا أخيَّ من دعائك فقال كلمة ما يسرني أن لي بها الدنيا قال شعبة ثم لقيت عاصماً بعد بالمدينة فحدثته وقال أشركنا يا أخي في دعائك ." رواه أبوداود والترمذي

ʿUmar ibn al-Khaṭṭāb ؓ said, "I asked permission of the Prophet ﷺ to perform the lesser pilgrimage and he gave me permission, saying, 'Include us in your supplication, my brother, and do not forget us.' And these words he said to me I would not be willing to exchange for the whole world. " (Tirmidhī & Abū Dāʾūd)

عن أبي سعيد الخدري – رضي الله عنه– أن النبي – صلى الله عليه وسلم – قال: " ما من مسلم يدعو بدعوة ليس فيها إثم، ولا قطيعة رحم إلا أعطاه الله بها

إحدى ثلاث: إما أن تعجل له دعوته، و إما أن يدخرها له في الآخرة، و إما أن يصرف عنه من السوء مثلها." قالوا: إذن نكثر. قال " الله أكثر." رواه أحمد

Abū Saʿīd al-Khudrī ﵇ reported that the Messenger of God ﷺ said, "Any Muslim who makes a supplication that does not contain anything sinful and does not involve severing the ties of mercy will be given by God one of three things: a speedy response to his prayer, or He will keep it for him in the other world, or He will turn away from him an equivalent amount of evil." Those who heard this said, "Then we will increase our supplications." He replied, "God is able to answer more than you can ask." (Aḥmad)

عن أبي موسى – رضي الله عنه– قال: قال رسول الله – صلى الله عليه وسلم– : " مثل الذي يذكر ربه، و الذي لا يذكر ربه ، مثل الحي و الميت." رواه البخاري ومسلم

Abū Mūsā ﵇ related that the Messenger of God ﷺ said, "One who remembers one's Lord and one who does not are like the living and the dead." (Bukhārī & Muslim)

عن أبي هريرة – رضي الله عنه– قال: قال رسول الله – صلى الله عليه وسلم– : " يقول الله تعالى: أنا عند ظن عبدي بي، و أنا معه إذا ذكرني، فإن ذكرني في نفسه ذكرته في نفسي، و إن ذكرني في ملأ، ذكرته في ملأ خير منهم وإن تقرب إليّ بشبر تقربت إليه ذراعاً وإن تقرب إليّ ذراعاً تقربت إليه باعا وإن أتاني يمشي أتيته هرولة ." رواه البخاري ومسلم

Abū Hurayrah ﵇ reported that the Messenger of God ﷺ said that God says, "I am as My servant thinks of Me. I am with him when He remembers Me. If he remembers Me inwardly, I shall remember him inwardly; and if he remembers Me among people, I shall remember him among people who are better than those he remembers Me among. Whoever draws the length of a span near Me, I draw the length of a cubit near him; and whoever draws the length of a cubit near Me, I draw the length of a fathom near him, and if he comes to me walking, I come to him running. " (Bukhārī & Muslim)

عن أبي ذر – رضي الله عنه– قال: قال رسول الله – صلى الله عليه وسلم– : " يقول الله عز وجل : من جاء بالحسنة فله عشر أمثالها، و أزيد، و من جاء بالسيئة فجزاؤه سيئة مثلها، أو أغفر، و من تقرب مني شبرا، تقربت منه ذراعا، و من تقرب مني ذراعا، تقربت منه باعا، و من أتاني يمشي أتيته هرولة، و من لقيني بقراب الأرض خطيئة لا يشرك بي شيئا لقيته بمثلها مغفرة." رواه مسلم

Abū Dharr ﷺ related that the Messenger of God ﷺ said that Allāh says, "Whoever comes to Me with a good deed shall receive ten times or more in return. Whoever comes to Me with a bad deed shall receive as much or My forgiveness in return. Whoever draws the length of a span near Me, I shall draw the length of a cubit near him; and whoever draws the length of a cubit near Me, I shall draw the length of a fathom near him. Whoever comes to Me walking, I shall come to him running. And whoever meets Me with enough sins to fill the earth, but has not associated[1] anything with Me, I shall meet him with a similar amount of forgiveness." (Muslim)

عن أبي هريرة – رضي الله عنه– قال: قال رسول الله – صلى الله عليه وسلم– : " إن الله قال: من عادى لي وليا فقد آذنته بالحرب، و ما تقرب إلي عبدي بشيء أحبَّ إلي مما افترضتُ عليه، و مازال عبدي يتقرب إلي بالنوافل حتى أحبه، فإذا أحببته: كنت سمعه الذي يسمع به، و بصره الذي يبصر به، و يده التي يبطش بها، و رجله التي يمشي بها، و لئن سألني لأعطينه، و لئن استعاذني لأعيذنه، و ما ترددت عن شئ أنا فاعله ترددي عن نفس المؤمن، يكره الموت و أنا أكره مساءته ." رواه البخاري

Abū Hurayrah ﷺ told that the Messenger of God ﷺ said that God has said, "Whoever is an enemy to one of My friends, I have declared war against him. My servant cannot come close to Me with anything dearer to Me than what I have made incumbent upon him. And My servant continues to draw nearer to Me by giving more and more without expectation so that I shall love him, and when I love him I shall be the hearing with which he hears, the sight with which he sees, the hand with which he grasps, and the foot with which he walks. If he asks from Me, I shall certainly give him, and if he seeks refuge in Me I shall certainly give

[1] i.e. attributing divinity to anything else.

him refuge. I have not hesitated about anything I do as I hesitate about taking the soul of a believer who dislikes death, for I dislike grieving him." (Bukhārī)

عن أبي هريرة رضي الله عنه قال : قال رسول الله – صلى الله عليه وسلم– : "إن لله ملائكة، يطوفون في الطرق يلتمسون أهل الذكر، فإذا وجدوا قوما يذكرون الله تنادوا: "هلُمُّوا إلى حاجتكم " قال: فيحفّونهم بأجنحتهم إلى السماء الدنيا." رواه البخاري

The Messenger of God ﷺ said, "God has angels who go about the paths seeking those who remember God, and when they find people doing so they call to one another, 'Come to what you are seeking!' And they surround them with their wings up to the lowest heaven." (Bukhārī)

عن أنس بن مالك – رضي الله عنه– قال: قال رسول الله – صلى الله عليه وسلم– : " إذا مررتم برياض الجنة، فارتعوا." قالوا: و ما رياض الجنة ؟. قال: " حِلَقُ الذكر." رواه الترمذي

Anas ﷺ related that the Messenger of God ﷺ said, "When you come upon the pastures of Paradise feed on them!" On being asked what these were, he replied, "The *Dhikr*[2] Circles." (Tirmidhī)

عن ابن عمر – رضي الله عنهما– قال: قال رسول الله – صلى الله عليه وسلم– : " لا تكثروا الكلام بغير ذكر الله، فإن كثرة الكلام بغير ذكر الله قسوة للقلب، و إن أبعد الناس من الله القلب القاسي." رواه الترمذي

Ibn ʿUmar ﷺ related that the Messenger of God ﷺ said, "Do not speak much without remembering God, for much talk without remembrance of God is hardness of the heart, and the one who is farthest from God is one whose heart is hard." (Tirmidhī)

---

[2] Remembrance of God.

عن ثوبان – رضي الله عنه– قال: لما نزلت " والذين يكنزون الذهب والفضة" كنا مع النبي – صلى الله عليه وسلم – في بعض أسفاره، فقال بعض أصحابه: نزلت في الذهب و الفضة، ما أنزل لو علمنا أي المال خير فنتخذه؟. فقال: " أفضله لسان ذاكر، و قلب شاكر، و زوجة مؤمنة تعينه على إيمانه." رواه أحمد والترمذي

When the verse, *Those who hoard gold and silver…* (*Sūrah at-Tawbah* 9:34), was revealed, the Companions asked the Prophet ﷺ what wealth was better to seek than gold and silver. He replied, "A tongue which remembers God, a grateful heart, and a believing spouse who is supportive of one's faith." (Aḥmad, Tirmidhī)

عن عبد الله بن عمر – رضي الله عنهما– عن النبي – صلى الله عليه وسلم – أنه كان يقول: " إن لكل شيء سقالة، وإن سقالة القلوب ذكر الله، و ما من شيء أنجى من عذاب الله من ذكر الله." قالوا: ولا الجهاد في سبيل الله ؟. قال: " ولو أن تضرب بسيفك حتى ينقطع." رواه البيهقي

ᶜAbdullāh ibn ᶜUmar ؓ related that the Messenger of God ﷺ said, "For everything there is a polish, and the polish of the heart is the remembrance of God. Remembrance of God is the best refuge from God's torment." They asked him, "Even better than *jihād* in the cause of God?" He replied, "Even if you wield your sword and strike with it until it is broken to bits!" (Bayhaqī)

عن أبي هريرة – رضي الله عنه– قال: قال رسول الله – صلى الله عليه وسلم– : " قال الله تعالى : أنا مع عبدي حيثما ذكرني، و تحركت بي شفتاه." رواه البخاري

Abū Hurayrah ؓ reported that the Messenger of God ﷺ stated that God has said; "I am with My servant when he remembers Me and his lips are moved by Me." (Bukhārī)

عن أبي موسى، قال: " كنا مع رسول الله – صلى الله عليه وسلم – في سفر، فكنا إذا علونا كبَّرنا، فقال النبي – صلى الله عليه وسلم– : " أيها الناس، أربعوا على أنفسكم، فإنكم لا تدعون أصم، ولا غائبا، ولكن تدعون سميعا بصيراً ثم أتى عليَّ وأنا أقول في نفسي لا حول ولا قوة إلا بالله. فقال : "يا عبد الله بن قيس، قل لا حول ولا قوة إلا بالله فإنها كنز من كنوز الجنة أو قال: ألا أدلك على كلمة هي كنز من كنوز الجنة ، لا حول ولا قوة إلا بالله ." أخرجه البخاري ومسلم

On a journey the people began to say aloud, "God is Most Great!" The Messenger of God ﷺ said, "Restrain yourselves; you are not calling one who is deaf or absent, you are calling One who is All-Hearing, and close to you. He is with you." A Companion, Abū Mūsā, was riding behind him and saying to himself, "There is no power or ability except through God," whereupon the Prophet ﷺ turned around and said to him, "O ʿAbdullāh ibn Qays, shall I guide you to one of the treasures of Paradise?" ʿAbdullāh said, "Yes, Messenger of God!" He told him, "Keep saying 'There is no power or ability except through God.'" (Bukhārī & Muslim)

عن أبي ذر – رضي الله عنه– عن النبي – صلى الله عليه وسلم– روى عن الله تبارك و تعالى أنه قال: "يا عبادي: إني حرمت الظلم على نفسي، و جعلته بينكم محرما، فلا تظالموا، يا عبادي: كلكم ضال إلا من هديته، فاستهدوني أهدكم، يا عبادي: كلكم جائع إلا من أطعمته، فاستطعموني أطعمكم، يا عبادي: كلكم عار إلا من كسوته، فاستكسوني أكسكم، يا عبادي: إنكم تخطئون بالليل و النهار، و أنا أغفر الذنوب جميعا، فاستغفروني أغفر لكم، يا عبادي: إنكم لن تبلغوا ضري فتضروني، و لن تبلغوا نفعي فتنفعوني، يا عبادي: لو أن أولكم، و آخركم، و إنسكم، و جنكم كانوا على أتقى قلب رجل واحد منكم، ما زاد ذلك في ملكي شيئا، يا عبادي: لو أن أولكم و آخركم و إنسكم و جنكم كانوا على أفجر قلب رجل واحد منكم، ما نقص ذلك من ملكي شيئا، يا عبادي: لو أن أولكم و آخركم و إنسكم و جنكم قاموا في صعيد واحد فسألوني، فأعطيت كل إنسان مسألته، ما نقص ذلك مما عندي إلا كما ينقص المخيط إذا أدخل البحر، يا عبادي: إنما هي أعمالكم أحصيها عليكم ثم أوفيكم إياها، فمن وجد خيرا، فليحمد الله، و من وجد غير ذلك فلا يلومن إلا نفسه." رواه مسلم

Abū Dharr ؓ related that the Messenger of God ﷺ said that God, most blessed and exalted, has said, "My servants, I have made oppression unlawful for Myself and I have made it unlawful between you, so do not oppress one another. My servants, each of you is lost except those whom

I guide, so seek My guidance and I will give it to you. My servants, each of you is hungry except for those that I feed, so seek My nourishment and I will give it to you. My servants, each of you is naked except for those I shelter, so seek My shelter and I will give it to you. My servants, each of you sins night and day, but I forgive all sins, so seek My forgiveness and I will forgive you. My servants, you can neither harm Me nor benefit Me. My servants, if the first and last of you, human and *jinn*, were as conscious of Me as the most God-conscious among you, this would not increase My Dominion at all. My servants, if the first and last of you, human and *jinn*, were as iniquitous as the most iniquitous among you, this would not decrease My Dominion at all. My servants, if the first and the last of you, human and *jinn*, were to stand in one plain and ask of Me, and if I were to give each one what he asked, that would not diminish what I possess any more than a needle would when put into the sea. My servants, I only keep your deeds for you and then I recompense you for them, so whoever finds Abundance let him praise God, and whoever finds other than this let him blame no other than himself." (Muslim)

عن أبي هريرة – رضي الله عنه – قال: قال رسول الله – صلى الله عليه وسلم – :" و الذي نفسي بيده، لو لم تذنبوا لذهب الله بكم، و لجاء بقوم يذنبون، فيستغفرون الله، فيغفر لهم." رواه مسلم

Abū Hurayrah ؓ said that the Messenger of God ﷺ said, "By the One who holds my soul in His Hand, if you did not sin God would have replaced you with people who sin so they would seek forgiveness from God and He would forgive them." (Muslim)

عن أنس بن مالك – رضي الله عنه – قال سمعت رسول الله – صلى الله عليه وسلم يقول : " قال الله تعالى: يا ابن آدم، إنك ما دعوتني و رجوتني، غفرت لك على ما كان فيك ولا أبالي، يا ابن آدم، لو بلغت ذنوبك عنان السماء ثم استغفرتني، غفرت لك ولا أبالي، يا ابن آدم، إنك لو أتيتني بقراب الأرض خطايا ثم لقيتني لا تشرك بي شيئا، لأتيتك بقرابها مغفرة." رواه الترمذي

Anas ؓ related that the Messenger of God ﷺ stated that God has said,

"O human! If you were to call for Me and put your hope in Me, I would forgive whatever you have done, no matter what you have done. O human! Even if your sins were as high as the sky and you sought My forgiveness I would forgive you no matter what you have done. O human! Even if you were to come to Me with so much sin as to fill the world, but you came to Me without associating anyone with Me, I would come to you with enough forgiveness to fill the world." (Tirmidhī)

عن أبي بكر الصديق – رضي الله عنه– قال: قال رسول الله – صلى الله عليه وسلم– : " ما أصَرَّ من استغفر، و إن عاد في اليوم سبعين مرة." رواه الترمذي وأبوداود

Abū Bakr Aṣ-Ṣādiq ﵁ reported that the Messenger of God ﷺ said, "The one who seeks forgiveness is not one bent on sinning, even if he were to relapse seventy times a day." (Tirmidhī & Abū Dāʾūd)

عن أبي هريرة – رضي الله عنه – أن رسول الله – صلى الله عليه وسلم– قال : "إن المؤمن إذا أذنب، كانت نكتة سوداء في قلبه، فإن تاب ونزع و استغفر صُقِلَ قلبه، فإن زاد زادت ، فذلك الرَّان الذي ذكر الله في كتابه : "كلا بل ران على قلوبهم ما كانوا يكسبون." رواه أحمد و الترمذي و ابن ماجه

Abū Hurayrah ﵁ related that the Messenger of God ﷺ said, "When a believer sins, a black spot is imprinted on his heart, and if he repents and asks forgiveness his heart is polished. But if he increases in his sinning, the spot increases until it gains ascendancy over his heart. That is the rust mentioned by God most high: *Nay, but what they have gained has caused rust to come upon their hearts* (*Sūrah al-Muṭaffifīn* 83:14)." (Aḥmad & Tirmidhī)

عن عبد الله بن عباس – رضي الله عنهما– قال: قال رسول الله – صلى الله عليه وسلم– : "ما الميت في القبر إلا كالغريق المتغوث، ينتظر دعوة تلحقه من أب أو أم أو أخ أو صديق، فإذا لحقته كان أحب إليه من الدنيا و ما فيها، و إن الله

عز وجل ليُدخل على أهل القبور من دعاء أهل الأرض أمثال الجبال، و إن هدية الأحياء إلى الأموات الاستغفار لهم." رواه البيهقي

ᶜAbdullāh ibn ᶜUmar ﷺ reported that the Messenger of God ﷺ said, "A dead man in his grave is just like a drowning man calling for help. He waits for a prayer from a father, mother, sibling, or friend to reach him, and if one does, it is dearer to him than the world and what is in it. Truly, God makes the prayers of the people of the world as great as mountains for the people of the graves. The gift of the living to the dead is to ask forgiveness for them." (Bayhaqī)

عن الحارث بن سويد – رضي الله عنهما – قال: حدثنا عبد الله بن مسعود حديثين: أحدهما عن النبي – صلى الله عليه وسلم – و الآخر عن نفسه، قال: "إن المؤمن يرى ذنوبه كأنه قاعد تحت جبل، يخاف أن يقع عليه، و إن الفاجر يرى ذنوبه كذباب مر على أنفه." فقال: به هكذا بيده فوق أنفه ثم قال لله أفرح بتوبة عبده من رجل نزل منزلاً وبه مهلكة ومعه راحلته عليها طعامه وشرابه فوضع رأسة فنام نومة فاستيقظ وقد ذهبت راحلته حتى إذا إشتد عليه الحر والعطش أو ما شاء الله قال أرجع إلى مكاني فرجع فنام نومة ثم رفع رأسه فإذا راحلته عنده . رواه البخاري

Al-Ḥārith bin Suwaīd ﷺ said that the Messenger of God ﷺ said, "The faithful one sees his sins as if they were a mountain which he fears may fall on him; but the unrighteous one sees his sins as if they were just a fly passing over his nose and which he brushes away with his hand without much concern. God is happier with the repentance of His servant than a traveler on a dangerous path who loses his mount with all his provisions and, suffering from heat and thirst, goes to sleep and wakes up to find his mount next to him." (Muslim)

عن ثوبان – رضي الله عنه– قال: سمعت رسول الله – صلى الله عليه وسلم – يقول: "ما أحب أن لي الدنيا وما فيها بهذه الآية :" يا عبادي الّذين أسرفوا على أنفسهم لا تقنطوا من رحمة الله "(1) رواه أحمد

Thawbān ﷺ reported that the Messenger of God ﷺ said, "I would not give this verse for the whole world: *O My servants who have transgressed against their souls, do not despair of God's Mercy.*" (*Sūrah az-Zumar* 39:53) (Aḥmad)

عن أبي هريرة – رضي الله عنه– أن رسول الله – صلى الله عليه وسلم– قال : " لمَّا قضى الله الخلق، كَتب عنده فوق عرشه " إن رحمتي سبقت غضبي." رواه البخاري ومسلم

Abū Hurayrah ؓ related that the Messenger of God ﷺ said, "When God completed the creation He wrote the following, which is with Him above His throne: 'My mercy takes precedence over My wrath.'" (Bukhārī & Muslim)

عن أبي هريرة – رضي الله عنه– أن رسول الله – صلى الله عليه وسلم– قال : " لو يعلم المؤمن ما عند الله من العقوبة، ما طمع بجنته أحد، و لو يعلم الكافر ما عند الله من الرحمة، ما قنط من جنته أحد." رواه البخاري ومسلم

Abū Hurayrah ؓ said that the Messenger of God ﷺ said, "If the believer knew the extent of God's punishment, no one would have any hope for His Paradise; and if the infidel knew the extent of His mercy, no one would despair of attaining His Paradise." (Bukhārī & Muslim)

عن ابن مسعود – رضي الله عنه– قال: قال النبي – صلى الله عليه وسلم– : " الجنة أقرب إلى أحدكم من شراك نعله، و النار مثل ذلك." رواه البخاري

Ibn Masʿūd ؓ told of the Messenger of God ﷺ saying, "Paradise is nearer to you than the thong of your sandals, and so is Hell." (Bukhārī & Muslim)

عن عمر بن الخطاب – رضي الله عنه– قال: قدم على النبي – صلى الله عليه وسلم – سَبي، فإذا امرأة من السبي قد تحلب ثديها تَسْقِي، إذا وجدت صبيا في السبي أخذته فألصقته ببطنها و أرضعته، فقال لنا النبي صلى الله عليه وسلم– :" أترون هذه طارحة ولدها في النار؟." فقلنا: لا، و هي تقدر على أن لا تطرحه. فقال: " الله أرحم بعباده من هذه بولدها." رواه البخاري ومسلم

ʿUmar ibn al-Khaṭṭāb ؓ said that captives were brought before the Prophet ﷺ, among them a woman whose breasts were full of milk. She was running and searching, and when she found an infant boy among the captives she took him, put him to her breast and suckled him. The Prophet said to us, "Do you think this woman would ever cast her child into the fire?" We replied, "No!" He said, "God is more merciful to His servants than this woman is to her child." (Bukhārī & Muslim)

عن أبي الدرداء – رضي الله عنه– أنه سمع النبي – صلى الله عليه وسلم – وهو يقص على المنبر : "و لمن خاف مقام ربه جنتان". فقلت: و إن زنى، و إن سرق يا رسول الله ؟. فقال رسول الله صلى الله عليه وسلم الثانية: " و لمن خاف مقام ربه جنتان ". فقلت الثانية: و إن زنى، و إن سرق يا رسول الله ؟. فقال النبي صلى الله عليه وسلم الثالثة: "و لمن خاف مقام ربه جنتان ". فقلت الثالثة: و إن زنى، و إن سرق يا رسول الله ؟. قال: " و إن، رغم أنف أبي الدرداء." رواه أحمد

Abū Dardāʾ ؓ told of his hearing the Prophet ﷺ deliver a sermon from the pulpit saying, "*He who fears the station of his Lord has two Paradises*" (*Sūrah ar-Raḥmān* 55:46). Abū Dardāʾ asked, "Even if he commits fornication and even if he steals, O Messenger of God?" But he said a second time, "*He who fears the station of his Lord has two Paradises.*" Abū Dardāʾ asked a second time, "Even if he commits fornication, and even if he steals, O Messenger of God?" But he said a third time, *"He who fears the station of his Lord has two Paradises.*" Abū Dardāʾ asked a third time, "Even if he commits fornication and even if he steals, O Messenger of God?" to which the Prophet finally replied, "Indeed, even in spite of Abū Dardāʾ!" (Aḥmad)

عن عامر الرام – رضي الله عنه– قال: فبينما نحن عنده إذ أقبل رجل عليه كساء و في يده شيء قد التف عليه، فقال: يا رسول الله، إني لما رأيتك أقبلت إليك فمررت بغيضة شجر فسمعت فيها أصوات فراخ طائر، فأخذتهن فوضعتهن في كسائي فجاءت أمُّهُنَّ، فاستدارت على رأسي، فكشفت لها عنهن فوقعت عليهن، فلففتهن بكسائي فهن أولاء معي . قال: " ضعهن عنك ." فوضعتهن، و أبت أمُّهُنَّ إلا لزومهن، فقال رسول الله – صلى الله عليه وسلم– لأصحابه : " أتعجبون لرحم أم الأفراخ فراخها ، قالوا نعم يا رسول الله ، قال فوالذي بعثني بالحق: لله أرحم بعباده من أم الأفراخ بفراخها، ارجع بهن حتى تضعهن من حيث أخذتهن، و أمُّهُنَّ معهن." فرجع بهن. رواه أبوداود

A man heard chirping in a thicket, found some young birds, and took them. Their mother came and flew around his head, so he uncovered them and, when she alighted on them, wrapped them up together in his garment and brought them to the Prophet ﷺ. He commanded the man to put them down and he did so. The mother would not leave them. The Prophet ﷺ said, "Do you wonder at the mercy of the chick's mother for her young? By Him who sent me with the truth, God shows more mercy to His servants than this mother shows to her young. Take them back and put them where you found them, and their mother with them." (Abū Dāʾūd)

عن حذيفة – رضي الله عنه– قال: كان النبي – صلى الله عليه وسلم – إذا أخذ مضجعه من الليل وضع يده تحت خده ثم يقول: "اللهم باسمك أموت و أحيا." و إذا استيقظ قال:"الحمد لله الذي أحيانا بعد ما أماتنا، و إليه النشور." رواه البخاري

Hudhayfa ﵁ related that when the Prophet ﷺ lay down on his bed at night he placed his hand under his cheek and would then say, "In Your name, O My God, I die and live!" When he awoke he would say, "Praise be to God who has given us life after causing us to die, and to Him shall be the resurrection." (Bukhārī)

عن أبي هريرة – رضي الله– قال: قال رسول – صلى الله عليه وسلم– :" من جلس في مجلس فكثر فيه لغطه، فقال قبل أن يقوم من مجلسه ذلك : سبحانك

اللهم و بحمدك، أشهد أن لا إله إلا أنت أستغفرك و أتوب إليك، إلا غفر له ما كان في مجلسه ذلك." رواه الترمذي والبيهقي

Abū Hurayrah ﷺ said that the Messenger of God ﷺ said, "If anyone sits in an assembly where there is much meaningless talk and says before getting up to leave, 'Glory and praise be to You, O God; I testify that there is no God but You; I ask Your pardon and turn to You in repentance,' he will be forgiven for what took place in that assembly." (Tirmidhī & Bayhaqī)

عن أبي بكر – رضي الله عنه– قال: قال رسول الله – صلى الله عليه وسلم– :" دعوات المكروب: اللهم رحمتك أرجو، فلا تكلني إلى نفسي طرفة عين، و أصلح لي شأني كله، لا إله إلا أنت." رواه أبوداود

Abū Bakr ﷺ reported that the Messenger of God ﷺ said, "In distress a man should say, 'O God, Your mercy is what I hope for. Do not abandon me to myself for even an instant! Make right all that concerns me. There is no God but You.'" (Abū Dā'ūd)

عن علي – رضي الله عنه– قال: قال لي رسول الله – صلى الله عليه وسلم– :" قل اللهم اهدني، و سددني، و اذكر بالهدى هدايتك الطريق، و بالسداد سداد السهم." رواه مسلم وأبوداود

ʿAlī ﷺ said that God's Messenger ﷺ told him to say, "O God, guide me and let me reach my aim. And remember that the guidance you seek is your being guided along the path, and that reach that you seek is how an arrow hits its mark." (Muslim)

عن عطاء بن السائب، عن أبيه – رضي الله عنه – قال: صلى بنا عمار بن ياسر صلاة فأوجز فيها فقال له بعض القوم: لقد خففت و أوجزت الصلاة فقال: أما على ذلك، لقد دعوت فيها بدعوات سمعتهن من رسول الله – صلى الله عليه وسلم– فلما قام تبعه رجل من القوم هو أبي، غير أنه كنى عن نفسه، فسأله عن

الدعاء ثم جاء فأخبر به القوم " اللهم بعلمك الغيب، و قدرتك على الخلق، أحيني ما علمت الحياة خيرا لي، و توفني إذا علمت الوفاة خيرا لي، اللهم و أسألك خشيتك في الغيب والشهادة، و أسألك كلمة الحق في الرضا و الغضب، وأسألك القصد في الفقر والغنى وأسألك نعيماً لا ينفذ وأسألك قرة عين لا تنقطع وأسألك الرضا بعد القضاء، و أسألك برد العيش بعد الموت، وأسألك لذة النظر إلى وجهك، و الشوق إلى لقائك في غير ضراء مضرة، ولا فتنة مضلة، اللهم زينا بزينة الإيمان، و اجعلنا هداة مهديين." رواه النسائي

One day ᶜAmmār ibn Yāssir was questioned by the congregation after a prayer that he led and made very short. He said he had chosen certain supplications he had learned from God's Messenger ﷺ. When asked about them he said they were, "O God, by Your knowledge of the unseen and Your power over creation, grant me life for as long as You know life to be best for me and take me back if You know that death is better for me. O God, I ask You for awe of You, both within my secret heart and openly. I ask You for truthfulness, both in contentment and anger. I ask You for moderation, both in poverty and riches. I ask You for a felicity which does not pass away. I ask You for a comfort which is not cut off. I ask You for satisfaction with what is decreed. I ask You for coolness of life after death. I ask You for the bliss of looking upon Your face, and I long to meet You in a state in which distress does not cause harm nor testing lead astray. O God, adorn us with the beauty of faith, and make us guides who are rightly guided." (Nasāʾī)

Pilgrimage (Ḥajj)

عن أبي هريرة – رضي الله عنه– قال: خطبنا رسول الله – صلى الله عليه وسلم – فقال:" يا أيها الناس قد فرض عليكم الحج فحجوا." فقال رجل: أكل عام يا رسول الله ؟. فسكت حتى قالها ثلاثا، فقال: " لو قلت نعم، لوجبت، و لما استطعتم." ثم قال: "ذروني ما تركتكم، فإنما هلك من كان قبلكم بكثرة سؤالهم، و اختلافهم على أنبيائهم، فإذا أمرتكم بشئ فأتوا منه ما استطعتم، و إذا نهيتكم عن شئ فدعوه." رواه مسلم

Abū Hurayrah ﷺ reported that in a sermon, the Messenger of God ﷺ said, "O people, pilgrimage has been made incumbent upon you, so undertake it." A man asked incessantly whether the pilgrimage should be made annually. In the end, the Prophet replied, "If I were to say that it should, it would be obligatory, and you would not be able to perform it." He then added, "Whenever I am silent (about a subject), let it be, for your predecessors perished from nothing other than their excessive questioning and their contention with their prophets. So when I direct you to do anything, do as much as you can of it; and when I stop you from anything, let it go." (Muslim)

عن أبي هريرة – رضي الله عنه– قال: قال رسول الله – صلى الله عليه وسلم– :" من حج لله فلم يرفث، و لم يفسق، رجع كيوم ولدته أمه." رواه البخاري و مسلم

Abū Hurayrah ﷺ related that the Messenger of God ﷺ said, "Whoever sets out earnestly on the pilgrimage seeking God, and refrains from obscene or lewd speech, and does not leave or forsake his quest, will return as pure as the day his mother gave him birth." (Bukhārī & Muslim)

عن ابن عباس – رضي الله عنهما– قال: قال رسول الله – صلى الله عليه وسلم– :" نزل الحجر الأسود من الجنة و هو أشد بياضا من الثلج حتى سودته خطايا أهل الشرك." رواه أحمد والترمذي

Ibn ʿAbbās ﵄ related that the Messenger of God ﷺ said, "The Black Stone descended from Paradise whiter than snow, but the sins of the people who associate others with God made it black." (Aḥmad & Tirmidhī)

عن وابصة بن معبد – رضي الله عنه– أن رسول الله – صلى الله عليه وسلم – قال:" يا وابصة، جئت تسأل عن البر و الإثم ؟ ". قلت: نعم. قال: فجمع أصابعه، فضرب بها صدره، و قال: "استفت نفسك، استفت قلبك يا وابصة " ثلاثا." البر ما اطمأنت إليه النفس، و اطمأن إليه القلب، و الإثم ما حاك في النفس، و تردد في الصدر، و إن أفتاك الناس وأفتوك ." رواه أحمد والدارمي

The Messenger of God ﷺ said to Wābiṣah ibn Maᶜbad ؓ, "Have you come to ask me about right and wrong?" Then he struck his breast with his fingers and said, "Consult yourself. Consult your heart. Consult your heart. Consult your heart. Right is what your inner self *(nafs)* and heart feel secure with, and wrong is what agitates your inner self (*nafs*) and brings doubt to the heart, no matter how much advice people give you." (Aḥmad & Dārimī)

عن أبي قتادة – رضي الله عنه– قال: قال رسول الله – صلى الله عليه وسلم– :" من سَرَّه أن ينجيه الله من كرب يوم القيامة، فلينَفِّس عن معسر، أو يضع عنه." رواه مسلم

Abū Qatādah ؓ related that the Messenger of God ﷺ said, "If anyone would like God to save him from the anxieties of the Day of Resurrection, he should grant a respite to one who is in straitened circumstances, or relieve him of his burden." (Muslim)

عن أبي هريرة – رضي الله عنه– أن رجلا تقاضى رسول الله – صلى الله عليه وسلم – فأغلظ له، فهم أصحابه، فقال: " دعوه فإن لصاحب الحق مقالا، و اشتروا له بعيرا، فأعطوه إياه." قالوا لا نجد إلا أفضل من سنه، قال: "اشتروه فأعطوه إياه، فإن خيركم أحسنكم قضاء." رواه البخاري ومسلم

Abū Hurayrah ؓ reported that a man demanded payment of a debt from God's Messenger ﷺ in a most uncivil manner. The Companions were incensed and were about to retaliate, but the Prophet said, "Leave him alone, for one who has a right is entitled to speak. Buy a camel and give it to him." When they told him that all they could find was one more excellent than the man was entitled to, he said, "Buy it and give it to him, for the best person among you is he who discharges his debt in the best manner." (Bukhārī & Muslim)

عن أبي هريرة – رضي الله عنه– قال: قال رسول الله – صلى الله عليه عن
معاوية بن الحكم – رضي الله عنه– قال: كانت لي جارية ترعى غنما لي قبل
أحد و الجوانية، فاطلعت ذات يوم فإذا الذئب قد ذهب بشاه من غنمها، و أنا رجل
من بني آدم آسف كما يأسفون، لكني صككتها صكة، فأتيت رسول الله – صلى الله
عليه وسلم– ، فعظم ذلك علي. قلت: يا رسول الله، أفلا أعتقها ؟ قال:"ائتني بها."
. فأتيته بها، فقال لها: " أين الله ؟." قالت: في السماء قال: "من أنا ؟." قالت: أنت
رسول الله، قال: "أعتقها فإنها مؤمنة." رواه مسلم

ᶜUmar ibn Al-Ḥakam ؓ said, "I had a slave girl who was herding sheep of mine, and one day I looked and saw that a wolf had gone off with one of the sheep. Now I am a man who becomes annoyed just as others do, so I gave her a blow (on the face). I then went to God's Messenger ﷺ, who let me know that this was a great offense on my part, so I asked whether I should set her free. He told me to bring her to him. When I did, he asked her where God was, and she said, 'In heaven.' He asked her who he was, and she replied that he was God's Messenger. He then told me to set her free, for she was a believer." (Muslim)

وسلم– :" نفس المؤمن معلقة بدينه حتى يقضي عنه." رواه أحمد والترمذي

Abū Hurayrah ؓ said that the Messenger of God ﷺ said, "A believer's soul is attached to his debt until it is paid." (Aḥmad, Tirmidhī)

عن رافع بن عمرو الغفاري – رضي الله عنه– قال: كنت غلاما أرمي نخل الأنصار، فأتي بي النبي – صلى الله عليه وسلم – فقال: " يا بني، لم ترمي النخل ؟." قال قلت: آكل. قال: "فلا ترم النخل ، و كُلْ مما يسقط في أسفلها." ثم مسح رأسي فقال: " اللهم أشبع بطنه." رواه الترمذي وأبوماجه

Rāfi^c ibn ^cAmrū Al-Ghifārī ﷺ said, "When I was a boy I used to throw stones at the palm-trees belonging to the Anṣār, so I was brought before the Prophet ﷺ. He asked, 'Child, why do you throw stones at the palm-trees?' I replied that it was to get something to eat. He said, 'Do not throw stones, but eat from whatever falls from them.' Then, passing his hand over my head, he said, 'O God, fill his belly!'" (Tirmidhī)

عن عائشة – رضي الله عنها– أنها قالت: يا رسول الله، ما الشئ الذي لا يحل منعه؟ قال: " الماء، و الملح، و النار." قالت: قلت يا رسول الله، هذا الماء قد عرفناه، فما بال الملح، و النار؟ قال: " يا حميراء، من أعطى نارا، فكأنما تصدق بجميع ما أنضجت تلك النار، و من أعطى ملحا، فكأنما تصدق بجميع ما طيبت تلك الملح، و من سقى مسلما شربة من ماء حيث يوجد الماء، فكأنما أعتق رقبة، و من سقى مسلما شربة من ماء حيث لا يوجد الماء، فكأنما أحياها." أخرجه ابن ماجه

^cĀ^3ishah ﷺ asked God's Messenger what thing was unlawful to refuse to anyone, and he replied, "Water, salt, and fire." She said, "Messenger of God, we know about water, but what about salt and fire?" He replied, "Little rosy one, the one who gives fire, it is as though he has given in charity all that the fire cooks. And the one who gives salt, it is as though he has given in charity all that salt flavors. And the one who gives a Muslim a drink of water where water is found, it is as though he has set a slave free; and the one who gives a Muslim a drink of water where water is not found, it is as though he has brought a soul to life." (Ibn Mājah)

عن أنس – رضي الله عنه– أن النبي – صلى الله عليه وسلم – :" كان لا يرد الطيب." رواه البخاري

Anas ﷺ said that the Prophet ﷺ never rejected a gift of perfume. (Bukhārī)

عن أبي هريرة – رضي الله عنه– قال: قال رسول الله – صلى الله عليه وسلم– :" من لم يشكر الناس، لم يشكر الله." رواه أحمد والترمذي

Abū Hurayrah ﵁ related that the Messenger of God ﷺ said, "The one who does not thank people does not thank God." (Aḥmad & Tirmidhī)

عن أبي هريرة – رضي الله عنه– عن النبي – صلى الله عليه وسلم – قال:" تهادوا، فإن الهدية تُذهِبُ وَحَرَ الصدر، ولا تَحقِرَنَّ جارة لجارتها و لو شقَّ فرسنَ شاة." رواه الترمذي

According to Abū Hurayrah ﵁, the Prophet ﷺ said, "Give presents to one another, for a present removes rancor from the breast; and let not a neighbor denigrate the gift of her neighbor, even if it is just a part of a sheep's shank." (Tirmidhī)

عن عمر بن الخطاب – رضي الله عنه– أن رجلا اسمه عبد الله كان يلقب حمارا، كان يُضحِّكُ رسول الله – صلى الله عليه وسلم – و كان النبي – صلى الله عليه وسلم – قد جلده في الشراب، فأُتِيَ به يوما فأمر به فجلد، فقال رجل من القوم: اللهم العنه، ما أكثر ما يُؤتَى به؟ فقال النبي – صلى الله عليه وسلم– : " لا تلعنوه فوالله ما علمت إلا أنه يحب الله و رسوله." رواه البخاري

ᶜUmar ibn al-Khaṭṭāb ﵁ related that there was a man named ᶜAbd Allāh whom they used to call the Donkey. He used to make the Prophet ﷺ laugh a lot, but the Prophet had to order him whipped several times for drunkenness. One day he was brought before the Prophet ﷺ drunk and he ordered him whipped yet again, which prompted someone to say, "May God curse him, how frequently he commits this offense!" To which the Prophet replied, "Do not curse him! For by God, do you not know that he loves God and His Messenger?" (Bukhārī)

عن عبد الرحمن بن سمرة قال : رسول الله صلى الله عليه وسلم "لا تسال
الامارة فانك ان اعطيتها عن مسألة وكلت اليها و ان اعطيتها عن غير مسألة
اعنت عليها" رواه مسلم

The Messenger of God ﷺ said, "Do not ask for authority, for if you are given it as a result of asking you will be left to deal with it yourself; but if you are given it without asking, you will be helped in undertaking it." (Muslim)

Marriage

عن عبد الله بن عمرو – رضي الله عنهما– قال: قال رسول الله – صلى الله عليه وسلم– : " إن الدنيا كلها متاع، و خير متاع الدنيا المرأة الصالحة." سنن النسائي

ʿAbdullāh ibn ʿUmar ؓ related that the Messenger of God ﷺ said, "The whole world is a joy, and the best joy in the world is a righteous woman." (Nisāʾī)

تابع– عن أسامة بن زيد – رضي الله عنهما– قال: قال رسول الله – صلى الله عليه وسلم– :" ما تركت بعدي فتنة أضَرُّ على الرجال من النساء." رواه البخاري ومسلم

Usāmah bin Zayd ؓ related that the Messenger of God ﷺ said, "I have not left after me a source of trial more harmful for men than women." (Bukhārī & Muslim)

عن أنس – رضي الله عنه– قال: قال رسول الله – صلى الله عليه وسلم– : " إذا تزوج العبد فقد أكمل نصف الدين، فليتَّقِ الله في النصف الباقي." رواه البيهقي

Anas ؓ reported that the Messenger of God ﷺ said, "When a servant marries he fulfills half the religion; so let him be conscious of God regarding the other half." (Bayhaqī)

عن أبي هريرة – رضي الله عنه– قال: قال رسول الله – صلى الله عليه وسلم– : "كل أمر ذي بال لا يُبدَأ فيه بالحمد أقطَع." رواه ابن ماجه

Abū Hurayrah ﵁ said that the Messenger of God ﷺ said, "Every important matter which is not begun by an expression of praise to God is incomplete." (Ibn Mājah)

عن ابن عباس – رضي الله عنهما– قال: أن زوج بريرة كان عبدا أسودا يقال له مغيث، كأني أنظر إليه يطوف خلفها و يبكي، و دموعه تسيل على لحيته، فقال النبي – صلى الله عليه وسلم – للعباس: "يا عباس، ألا تعجب من حب مغيث لبريرة ؟ و من بغض بريرة مغيثا ؟." فقال النبي – صلى الله عليه وسلم– : "لوراجَعَته." قالت: يا رسول الله تأمرني؟ قال: " إنما أشفع." قالت: لا حاجة لي فيه. رواه البخاري

Ibn ʿAbbās ﵄ related that the Prophet ﷺ saw a man named Mughīth following his wife, Barīrah, who had rejected him, through the streets of Medina with tears flowing down his beard. The Prophet ﷺ turned to ʿAbbās and said, "O ʿAbbās, are you not amazed at how much Mughīth loves Barīrah and how much she detests him?" Then he told Barīrah, "If only you would take him back." She said, "Are you commanding me, Messenger of God?" To which he replied, "I am only interceding on his behalf." Whereupon she responded, "I have no need for him!" (Bukhārī)

عن عائشة – رضي الله عنها– قالت: قال لي رسول الله – صلى الله عليه وسلم– : " إني لأعلم إذا كنت عني راضية، و إذا كنت علي غضبَى." قالت فقلت: من أين تعرف ذلك ؟ فقال: " أما إذا كنت عني راضية فإنك تقولين: لا و رب محمد، و إذا كنت علي غضبَى قلت: لا و رب إبراهيم." قالت: قلت أجل، و الله يا رسول الله، ما أهجر إلا اسمك. رواه البخاري ومسلم

The Messenger of God ﷺ said to ʿĀʾishah ﵂, "I know when you are pleased with me and when you are angry with me!" She asked how he knew, and he replied that when she was pleased she would say, "No, by

Muḥammad's Lord!"; and when she was angry with him she would say, "No, by the Lord of Abraham!" And ᶜĀʾishah replied, "Yes, but by God, O Messenger of God, I can only abandon your name!" (Bukhārī & Muslim)

عن عاشة – رضي الله عنها – قالت: " كان نبي الله – صلى الله عليه وسلم – يَستاك، فيعطيني السواك لأغسله، فأبدأ به فأستاك، ثم أغسله و أدفعه إليه." رواه أبوداود

ᶜĀʾishah ﷺ said, "The Prophet ﷺ used the tooth-stick. He would then give it to me to wash it. I would first use it myself, then wash it and hand it to him." (Abū Dāʾūd)

قالت عائشة – رضي الله عنها – : "كنت أغتسل أنا و رسول الله – صلى الله عليه وسلم – من إناء واحد فيُبادرني حتى أقول: دع لي دع لي. قالت: و هما جنبان." رواه البخاري ومسلم

ᶜĀʾishah ﷺ said, "After intercourse, God's Messenger ﷺ and I used to wash from one vessel, and he would get ahead of me, so that I would say, 'Give me a chance, give me a chance!'" (Bukhārī & Muslim)

عن أبي هريرة – رضي الله عنه– أن أعرابيا أتى رسول الله – صلى الله عليه وسلم – فقال: إن امرأتي ولدت غلاما أسودا و إني أنكرته، فقال له رسول الله – صلى الله عليه وسلم– : " هل لك من إبل ؟." قال: نعم. قال: " فما ألوانها ؟." قال: حمر. قال:" هل فيها من أورق ؟." قال: إن فيها لوُرقا. قال: " فأنى ترى ذلك جاءها ؟." قال: يارسول الله عِرق نزعها، قال: " ولعل هذا عِرق نزعه." و لم يُرخِّص له في الانتفاء منه . أخرجه البخاري ومسلم

Abū Hurayrah ﷺ related that a desert Arab came to the Prophet ﷺ and told him, "My wife has given birth to a black son and I have denied that he is mine." The Prophet ﷺ asked him, "Do you have any camels?" He replied that he had. He then asked, "What color are they?" and the man said that they were reddish. He asked him, "Is there a dark one among them?" and the man said that there was one who was dark. He asked him, "How do you think this came about?" The man told him that he thought it was a strain to which they had reverted. At this the Prophet said, "Well this, too, may be a strain to which the child has reverted," and he would not permit the man to disown the child. (Bukhārī & Muslim)

Animals

عن ابن عمر – رضي الله عنهما– قال: سمعت رسول الله – صلى الله عليه وسلم – نهى أن تُصبَر بهيمة أو غيرها للقتل. رواه البخاري ومسلم
تابع– عن ابن عمر – رضي الله عنهما– أن النبي – صلى الله عليه وسلم – لعن من اتخذ شيئا فيه الروح غرضا . رواه البخاري ومسلم

Ibn ᶜUmar ﵄ said that he heard God's Messenger ﷺ prohibit keeping an animal or any creature waiting to be killed (for food). Ibn ᶜUmar ﵄ also told that the Prophet cursed those who used a living creature as a target. (Bukhārī & Muslim)

عن جابر – رضي الله عنه– قال: أن النبي – صلى الله عليه وسلم – مَرَّ عليه حمار قد وُسِمَ في وجهه. فقال: " لعن الله الذي وَسَمَه." رواه مسلم

Jābir ﵁ said that when the Prophet ﷺ saw a donkey which had been branded on the face, he said, "God has cursed the one who branded it!" (Muslim)

عن أبي هريرة – رضي الله عنه– قال: سمعت رسول الله – صلى الله عليه وسلم– يقول : " قرصت نملة نبيا من الأنبياء، فأمر بقرية النمل فأحرقت، فأوحى الله تعالى إليه: " أن قرصتك نملة أحرقت أمة من الأمم تسبح ؟." رواه البخاري ومسلم

Abū Hurayrah ﵁ related that the Messenger of God ﷺ said, "Once an ant bit one of the prophets, so he ordered the entire ant colony to be burned. Later God revealed to him, 'Would you burn an entire community that glorifies me just because one ant bit you?'" (Bukhārī & Muslim)

Food

عن عمر بن أبي سلمى – رضي الله عنه– قال: كنت في حجر رسول الله – صلى الله عليه وسلم– و كانت يدي تطيش في الصَّحْفة. فقال لي– : " يا غلام، سَمِّ الله، و كُلْ بيمينك، و كُلْ مما يليك." رواه البخاري ومسلم

ᶜUmar ibn Abū Salmah ﷺ said, "When I was a small boy I was in the house of the Messenger of God ﷺ and during the meal, my hands would roam all over the serving dish. The Messenger of God ﷺ said to me, 'My boy, begin with God's name, eat with your right hand, and eat from what is closest to you." (Bukhārī)

عن أبي هريرة – رضي الله عنه– قال: ما عاب النبي – صلى الله عليه وسلم – طعاما قط ، كان إذا اشتهى شيئاً أكله، و إن كرهه تركه. رواه البخاري ومسلم

Abū Hurayrah ﷺ said, "The Prophet ﷺ never expressed criticism of any food. If he liked it he ate it, and if he disliked it he left it alone." (Bukhārī & Muslim)

عن عائشة – رضي الله عنها– قالت: كان رسول الله – صلى الله عليه وسلم – يحب الحلواء و العسل . رواه البخاري

ᶜĀʾishah ﷺ said, "God's Messenger ﷺ liked sweets and honey." (Bukhārī)

عن أبي هريرة – رضي الله عنه– قال: قال رسول الله – صلى الله عليه وسلم– : " الطاعم الشاكر، بمنزلة الصائم الصابر." رواه الترمذي

According to Abū Hurayrah ؓ, the Messenger of God ﷺ said, "The one who eats and gives thanks is like the one who fasts and shows patience." (Tirmidhī)

عن أبي أيوب الأنصاري – رضي الله عنه– قال: كان رسول الله – صلى الله عليه وسلم – إذا أكل أو شرب قال: " الحمد لله الذي أطعم ،و سقى، و سَوَّغه، و جعل له مَخرَجا." رواه أبوداود

Abū Ayyūb ؓ related that the Messenger of God ﷺ used to say after he finished eating and drinking, "Praise be to God who has given food and drink, made it easy to swallow and made a way out for it." (Abū Dāʾūd)

عن أبي هريرة – رضي الله عنه– قال: قال رسول – صلى الله عليه وسلم– : " من كان يؤمن بالله و اليوم الآخرفلا يؤذ جاره، و من كان يؤمن بالله و اليوم الآخر فليكرم ضيفه، و من كان يؤمن بالله و اليوم الآخر فليقل خيرا أو ليصمت." رواه البخاري ومسلم

Abū Hurayrah ؓ related that the Messenger of God ﷺ said, "Whoever believes in God and the Last Day, let him honor his guest, let him not harm his neighbors, and let him say what is good or else be silent." (Bukhārī & Muslim)

عن أبي الأحوص الجشمي عن أبيه، قال: قلت يا رسول الله، أرأيت إن مررت برجل فلم يَقرني، و لم يُضيفني ثم مَرَّ بعد ذلك، أقريه أم أجزيه ؟ قال " بل أقرِه." السنن الكبرى للبيهقي

Abū Al-Aḥwaṣ Al-Jashmī related that his father once asked the Messenger of God, "If I pass by someone who does not offer me a place to rest or show me hospitality and then he later comes my way, should I offer him hospitality or treat him as he treated me?" He replied, "You should offer him hospitality." (Tirmidhī)

عن أبي سعيد الخدري – رضي الله عنه– عن النبي – صلى الله عليه وسلم – قال: " مثل المؤمن و مثل الإيمان، كمثل الفرس في أخبيته يجول حتى يرجع الى خبته، و إن المؤمن يسهو ثم يرجع إلى الإيمان، فأطعموا طعامكم الأتقياء، وولوا معروفكم المؤمنين." رواه البيهقي

Abū Saᶜīd ﵁ related that the Messenger of God ﷺ said, "The faithful's relationship to faith is as a horse's relationship to the stake to which it is tethered; it wanders around but always returns to its stake. Verily, the faithful falls into heedlessness, then returns to faith. Feed the pious with your food, and confer your kindness upon the faithful." (Bayhaqī)

Matters of Dress and Appearance

عن أبي سعيد الخدري – رضي الله عنه– قال: كان رسول الله – صلى الله
عليه وسلم – إذا استجد ثوبا سماه باسمه: عمامة، أو قميصا، أو رداء، ثم يقول:"
اللهم لك الحمد أنت كسوتنيه، أسألك خيره و خير ما صُنِعَ له، و أعوذ بك من
شره و شر ما صُنِعَ له." رواه الترمذي و أبوداود

Abū Saʿīd al-Khudrī ؓ related that when God's Messenger ﷺ put on a new garment he would say, "O God, praise be to You! As You have clothed me with it, I ask You for its good and the good of that for which it was made, and I seek refuge in You from its evil and from the evil of that for which it was made." (Tirmidhī & Abū Dāʾūd)

عن ابن عمر – رضي الله عنهما– قال: قال رسول الله – صلى الله عليه وسلم– :
" من تشبَّه بقوم فهو منهم." رواه أبوداود

Ibn ʿUmar ؓ reported that the Messenger of God ﷺ said, "Whoever imitates a people becomes one of them." (Abū Dāʾūd)

عن عمرو بن شعيب، عن أبيه، عن جده، قال: قال رسول الله – صلى الله
عليه وسلم– : " إن الله يحب أن يرى أثر نعمته على عبده." رواه الترمذي

The Messenger of God ﷺ said, "God likes the evidence of His bounty to be seen on His servant." (Tirmidhī)

عن عائشة – رضي الله عنها– قالت كان رسول الله صلى الله عليه وسلم إذا أراد أن يحرم يتطيب بأطيب ما يجد ثم أرى وبيص الدهن في رأسه ولحيته بعد ذلك . رواه البخاري ومسلم

ᶜĀʾishah ﷺ said that when the Prophet ﷺ entered the state of sanctity before pilgrimange he would anoint himself with the sweetest perfume until she saw its oil shining on his head and beard. (Bukhārī & Muslim)

عن عائشة – رضي الله عنها– قالت: كنت أغتسل أنا و رسول الله – صلى الله عليه وسلم – في إناء واحد، و كان له شعر فوق الجُمَّة و دون الوفرة . رواه الترمذي

ᶜĀʾishah ﷺ said, "God's Messenger ﷺ and I used to wash from one vessel, and he had hair which did not reach the shoulder, but came lower than the ear." (Tirmidhī)

عن كريمة بنت همام: أن امرأة سألت عائشة – رضي الله عنها – فسألتها عن خِضاب الحنَّاء، فقالت: لا بأس به ، و لكن أكرهه كان حبيبي رسول الله صلى الله عليه وسلم يكره ريحه . رواه أبو داود و النسائي

A woman asked ᶜĀʾishah ﷺ about dyeing with henna and she replied, "It's acceptable to use but I do not like it. My beloved disliked its odor." (Abū Dāʾūd)

عن عائشة – رضي الله عنها– قالت: سأل أناس رسول الله – صلى الله عليه وسلم – عن الكُهَّان، فقال لهم رسول الله – صلى الله عليه وسلم– : " ليسوا بشئ." قالوا: يا رسول الله، فإنهم يحدثون أحيانا الشئ يكون حقا. قال رسول الله – صلى الله عليه وسلم– : " تلك الكلمة من الجن يخطفها الجني، فيَقرُّها في أذن وَليِّه قَرَّ الدجاجة، فيخلطون فيها أكثر من مائة كذبة." رواه البخاري ومسلم

ʿĀʾishah ﷺ said that when people asked the Messenger of God ﷺ about fortune-tellers, he replied, "They are not reliable." The people said, "Messenger of God ﷺ, they sometimes tell a thing which turns out to be true!" He replied, "That relates to a truth which a *jinn* has snatched and cackles into the ear of his friend as a hen does; then they mix more than a hundred lies with it." (Bukhārī & Muslim)

عن أبي هريرة رضي الله عنه قال : قال رسول الله – صلى الله عليه وسلم– : " الرؤيا الصالحة جزء من ستة و أربعين جزءا من النبوة." رواه البخاري ومسلم

Anas ﷺ related that the Messenger of God ﷺ said, "A true dream is just one part of forty-six parts of prophethood." (Bukhārī & Muslim)

عن أبي هريرة – رضي الله عنه– أن رسول الله – صلى الله عليه وسلم – قال: " من رآني في المنام، فقد رآني، فإن الشيطان لا يتمثل بي ." رواه البخاري ومسلم

Abū Hurayrah ﷺ related that the Messenger of God ﷺ said, "Whoever sees me in a dream has truly seen me, for Satan does not appear in my form." (Bukhārī & Muslim)

عن أبي رَزِين العُقَيلي – رضي الله عنه– قال: قال رسول الله – صلى الله عليه وسلم– : " رؤيا المؤمن جزء من أربعين جزءا من النبوة، و هي على رجل طائر ما لم يتحدث بها، فإذا تحدث بها وقعت." قال و أحسبه قال: " ولا يُحدث بها إلا لبيباً أو حبيبا ." رواه الترمذي

The Messenger of God ﷺ said, "The vision (or dream) of the faithful one is but one part of forty parts of prophethood. And it is borne upon the leg of a bird as long as he speaks of it to no one. But once he does, it descends; so do not speak of it, except to a beloved one or to one of inner understanding." (Tirmidhī & Abū Dā'ūd)

عن أبي هريرة – رضي الله عنه– عن النبي – صلى الله عليه وسلم قال– : " إنكم ستحرصون على الإمارة، و ستكون ندامة يوم القيامة، فنِعمَ المرضعة، و بَئِسَتْ الفاطمة." رواه البخاري

Abū Hurayrah ﷺ related that the Prophet ﷺ said, "You are eager to have authority, but it will be your regret on the Day of Resurrection, for power is the best of breasts to suckle, but it is the worst to be weaned from!" (Bukhārī)

عن أبي سعيد الخدري – رضي الله عنه– قال: قال رسول الله – صلى الله عليه وسلم– : " أفضل الجهاد كلمة عدل ، عند سلطان جائر." رواه الترمذي و أبو داود

Ibn Saʿīd ﷺ reported that the Messenger of God ﷺ said, "The best *jihād* is when one speaks the truth in the presence of a tyrannical ruler." (Tirmidhī, Abū Dāʾūd)

عن عبد الله ابن مسعود – رضي الله عنه– قال: قال رسول الله – صلى الله عليه وسلم– : " خير الناس قرني، ثم الذين يَلونهم، ثم الذين يَلونهم، ثم يجئ قوم تسبق شهادة أحدهم يمينه، و يمينه شهادته." أخرجه البخاري

Ibn Masʿūd ﷺ said that the Messenger of God ﷺ said, "The best of men are my generation, then those who come after them, then those who come after them, then there will come a people whose testimonies will contradict their oaths and whose oaths will contradict their testimonies!" (Bukhārī)

عن عبد الرحمن بن حبر – رضي الله عنه– قال: قال رسول الله – صلى الله عليه وسلم– :" ما أغبَرَّتْ قدَما عبد في سبيل الله، فتَمسَّه النار." رواه البخاري

The Messenger of God ﷺ said to Ibn ʿAbbās ؓ that, "No servant who travels in God's way will be touched by the fire." (Bukhārī)

عن ابن عباس – رضي الله عنه– قال: سمعت رسول الله – صلى الله عليه وسلم– يقول : "عينان لا تَمسَّهما النار: عين بكت من خشية الله، و عين باتت تحرس في سبيل الله." رواه الترمذي

Ibn ʿAbbās ؓ said that the Messenger of God ﷺ said, "There are two eyes that will not be touched by the fire: an eye that weeps from awe of God and an eye that spends the night in vigil in God's way." (Tirmidhī)

عن أبي سعيد – رضي الله عنه– أن رسول الله – صلى الله عليه وسلم – قال: يا أبا سعيد " من رضي بالله ربا، و بالإسلام دينا، و بمحمد نبياً وَجَبَت له الجنة فعجب لها أبو سعيد فقال أعدها عليَّ يا رسول الله ففعل ثم قال وأخرى يرفع بها العبد مائة درجة في الجنة مابين كل درجتين كما بين السماء والأرض قال وما هي يا رسول الله قال الجهاد في سبيل الله الجهاد في سبيل الله." رواه مسلم

The Messenger of God ﷺ said to Abu Saʿīd ؓ, "Whoever is content with God as his Lord, and with Islām as his religion, and with Muḥammad as his Messenger, the garden is made ready for him." Abū Saʿīd was pleased with this and asked the Prophet to repeat it which he did and added, "And another by which a servant is elevated a hundred degrees in Paradise, the distance between each degree is as between heaven and earth." He asked him, "And what is it, O Messenger of God?" He replied, "Striving in the way of God, striving in the way of God!" (Muslim)

عن أنس – رضي الله عنه– قال: كانت ناقة لرسول الله – صلى الله عليه وسلم – تسمى العضباء، و كانت لا تسبق فجاء أعرابي على قعود له فسبقها، فاشتد ذلك على المسلمين، وقالوا سُبقت العضباء فقال رسول الله – صلى الله عليه وسلم– : " إن حقا على الله، أن لا يرفع شيئاً من الدنيا إلا وضعه." رواه البخاري

Anas reported that the Messenger of God ﷺ had a camel named Aḍbā᾽ (the split-eared one) which could not be beaten in a race. Then one day a Bedouin came with a camel and he won the race with her. This was hard on the Muslims, but the Prophet ﷺ said to them, "It is God's right that whatever becomes exalted in the world, He eventually causes it to be brought low." (Bukhārī)

عن أبي رافع – رضي الله عنه– قال: بعثتني قريش إلى رسول الله – صلى الله عليه وسلم – فلما رأيت رسول الله – صلى الله عليه وسلم– ألقي في قلبي الإسلام، فقلت: يا رسول الله، إني و الله لا أرجع إليهم أبدا. فقال رسول الله صلى الله عليه وسلم: " إني لا أخيس بالعهد ولا أحبس البُرُدَ، و لكن ارجع، فإن كان في نفسك الذي في نفسك الآن فارجع." قال: فذهبت ثم أتيت النبي – صلى الله عليه وسلم – فأسلمت. رواه أبوداود

Abū Rāfiʿ said, "The Quraysh sent me on a mission to the Messenger of God ﷺ and when I saw him, Islām entered my heart. So I told him, 'O Messenger of God, I swear by God that I shall never go back to them!' But the Prophet ﷺ told me, 'Indeed, I do not break a covenant nor do I imprison envoys. Go back for a while, and if later you find in your soul what you find in it now, then return to me.' So I left for Mecca and later returned to the Prophet and entered Islām." (Abū Dā᾽ūd)

عن أبي هريرة – رضي الله عنه– قال: قال رسول الله – صلى الله عليه وسلم– : " لا تدخلوا الجنة حتى تؤمنوا، ولا تؤمنوا حتى تحابوا، أوَلا أدلكم على شئ إذا فعلتموه تحاببتم ؟ أفشوا السلام بينكم." رواه مسلم

Abū Hurayrah said that the Messenger of God ﷺ said, "You will not enter Paradise until you attain to faith, and you will not attain to faith until you love one another. Shall I tell you of a thing to do that will make you love one another? Spread peace among yourselves." (Muslim)

عن أبي هريرة – رضي الله عنه– قال: قبل رسول الله – صلى الله عليه وسلم – الحسن بن علي و عنده الأقرع بن حابس التميمي جالساً ، فقال الأقرع: إن لي عشرة من الولد ما قبّلت منهم أحدا. فنظر إليه رسول الله – صلى الله عليه وسلم – ثم قال: " من لا يَرْحَم لا يُرحم." رواه البخاري ومسلم

Abū Hurayrah ﷺ reported that God's Messenger ﷺ kissed (his grandson) al-Ḥasan while Al-Aqra[c] ibn Ḥābis was with him. Al-Aqra[c] said, "I have ten children, and I have never kissed any of them!" God's Messenger ﷺ looked at him and said, "The one who shows no mercy receives no mercy." (Bukhārī & Muslim)

عن البَرَّاء بن عازب – رضي الله عنه– قال: قال النبي – صلى الله عليه وسلم– : " ما من مسلمَين يلتقيان فيتصافحان إلا غُفِرَ لهما قبل أن يتفرَّقا." رواه أحمد والترمذي و ابن ماجه

The Prophet ﷺ said, "Any two Muslims who meet and greet each other will have their sins forgiven before they separate." (Aḥmad, Tirmidhī, Ibn Mājah)

عن أيوب بن بشير بن كعب العدوي ، عن رجل من عنزة أنه قال لأبي ذر حيث سُيِّر من الشام إني أريد أن أسألك عن حديث من حديث رسول الله صلى الله عليه وسلم قال : إذا أخبرك به إلا أن يكون سراً قلت إنه ليس بسر: هل كان رسول الله – صلى الله عليه وسلم يصافحكم إذا لقيتموه ؟ قال : ما لقيته قط إلا صافحني، و بعث إلي ذات يوم و لم أكن في أهلي، فلما جئت أخبرت أنه أرسل لي فأتيته و هو على سريره، فالتزمني فكانت تلك أجوَد و أجوَد . رواه أبوداود

A man from the tribe of [c]Anza asked Abū Dharr ﷺ, "Did the Prophet ﷺ shake hands with you when you met him?" He said, "I never met him (the Prophet) without his shaking hands with me. One day he sent for me when I was not at home, and, being informed after I returned, I went to him and found him on a couch. He embraced me, and that was better still!" (Abū Dāʾūd)

عن أسيد بن خضير – رضي الله عنه – رجل من الأنصار – قال: بينما هو يحدث القوم – و كان فيه مزاح – بينا يضحكهم، فطعنه النبي – صلى الله عليه وسلم – في خاصرته بعود، فقال: أصبرني، فقال: " اصطبر." قال : إن عليك قميصا و ليس علي قميص، فرفع النبي – صلى الله عليه و سلم عن قميصه، فاحتضنه و جعل يُقَبِّل كَشْحَهُ، قال : إنما أردت هذا يا رسول الله . رواه أبوداود

ʾUsayd ibn Khuḍayr ﷺ said that one of the Anṣār who was given to jesting was talking to the people and making them laugh. The Prophet ﷺ poked him in the ribs with a stick, whereupon the man said, "Let me take retaliation!" The Prophet told him to do so, and he said, "You are wearing a shirt, but I am not." The Prophet ﷺ raised his shirt, and the man embraced him and began to kiss his side. Then he said, "This is all I wanted, Messenger of God!" (Abū Dāʾūd)

عن أبي هريرة – رضي الله عنه– قال: قال رسول الله – صلى الله عليه وسلم– : " لا يَسُبّ أحدكم الدهر، فإن الله هو الدهر ولا يقولن أحدكم للعنب : الكَرم فإن الكَرم الرجلُ المسلم." رواه مسلم

Abū Hurayrah ﷺ related that the Messenger of God ﷺ said, "Do not curse time, for God is time!" (Muslim)

عن سهل بن سعد – رضي الله عنه– قال : قال رسول الله – صلى الله عليه وسلم– : " من يضمن لي ما بين لِحيِيه، و ما بين رجليه أضمن له الجنة." رواه البخاري

Sahl bin Saʿd ﷺ reported that the Messenger of God ﷺ said, "Anyone who guarantees me what is between his jaws and what is between his legs, I will guarantee him Paradise!" (Bukhārī)

عن عبدالله بن مسعود – رضي الله عنه– قال : قال رسول الله – صلى الله عليه وسلم– : "سباب المسلم فسوق، و قتاله كفر." رواه البخاري ومسلم

ʿAbdullāh ibn Masʿūd ﵁ related that the Messenger of God ﷺ said, "Reviling a Muslim is disobedience to God, and fighting with him is infidelity." (Bukhārī & Muslim)

عن أبي ذر – رضي الله عنه– قال : قال رسول الله – صلى الله عليه وسلم– : " لا يرمي رجل رجلا بالفسوق، ولا يرميه بالكفر إلا ارتدت عليه، إن لم يكن صاحبه كذلك." رواه البخاري

Abū Dharr ﵁ reported that the Messenger of God ﷺ said, "No one accuses another of disobedience to God or of infidelity without it recoiling on him, if the other is not as he said." (Bukhārī)

عن أبي هريرة – رضي الله عنه– قال : قال رسول الله – صلى الله عليه وسلم– :" تجد من شرار شر الناس يوم القيامة عند الله ذا الوجهين، الذي يأتي هؤلاء بوجه، و هؤلاء بوجه." رواه البخاري ومسلم

Abū Hurayrah ﵁ said that the Messenger of God ﷺ said, "You will find that the worst people on the Day of Resurrection will be those with two faces: who present one face to some and another face to others." (Bukhārī & Muslim)

عن أبي هريرة – رضي الله عنه– أن رسول الله – صلى الله عليه وسلم – قال:" أتدرون ما الغيبة ؟." قالوا : الله و رسوله أعلم . قال " ذِكرُكَ أخاك بما يكره." قيل : أفرأيت إن كان في أخي ما أقول ؟. قال :" إن كان فيه ما تقول فقد اغتبته، و إن لم يكن فيه ما تقول فقد بَهتَّه." رواه مسلم

It was reported by Abū Hurayrah ﵁ that the Messenger of God ﷺ asked, "Do you know what gossip is?" They replied, "God and His Messenger know best." He said, "Saying something about your brother that he would dislike." They asked, "What if he is as we say?" He replied, "If what you say is true, you have gossiped about him; if it is not true, you have slandered him!" (Muslim)

عن عائشة – رضي الله عنها– أن رجلا استأذن على النبي – صلى الله عليه وسلم – فقال: "ائذنوا له، فبئس أخو العشيرة أو إبن العشيرة فلما دخل ألان له الكلام قلت يا رسول الله قلت الذي قلت ثم ألنت له الكلام قال : أي عائشة ان شر الناس من تركه الناس او وَدَعَهُ الناس إتقاء فحشه ." جلس تطلق النبي – صلى الله عليه وسلم– في وجهه و انبسط اليه، فلما انطلق الرجل قالت عائشة : يا رسول الله، قلت له كذاو كذا، ثم تطلقت في وجهه، و انبسطت إليه، فقال رسول الله – صلى الله عليه وسلم– :" متى عهدتني فحاشا ؟ إن شر الناس عند الله منزلة يوم القيامة من تركه الناس اتقاء شره." رواه البخاري ومسلم

ʿĀʾishah ﷺ related that a man asked permission to visit the Prophet ﷺ and he gave the permission saying, "Let him in, this worst of companions!" But when the man sat down with him, he smiled at him and relaxed in his company. When the man left, ʿĀʾishah asked the Prophet ﷺ, "You said what you said about him and then you behaved in such a good way with him?" The Messenger of God ﷺ replied, "Do you know me to be an evil-doer? The one who will be in the worst position in God's estimation on the Day of Resurrection will be the one whom people avoided for fear of the harm he might do (them)." (Bukhārī & Muslim)

عن أبي هريرة – رضي الله عنه– قال: قال رسول الله – صلى الله عليه وسلم–:" كل أمتي معافىَ إلاّ المجاهرين، و إن من المجاهرة أن يعمل الرجل بالليل عملا ثم يصبح و قد ستره الله، فيقول : يا فلان عملت البارحة كذا و كذا، و قد بات يستره ربه، و يصبح يكشف ستر الله عنه." رواه البخاري ومسلم

Abū Hurayrah ﷺ related that the Messenger of God ﷺ said, "Every one of my community is pardoned except the flaunters. Flaunting is when one commits an act of disobedience during the night and then, although God has concealed it for him, brags to someone in the morning that he did such-and-such the previous night. He slept under the protection of

God and in the morning he removes God's protection from him." (Bukhārī & Muslim)

عن علي بن حسين بن علي بن أبي طالب – رضي الله عنهم– قال رسول الله – صلى الله عليه وسلم– :" من حسن إسلام المرء، تركه ما لا يَعنِيه." رواه مالك وأحمد و الترمذي

According to ʿAlī ibn Ḥusayn ﷺ (Zayn Al-Abideen), the Prophet ﷺ said, "Among the beautiful qualities of a person's Islām is to leave alone what does not concern him." (Mālik, Aḥmad, & Tirmidhī)

عن صفوان بن سليم، أنه قيل لرسول الله – صلى الله عليه وسلم– : أيكون المؤمن جبانا ؟ قال "نعم." قيل : أيكون المؤمن بخيلا ؟ قال:" نعم." فقيل له أيكون المؤمن كذابا ؟ قال : " لا." رواه مالك والبيهقي

The Messenger of God ﷺ was asked, "Can a believer be a coward?" He replied, "Yes." He then was asked, "Can a believer be a miser?" Again he said, "Yes." He was then asked, "Can a believer be a liar?" He replied, "No!" (Mālik & Bayhaqī)

عن أبي ذر – رضي الله عنه – قال : دخلت على رسول الله – صلى الله عليه وسلم – فذكر الحديث بطوله إلى أن قال : قلت : يا رسول الله، أوصني. قال : " أوصيك بتقوى الله عز وجل، فإنه أزيَنُ لأمرك كله." قلت : زدني. قال :" عليك بتلاوة القرآن، و ذكر الله عز وجل، فإنه ذكر لك في السماء، و نور لك في الأرض." قلت: زدني. قال: "عليك بطول الصمت، فإنه مَطرَدة للشيطان، و عَون لك على أمر دينك." قلت :زدني. قال:"إيَّاك و كثرة الضحك، فإنه يميت القلب، و يُذهب بنور الوجه قلت : زدني قا ل: قل الحق وإن كان مرًّا قلت : زدني قال: لا تخف في الله لومة لائم قلت : زدني قال : ليحجزك عن الناس ما تعلم من نفسك ." شعب الايمان للبيهقي

Abū Dharr ﷺ asked the Prophet ﷺ to advise him. He told him, "I advise you to be conscious of God, for this is the best adornment to all of your matters." He asked for more. "Continue the recital of the Qur'ān and the remembrance of God, for it is a remembrance for you in Heaven and a light for you on earth." He still asked for more. "Prolong your silence, for it repels Satan and is a great help for you in the matters of your religion." He asked for more. "Avoid excessive laughter, for it kills the heart and removes the light of the countenance." He asked for more. "Speak the truth even if it is bitter." He asked for more. "Do not fear in the matters of God the blame of any blamer." He asked for more. "Let what you know about yourself deter you from criticizing people." (Bayhaqī)

عن أنس – رضي الله عنه– أن رجلا استحمل رسول الله – صلى الله عليه وسلم– فقال:" إني حاملك على ولد الناقة؟." فقال يا رسول الله : ما أصنع بولد الناقة ؟. فقال رسول الله – صلى الله عليه وسلم – :" و هل تلد الإبل إلا النوق ؟."
رواه الترمذي وأبو داود

Anas ﵁ reported that a man asked God's Messenger ﷺ for a mount. "I shall give you a she-camel's child to ride upon," said the Prophet ﷺ. "What am I to do with a she-camel's child?" demanded the man. "Do she-camels give birth to anything other than camels?" (Tirmidhī & Abū Dā'ūd)

عن أنس – رضي الله عنه– أن رجلا من أهل البادية كان اسمه زاهراً ، كان يهدي للنبي – صلى الله عليه وسلم– الهدية من البادية، فيجهزه رسول الله – صلى الله عليه وسلم – إذا أراد أن يخرج، فقال النبي – صلى الله عليه وسلم– :" إن ز اهرا باديتنا، و نحن حاضروه." و كان النبي – صلى الله عليه وسلم – يحبه و كان رجلاً دميما، فأتى النبي – صلى الله عليه وسلم– يوما و هو يبيع متاعه، فاحتضنه من خلفه، و هو لا يبصره، فقال الرجل : أرسلني, من هذا ؟ فالتفت، فعرف النبي – صلى الله عليه وسلم– فجعل لا يألو ما ألصق ظهره بصدر النبي – صلى الله عليه وسلم – حين عرفه، و جعل النبي – صلى الله عليه وسلم– يقول : " من يشتري العبد." فقال: يا رسول الله، إذاً و الله تجدني كاسدا،فقال النبي – صلى الله عليه وسلم– " لكن عند الله لست بكاسد أو قال لكن عند الله أنت غالٍ ."
مسند أحمد

It was related by Anas ﷺ that a Bedouin named Zāhir used to come to the Prophet ﷺ for provisions on a regular basis. He was a very ugly man, but the Prophet ﷺ loved him and used to say, "Zāhir is our wilderness and we are present with him." The Prophet ﷺ came upon him one day when he was selling goods and put his arms around him from behind. "Let me go! Who is this?" he cried. Then, turning round, recognized the Prophet ﷺ and remained close against the Prophet's ﷺ chest. The Prophet ﷺ playfully called out, "Who will buy this slave?" To which Zāhir responded, "Messenger of God, you will find me to be worthless goods, I swear by God." The Prophet ﷺ said to him, "But in God's sight you are not worthless goods!" (Aḥmad)

عن النعمان بن بشير – رضي الله عنه– قال : استأذن أبوبكر رحمة الله عليه على النبي – صلى الله عليه وسلم– فسمع صوت عائشة عاليا, فلما دخل تناولها ليلطمها, و قال: ألا أراك ترفعين صوتك على رسول الله – صلى الله عليه وسلم– فجعل النبي صلى الله عليه وسلم يحجزه، و خرج أبو بكر مغضبا، فقال النبي – صلى الله عليه وسلم – حين خرج أبو بكر" كيف رأيتني أنقذتك من الرجل ؟." قال: فمكث أبو بكر أياما ثم استأذن على رسول الله صلى الله عليه وسلم فوجدهما قد اصطلحا، فقال لهما : أدخلاني في سلمكما كما أدخلتماني في حربكما، فقال النبي – صلى الله عليه وسلم– :" قد فعلنا، قد فعلنا." رواه أبو داود

An-Nuᶜmān bin Bashīr ﷺ related that coming into the Prophet's ﷺ house, Abū Bakr heard his daughter, ᶜĀ᾿ishah, speaking in a loud voice. So when he entered, he caught hold of her to slap her, and said, "Don't let me ever find you raising your voice to God's Messenger!" The Prophet ﷺ prevented him from slapping her, and Abū Bakr walked out of the house angry. After he had gone, the Prophet ﷺ said to ᶜĀ᾿ishah, "You see, I rescued you from him!" Some days later, Abū Bakr came back and, finding they had made peace with one another, said to them, "Bring me into your peace as you brought me into your war!" The Prophet ﷺ replied, "We have done so, we have done so!" (Abū Dāwūd)

عن عقبة بن عامر – رضي الله عنه– قال : قال رسول الله – صلى الله عليه وسلم– :" أنسابكم هذه ليست بمسبَّة على أحدكم ، كلكم بنو آدم، ، ليس لأحد

على أحد فضل بالدين أو تقوى، وكفى بالرجل أن يكون بذيا، فاحشا، بخيلا."
رواه أحمد والبيهقي

ᶜAqabah ibn ᶜAmr ﷺ related that the Messenger of God ﷺ said, "These lineages of yours do not make you superior to anyone. You are all human. No one has superiority over another except in piety and consciousness. It is sufficient shame for one to be foul, evil, or stingy." (Aḥmad & Bayhaqī)

عن أبي بكرة – رضي الله عنه– قال: قال رسول الله – صلى الله عليه وسلم– :" ما من ذنب أجدر أن يُعجِّل الله لصاحبه العقوبة في الدنيا مع ما يدخر له في الآخرة من البغي، و قطيعة الرحم." رواه الترمذي وأبوداود

Abū Bakr ﷺ said that the Messenger of God ﷺ said, "There is no sin more fitting for God to hasten the punishment to its perpetrator in this world, along with what He has stored for him in the next world, than oppression and the severing of ties of mercy." (Tirmidhī & Abū Dā'ūd)

عن ابن عمر – رضي الله عنهما– أن رجلا أتى رسول الله – صلى الله عليه وسلم – فقال: يا رسول الله، إني أصبت ذنبا عظيما، فهل لي توبة ؟ قال :"هل لك من أم ؟." قال : لا. قال:" هل لك خالة ؟." قال: نعم. قال:" فبِرَّها."
رواه الترمذي

Ibn ᶜUmar ﷺ related that a man came to the Prophet ﷺ and said, "I have committed a serious sin. Is there a way for me to repent for it?" The Prophet asked him, "Is your mother alive?" He replied that she was not. Then he asked, "Do you have a maternal aunt?" And he said yes. The Prophet told him, "Then go and be kind to her." (Tirmidhī)

عن أبي أسَيدٍ مالك بن ربيعة السَّاعِدِي – رضي الله عنه– قال: بينما نحن عند رسول الله – صلى الله عليه وسلم– إذ جاءه رجل من بني سلمة فقال : يا رسول الله، هل بقي من برِّ أبوي شئ أبرهما به بعد موتهما ؟ قال :" نعم الصلاة

عليهما و الاستغفار لهما وإنفاذ عهدهما من بعدهما، و صلة الرحم التي لا توصل إلا بهما، و إكرام صديقهما." رواه أبوداود و ابن ماجه

A man came to the Messenger of God ﷺ and said, "O Messenger of God, is there any kindness left that I can do to my parents after their death?" He replied, "Yes, you can invoke blessings on them, ask forgiveness for them, carry out whatever commitments they had made, uphold the relationships of mercy which could only have been maintained by them, and honor their friends." (Abū Dā᾿ūd & Ibn Mājah)

عن معاوية بن جاهمة السلمي – رضي الله عنه– أن جاهمة جاء إلى النبي صلى الله عليه وسلم – فقال : يا رسول الله، أردت أن أغزو، و قد جئت أستشيرك، فقال :" هل لك من أم ؟." قال: نعم. قال: "فالزمها، فإن الجنة تحت رجليها." رواه أحمد والنسائي والبيهقي

Muᶜāwiyah ibn Jāhimah ؓ said that Jāhimah came to the Prophet ﷺ and said, "Messenger of God, I want to go on a military expedition and I have come to consult you." The Prophet ﷺ asked if his mother was alive. When he replied that she was, he said to him, "Stay with her, for Paradise is at her feet." (Aḥmad)

عن جرير بن عبد الله – رضي الله عنه– قال : قال رسول الله – صلى الله عليه وسلم– : "لا يرحم الله من لا يرحم الناس." رواه البخاري ومسلم

Jarīr ibn ᶜAbdullāh ؓ reported that the Messenger of God ﷺ said, "God does not show mercy to those who do not show mercy to people." (Bukhārī & Muslim)

عن عائشة – رضي الله عنها– قالت: جاء أعرابي إلى النبي – صلى الله عليه وسلم – فقال : تقبلون الصبيان؟ فما نقبلهم، فقال النبي – صلى الله عليه وسلم – :" أوَ أملك لك أن نزع الله من قلبك الرحمة ؟." رواه البخاري ومسلم

ᶜĀʾishah ﷺ told that a Bedouin came to the Prophet ﷺ and asked, "Do you kiss your male children? We do not kiss them!" and the Prophet ﷺ replied, "What can I do for you if God has deprived your heart of mercy?" (Bukhārī & Muslim)

عن أبي هريرة – رضي الله عنه– قال: قال رسول الله – صلى الله عليه وسلم – :" الساعي على الأرملة، و المسكين كالمجاهد في سبيل الله او القائم الليل الصائم النهار ." رواه البخاري ومسلم

Abū Hurayrah ﷺ related that the Messenger of God ﷺ said, "The one who strives on behalf of a widow or a poor person is like one who strives in God's path or the one who stays up the night in prayer and fasts by day." (Bukhārī & Muslim)

عن النعمان بن بشير– رضي الله عنهما– قال: قال رسول الله – صلى الله عليه وسلم– :" ترى المؤمنين في تراحمهم، و توادهم و تعاطفهم كمثل الجسد إذا اشتكى عضو، تداعى له سائر الجسد بالسهر و الحمى." رواه البخاري ومسلم

An-Nuᶜmān bin Bashīr ﷺ related that the Messenger of God ﷺ said, "You see the believers in their mutual mercy, love, and affection, like one body. When one member suffers, the rest of the body inclines towards it with sleeplessness and fever." (Bukhārī & Muslim)

عن عبد الله ابن عمر – رضي الله عنهما– أن رسول الله – صلى الله عليه وسلم – قال :" المسلم أخو المسلم، لا يظلمه ولا يَسْلِمه، و من كان في حاجة أخيه كان الله في حاجته، و من فَرَّج عن مسلم كربةَ فَرَّج الله عنه كُرُبَةَ من كربات يوم القيامة، و من ستر مسلما ستره الله يوم القيامة." رواه البخاري ومسلم

Ibn ᶜUmar ﷺ said that the Messenger of God ﷺ said, "A Muslim is a Muslim's brother; he does not wrong him or abandon him. If anyone cares for his brother's need, God will care for his need. If anyone eases his brother's distress, God will ease for him one of the distresses of the Day of Resurrection. And if anyone protects a Muslim's secrets, God will protect his secrets on the Day of Resurrection." (Bukhārī & Muslim)

عن أنس – رضي الله عنه– قال : قال رسول الله – صلى الله عليه وسلم –: " و الذي نفسي بيده، لا يؤمن عبد حتى يحب لجاره أو قال لأخيه ما يحب لنفسه." رواه البخاري ومسلم

Anas ﷺ related that the Messenger of God ﷺ said, "By the One who holds my soul in His hand, a man does not believe until he loves for his neighbor or brother what he loves for himself." (Bukhārī & Muslim)

عن عبد الله بن مسعود – رضي الله عنه– قال : قال رسول الله – صلى الله عليه وسلم –: " إذا كنتم ثلاثة، فلا يتناجى اثنان دون الآخر حتى تختلطوا بالناس، من أجل أن يحزنه." رواه البخاري ومسلم

ᶜAbdullāh ibn Masᶜūd ﷺ said that the Messenger of God ﷺ said, "When three of you are together, two of you must not talk privately without the third in order not to cause him sorrow." (Bukhārī & Muslim)

عن عبد الله بن عمرو – رضي الله عنهما– قال: قال رسول الله – صلى الله عليه وسلم –: " خير الأصحاب عند الله خيرهم لصاحبه، و خير الجيران عند الله خيرهم لجاره." رواه الترمذي والدارمي

ᶜAbdullāh ibn ᶜUmar ﷺ related that the Messenger of God ﷺ said, "The best companion in God's estimation is the one who is best to his companion, and the best neighbor in God's estimation is the one who is best to his neighbor." (Tirmidhī & Dārimī)

عن عبد الله – رضي الله عنه – قال: قال رسول الله – صلى الله عليه وسلم– : "الخلق عيال الله، فأحب الخلق إلى الله من أحسن إلى عياله." رواه البيهقي

Anas and ᶜAbdullāh ﷺ related that the Messenger of God ﷺ said, "All creatures are God's children, and those dearest to God are the ones who treat His children in the best way." (Bayhaqī)

عن أبي هريرة – رضي الله عنه– قال : قال رسول الله – صلي الله عليه وسلم – :" إن الله يقول يوم القيامة : أين المتحابون بجلالي ؟ اليوم أظلهم في ظِلِّي، يوم لا ظِلَّ إلا ظِلِّي." رواه مسلم

Abū Hurayrah ﷺ related that the Messenger of God ﷺ said, "On the Day of Resurrection, God will say, 'Where are those who love one another by My Majesty? Today I shall shelter them in My shade, when there is no shade but Mine!'" (Muslim)

عن معاذ بن جبل – رضي الله عنه– قال: سمعت رسول الله – صلى الله عليه وسلم – يقول: "قال الله تعالى : وَجَبَتْ محبتي للمتحابين فيَّ، و المتجالسين فيَّ، و المتزاورين فيَّ، و المتباذلين فيَّ." رواه مالك

Muᶜādh ibn Jabal ﷺ reported that the Messenger of God ﷺ said, "God, most exalted, said, 'My love belongs by right to those who love one another in Me, to those who sit together in Me, to those who visit one another in Me, and to those who give generously to one another in Me.'" (Mālik)

عن أنس – رضي الله عنه– قال: مر رجل بالنبي – صلى الله عليه وسلم – و عنده ناس، فقال رجل ممن عنده: إني لأحب هذا في الله، فقال النبي – صلى الله عليه وسلم– :" أأعلمته ؟." قال : لا. قال: " قُمْ إليه فأعلِمْه." فقام إليه فأعلَمه، فقال : أحبك الذي أحببتني له. قال : ثم رجع فسأله النبي – صلى الله عليه وسلم – فأخبره بما قال، فقال النبي – صلى الله عليه وسلم– :" أنت مع من أحببت، و لك ما احتسبت." رواه البيهقي

Anas رضي الله عنه related that a man came by the Prophet ﷺ while some people were with him. After the man left one of them said, "I love that man for God's sake." The Prophet ﷺ asked him, "Did you let him know?" The man said that he had not. He then said to the man, "Get up, go to him, and let him know." When the man did so, the other man said to him, "May the One for whose sake you love me, love you!" The companion returned to the Prophet ﷺ who asked him what happened. When he told him, the Prophet ﷺ said, "You are with the one you love and what you have offered will be yours." (Bayhaqī)

عن أسماء بنت يزيد – رضي الله عنها– أنها سمعت رسول الله – صلى الله
عليه وسلم – يقول:" ألا أنبئكم بخياركم ؟." قالوا: بلى، يا رسول الله. قال "
خياركم الذين إذا رُؤوا، ذكر الله." رواه ابن ماجه

ʾAsmāʾ bint Yazīd رضي الله عنها related that the Messenger of God ﷺ said, "Shall I tell you who the best among you are?" They replied, "Yes, O Messenger of God!" He told them, "The best among you are those who, when seen, remind one of God." (Ibn Mājah)

عن الزبير – رضي الله عنه– قال: قال رسول الله – صلى الله عليه وسلم–
:" دَبَّ إليكم داء الأمم قبلكم: الحسد، و البغضاء، و البغضاء هي الحالقة، لا أقول
تحلق الشعر و لكن تحلق الدين." رواه أحمد والترمذي

Az-Zubayr رضي الله عنه said that the Messenger of God ﷺ said, "The disease of the people before you, namely envy and hatred, has crept into you, and hatred is what shears things off. I do not say that it shears off the hair; but it shears off religion!" (Aḥmad, & Tirmidhī)

عن أبي هريرة – رضي الله عنه– عن النبي – صلى الله عليه وسلم
– قال :" إيَّاكم و الحسد، فإن الحسد يأكل الحسنات كما تأكل النار الحطب
أو قال العشب ." رواه أبوداود

Abū Hurayrah ﵁ reported that the Messenger of God ﷺ said, "Beware of envy! Envy devours good deeds just as fire devours firewood." (Abū Dāʾūd)

عن ابن عمر – رضي الله عنهما– قال : صعد رسول الله – صلى الله عليه وسلم– المنبر ، فنادى بصوت رفيع فقال:"يا معشر من أسلم بلسانه، و لم يفض الإيمان إلى قلبه : لا تؤذوا المسلمين، ولا تعيروهم، ولا تتبعوا عوراتهم، فإنه من يتبع عورة أخيه المسلم يتبع الله عورته، و من يتبع الله عورته يفضحه و لو في جوف رَحلِه." رواه الترمذي

Ibn ʿUmar ﵄ said one day the Messenger of God ﷺ ascended the pulpit and declared, "O you who are Muslims in word, but faith has not yet flowed into your hearts! Do not harm the Muslims, do not disparage them, and do not seek to find their faults, for anyone who seeks out the faults of his brother, God will seek out his faults. And if God seeks out your faults, you will be scandalized, even if your faults are well-concealed inside your saddle bags!" (Tirmidhī)

عن عائشة – رضي الله عنها– أن رسول الله – صلى الله عليه وسلم – قال يا عائشة :" إن الله رفيق يحب الرفق، و يعطي على الرفق ما لا يعطي على العنف، و ما لا يعطي على ما سواه." رواه مسلم

ʿĀʾishah ﵂ related that the Messenger of God ﷺ said, "God is gentle, and loves gentleness. He gives for gentleness what He does not give for violence, and He gives for it as He does for nothing else." (Muslim)

عن أبي هريرة – رضي الله عنه– قال : قال رسول الله – صلى الله عليه وسلم– :" الحياء من الإيمان، و الإيمان في الجنة، و البذاء من الجفاء، و الجفاء في النار." رواه أحمد والترمذي

Abū Hurayrah ﵁ said the Messenger of God ﷺ said, "Modesty is from faith, and faith is of Paradise. Obscenity is from hardness of the heart, and hardness is of Hell." (Aḥmad, & Tirmidhī)

عن حارثة بن وهب – رضي الله عنه– قال: قال رسول الله – صلى الله عليه وسلم–:" ألا أخبركم بأهل الجنة ؟ كل ضعيف متضعف لو أقسم على الله لأبره، ألا أخبركم بأهل النار ؟ كل عُتُلٍّ، جَوَّاظ، مستكبِر." رواه البخاري ومسلم

Ḥārithah bin Wahab ﷺ related that the Messenger of God ﷺ said, "Shall I tell you about the people of Paradise? They are all the meek ones who seek meekness. If they call upon God, He would respond with kindness to them. Shall I tell you about the people of Hell? They are all the harsh, voracious, unsharing ones, the false-speaking ones, and the proud ones!" (Bukhārī & Muslim)

عن ابن مسعود – رضي الله عنه– قال: قال رسول الله – صلى الله عليه وسلم– :" لا يدخل الجنة من كان في قلبه مثقال ذرة من كِبر." قال رجل : إن الرجل يحب أن يكون ثوبه حسنا و نعله حسنا، قال : " إن الله جميل يحب الجمال، الكِبرُ: بَطَرُ الحق، و غَمطُ الناس." رواه مسلم

Ibn Masʿūd ﷺ related that the Messenger of God ﷺ said, "No one shall enter Paradise who has even an atom's weight of pride in his heart." To this someone responded, "But a man likes to have beautiful clothes and beautiful shoes." The Prophet replied, "Indeed, God Most High is beautiful and loves beauty. This is not pride; pride is the rejection of truth and having contempt for people." (Muslim)

عن أسماء بنت عُمَيس – رضي الله عنها– قالت: سمعت رسول الله – صلى الله عليه وسلم – يقول :" بئس العبد عبد تخيَّل و اختال، و نسي الكبير المتعال، بئس العبد عبد تجبر و اعتدى، و نسي الجبار الأعلى، بئس العبد عبد سهى و لهى، و نسي المقابر و البلى، بئس العبد عبد عتا و طغى، و نسي المبتدأ و المنتهى، بئس العبد عبد يُختِّل الدنيا بالدين، بئس العبد عبد يُختِّل الدين بالشبهات، بئس العبد عبد طمع يقوده، بئس العبد عبد هوى يضله، بئس العبد عبد رغب يذله." رواه الترمذي والبيهقي

ʾAsmāʾ bint ʿAmīs ﷺ said that the Messenger of God ﷺ said, "How miserable is the one who forms a fanciful image of himself, thus becoming arrogant, and forgets the Great and Sublime One. How miserable is the one who becomes overbearing and transgresses, and forgets the Overpowering and Most High One. How miserable is the one who becomes heedless and distracted with his desires, and forgets the grave and its great trials. How miserable is the one who disobeys and oversteps his bounds, and forgets the beginning and the end. How miserable is the one who deceptively uses religion for worldly ends. How miserable is the one who deceptively casts doubts on religion. How miserable is the one who is led by greed. How miserable is the one who is misled by his passions. How miserable is the one who is brought low by what he desires!" (Tirmidhī & Bayhaqī)

عن حذيفة – رضي الله عنه– قال : قال رسول الله – صلى الله عليه وسلم– :" لا تكونوا إمَّعَة تقولون : إن أحَسَنَ الناس أحسنـَّا، و إن ظلموا ظلمنا، و لكن وطنوا أنفسكم: إن أحسن الناس أن تحسنوا، و إن أساءوا فلا تظلموا." رواه الترمذي

Ḥadhīfah ﷺ related that the Messenger of God ﷺ said, "Do not be people without minds of your own, saying that if others treat you well you will treat them well, and that if they do you wrong you will do them wrong. But rather accustom yourselves to reciprocate goodness and to avoid wronging those who do wrong to you." (Tirmidhī)

عن العُرس بن عميرة – رضي الله عنه– عن النبي – صلى الله عليه وسلم – قال :" إذا عملت الخطيئة في الأرض, من شهدها فكرهها كان كمن غاب عنها، و من غاب عنها فرضيها كان كمن شهدها." رواه أبوداود

The Messenger of God ﷺ said, "When sin is committed in the world, the one who witnesses it and then rejects it is like one who never saw it, while the one who never saw it but approves of it is like one who participated in it." (Abū Dā'ūd)

عن أبي ثعلبة – رضي الله عنه– في قوله تعالى: (عليكم أنفسكم لا يضركم
من ضل إذا اهتديتم). فقال : أما والله لقد سألت عنها رسول الله – صلى الله عليه
وسلم – فقال :" بل ائتمروا بالمعروف، و تناهوا عن المنكر، حتى إذا رأيت شحا
مطاعا، و هوى متبعا، و دنيا مؤثرة، و إعجاب كل ذي رأي برأيه ، فعليك نفسك
و دع العوام، فإن من ورائكم أياماً الصبر فيهن مثل القبض على الجمر، لـلعامل
فيهن أجر خمسين رجلا يعملون مثل عملكم ." قالوا: يا رسول الله، أجر خمسين
منّا أو منهم ؟ قال :" أجر خمسين رجلا منكم." رواه الترمذي و ابن ماجه

Abū Thaʿalabah ؓ asked the Prophet ﷺ about the verse in the Qurʾān that says, *You are responsible for yourselves; no one who is misguided can harm you if you seek guidance* (*Sūrah al-Māʿidah* 5:105). He said, "It is for you to be devoted to kindness and to avoid what is hateful even if you see people following greed and desire, even if you see people preferring this world, and even if you see people admiring their own opinions and ignoring the truth. When you find yourselves before a matter that you cannot avoid, then take responsibility for yourselves and abandon the general norms of the public, for beyond you lie the Days of Perseverance. The one who perseveres through them will be like one who grasps live coals. The one who acts rightly in those times will reap the benefit of fifty who act as he does." The people asked him, "The reward of fifty men of us or of them, O Messenger of God?" And he assured them, "The reward of fifty men like you!" (Tirmidhī & Ibn Mājah)

عن المُستَورِدِ بن شداد – رضي الله عنه– قال : سمعت رسول الله – صلى
الله عليه وسلم– يقول: " و الله ما الدنيا في الآخرة إلا مثل ما يجعل أحدكم إصبعه
وأشار يحيى بالسبابة في اليَمِّ، فلينظر بم يرجع ؟." رواه مسلم

Mustawrid ؓ reported that the Messenger of God ﷺ said, "By God, this world in comparison with the other world, is just like one of you putting his finger into the sea. Let him consider what he can take out of it!" (Muslim)

تابع – عن أبي هريرة – رضي الله عنه– قال : قال رسول الله – صلى الله عليه وسلم– : " حُجِبَت النار بالشهوات، و حُجِبت الجنة بالمكاره." رواه البخاري ومسلم

Abū Hurayrah ﷺ related that the Messenger of God ﷺ said, "Hell has been veiled by desirable things, and Paradise by disagreeable things!" (Bukhārī & Muslim)

عن أبي هريرة – رضي الله عنه– قال : قال رسول الله – صلى الله عليه وسلم– : " تَعِسَ عبد الدينار، و عبد الدرهم، و عبد الخميصة، إن أعطي رضي، و إن لم يُعط سخط ، تَعِسَ و انتكس، و إذا شيك فلا انتقش، طوبى لعبد آخذ بعنان فرسه في سبيل الله، أشعث رأسه، مغبرة قدماه، إن كان في الحراسة كان في الحراسة، و إن كان في الساقة كان في الساقة، إن استأذن لم يؤذن له، و إن شفع لم يشفع." رواه البخاري

Abū Hurayrah ﷺ said that the Messenger of God ﷺ said, "How wretched is one who is the slave of money and fine clothes! He is only content when he receives, and he is bitter when he does not receive. He is wretched and confused; and if he is afflicted in the slightest he cannot cope with his affliction. Blessed is the one who sets out with determination on God's path; with disheveled head and dusty feet, he carries out his duty with dedicated resolve. If he is assigned watch duty, he is on watch; and if he is assigned rear-guard duty, he is on guard. He does not shirk his responsibilities." (Bukhārī)

عن عبد الله بن عمرو بن العاص – رضي الله عنهما– قال : قال رسول الله – صلى الله عليه وسلم– :" قد أفلح من أسلم، و رُزِقَ كفافا، و قنّعه الله بما آتاه." رواه مسلم

ʿAbdullāh ibn ʿUmar ﷺ reported that the Messenger of God ﷺ said, "Successful is the one who has submitted (become Muslim), whose provisions are sufficient for him, and has been made content by God with what He has given him." (Muslim)

عن أبي هريرة – رضي الله عنه– قال : قال رسول الله – صلى الله عليه وسلم – : " يقول العبد مالي مالي، و إن ما له من ماله ثلاث: ما أكل فأفنى، أو لبس فأبلى،أو أعطىَ فاقتنى، و ما سوى ذلك فهو ذاهب، و تاركه للناس." رواه مسلم

Abū Hurayrah ﵁ related that the Messenger of God ﷺ said, "A person keeps saying, 'Mine, mine!' But what is theirs but three things? What he's eaten and consumed, what he's worn and worn out, and what he's given and that is what endures. Everything else is fleeting and must be given up eventually to others." (Muslim)

عن ابن عمر – رضي الله عنهما– قال : قال رسول الله – صلى الله عليه وسلم– : " إنما الناس كالإبل المائة، لا تكاد تجد فيها راحلة." رواه البخاري ومسلم

Ibn ʿUmar ﵄ said that the Messenger of God ﷺ said, "People are just like a hundred camels among which you can scarcely find a strong riding-beast." (Bukhārī & Muslim)

عن سهل بن سعد – رضي الله عنه– قال : قال رسول الله – صلى الله عليه وسلم – : " لو كانت الدنيا تَعدُل عند الله جناح بعوضة، ما سقى كافرا منها شربة." رواه أحمد والترمذي و ابن ماجه

Sahl bin Saʿd ﵁ said the Messenger of God ﷺ said, "If this world was worth even a gnat's wing in God's sight, He would not permit a denier of truth to have even a sip of it!" (Tirmidhī)

عن أبي موسى – رضي الله عنه– قال : قال رسول الله – صلى الله عليه وسلم– :" من أحب دنياه أضرَّ بآخرته، و من أحب آخرته أضرَّ بدنياه، فآثروا ما يبقى على ما يفنى." رواه أحمد والبيهقي

The Messenger of God ﷺ said to Abū Mūsā ﵁, "Whoever loves this world finds hardship in the other world, and whoever loves the other world finds hardship in this world; so prefer what is lasting to what is evanescent." (Aḥmad)

عن ابن مسعود – رضي الله عنه– أن رسول الله – صلى الله عليه وسلم– نام على حصير فقام و قد أثر في جنبه فقلنا يا رسول الله . لو أتخذنا لك وطاءً . فقال :" مالي و للدنيا؟ ما أنا في الدنيا إلا كراكب استظل تحت شجرة ثم راح و تركها." رواه أحمد والترمذي و ابن ماجه

Ibn Masᶜūd ﷺ related that the Messenger of God ﷺ slept on a reed mat and when he got up its imprint was on his body. Ibn Masᶜūd said to him, "O Messenger of God, if you had just told us, we would have prepared for you a comfortable bed." The Prophet told him, "What do I have to do with this world? My relationship to it is only as a rider who rests temporarily under the shade of a tree and then moves on and leaves it behind." (Aḥmad, Tirmidhī)

عن عبيد الله بن محصن – رضي الله عنه– قال : قال رسول الله – صلى الله عليه وسلم– : " من أصبح منكم آمنا في سربه، معافَى في جسده، عنده قوت يومه، فكأنما حِيزت له الدنيا." رواه الترمذي

The Messenger of God ﷺ said, "Whoever becomes secure within himself, given robustness of body, having his daily provision, is like someone towards whom the whole world inclines." (Tirmidhī)

عن أبي ذر – رضي الله عنه– أن رسول الله– صلى الله عليه وسلم – قال : " قد أفلح من أخلص الله قلبه للإيمان، و جعل قلبه سليما و لسانه صادقا، و نفسه مطمئنة، و خليقته مستقيمة، و جعل أذنه مستمعة، و عينه ناظرة، فأما الأذن فقمع، و أما العين فمُقرَّة لما يوعي القلب، و قد أفلح من جعل قلبه داعيا." رواه أحمد والبيهقي

Abū Dharr ﷺ related that the Messenger of God ﷺ said, "Successful indeed is the one whose heart God has made pure for faith, and made his heart sound and whole, and made his tongue truthful, and his soul tranquil, and his nature upright, and his ear capable of listening, and his eyes capable of seeing. Indeed the ear is a funnel and the eye shows what is contained within the heart. Successful is the one whose heart God has made full with supplication." (Aḥmad & Bayhaqī)

عن أنس – رضي الله عنه– قال : قال رسول الله – صلى الله عليه وسلم– :" هل من أحد مشى على الماء إلا ابتلت قدماه؟" قالوا : لا، يا رسول الله. قال: " كذلك صاحب الدنيا، لا يسلم من الذنوب." رواه البيهقي

Anas ﷺ said that the Messenger of God ﷺ asked, "Can anyone walk in water without getting his feet wet?" On being told that no one could, he said, "Similarly, the worldly person is not safe from sins." (Bayhaqī)

عن عائشة – رضي الله عنها– عن رسول الله – صلى الله عليه وسلم – قال : " الدنيا دار من لا دار له، و مال من لا مال له، و لها يجمع من لا عقل له." رواه أحمد و البيهقي

ʿĀʾishah ﷺ related that the Messenger of God ﷺ said, "The world is the home of the one who has no real home, and it is the wealth of the one who has no real wealth, and for its sake those who lack real understanding devote all of their efforts." (Aḥmad & Bayhaqī)

عن جابر– رضي الله عنه– قال : قال رسول الله – صلى الله عليه وسلم– :" إن أخوف ما أتخوف على أمتي : الهوى، وطول الأمل، فأما الهوى فيصد عن الحق، و أما طول الأمل فينسي الآخرة، و هذه الدنيا مرتحلة ذاهبة، و هذه الآخرة مرتحلة قادمة، و لكل واحدة منهما بَنون، فإن استطعتم أن لا تكونوا من بني الدنيا فافعلوا، فإنكم اليوم في دار العمل ولا حساب، و أنتم غدا في دار الحساب ولا عمل." رواه البيهقي

Jābir ﷺ reported that the Messenger of God ﷺ said, "What I fear most for my community is vain desire and wishful thinking. As for desire, it prevents you from the Truth. As for wishful thinking, it makes you forget the other world. Know that this world is in motion, and it is receding; and the other world is in motion, and it is approaching; and each world has its children. So if you are able to not be among the children of this world, then do so! For today you are in the abode of action without reckoning, and tomorrow you will be in the abode of reckoning without action." (Bayhaqī)

عن أبي أيوب الأنصاري – رضي الله عنه– قال : جاء رجل إلى النبي – صلى الله عليه وسلم – فقال : عظني و أوجز ، فقال:"إذا قمت في صلاتك، فصَلِّ صلاة مُودِّع، ولا تكلم بكلام تعتذر منه غدا، و اجمع الإياس مما في أيدي الناس." رواه أحمد

A man came to the Prophet ﷺ and told him, "Advise me and make it short!" He said to him, "When you pray, pray as if you are departing from this world. Don't say words today that you will regret tomorrow. And don't put your hope in what is in people's hands." (Aḥmad)

عن ابن مسعود – رضي الله عنه– قال: تلا رسول الله – صلى الله عليه وسلم– : (فمن يُرِدْ الله أن يهديه يشرح صدره للإسلام). فقال رسول الله – صلى الله عليه وسلم– : " أن النور إذا دخل الصدر، انفسح." فقيل: يا رسول الله، هل لذلك من علم يعرف به ؟ قال : " نعم، التجافي من دار الغرور، و الإنابة إلى دار الخلود، و الاستعداد للموت قبل نزوله." رواه البيهقي

Ibn Masᶜūd ؓ related that the Messenger of God ﷺ recited, "*When God wishes to guide someone, He broadens his breast for acceptance of submission (Islām)*" (*Sūrah al-Anᶜām* 6:125). Then he said, "When the Light enters the breast it expands." We asked him, "O Messenger of God, is there a way for us to know when this happens?" He told us, "Yes. Its signs are withdrawal from the abode of deception and turning to the abode of eternity, and preparing for death before it descends." (Bayhaqī)

عن محمود بن لبيد – رضي الله عنهما– أن النبي – صلى الله عليه وسلم – قال : " اثنتان يكرههما ابن آدم : الموت، و الموت خير للمؤمن من الفتنة، و يكره قلة المال، و قلة المال أقلُّ للحساب." رواه أحمد

Maḥmūd ibn Labīd ﷺ related that the Prophet ﷺ said, "There are two things which people hate. They hate death, but death is better for the believer than temptation. And they hate having little wealth, but less wealth means less reckoning." (Aḥmad)

عن أبي ذر – رضي الله عنه– قال: أوصاني حِبي بخمس : أرحم المساكين وأجالسهم وأنظر إلي من هو تحتي ولا أنظر إلي من هو فوقي، وأن أصل الرحم و إن أدبرت، وأن أقول الحق و إن كان مُرّا، وأن أقول: لا حول ولا قوة الا بالله ". رواه أحمد

Abū Dharr said, "My beloved ordered me to observe five things: He ordered me to love the helpless and to draw near to them; he ordered me to look at those who have less than me and not look at those who have more than me; he ordered me to join ties of mercy in relationship even if someone turns away; he ordered me not to ask anyone for anything; he ordered me to speak the truth even if it is bitter; and he ordered me to repeat often, 'There is no ability or strength except through God.'" (Aḥmad)

عن أبي هريرة – رضي الله عنه– عن النبي – صلى الله عليه وسلم– قال: " لا يزال قلب الكبير شابا في اثنين: في حب الدنيا، و طول الأمل." رواه البخاري ومسلم

Abū Hurayrah ﷺ reported that the Prophet ﷺ said, "The heart of the old man remains childish in two respects: love of this world and wishful thinking regarding the distant future." (Bukhārī & Muslim)

عن ابن عمر – رضي الله عنهما– قال : أخذ رسول الله – صلى الله عليه وسلم – بعض جسدي فقال: " كُنْ في الدنيا كأنك غريب، أو عابر سبيل ." رواه البخاري

Ibn ʿUmar related that the Messenger of God ﷺ took hold of him and said, "Be in the world as though you were a stranger or a wayfarer." (Bukhārī)

عن صهيب – رضي الله عنه– قال : قال رسول الله – صلى الله عليه وسلم– : "عجبا لأمر المؤمن، إن أمره كله خير، و ليس ذلك لأحد إلا للمؤمن، إن أصابته سراء شكر، فكان خيرا له، و إن أصابته ضراء صبر، فكان خيرا له." رواه مسلم

The Messenger of God ﷺ said, "The condition of the faithful one is a wonder! Everything turns out well for him, and this is only true for those who have faith. If happiness befalls him, he gives thanks and that is good for him; and if misfortune befalls him, he perseveres and that is good for him." (Muslim)

عن أبي هريرة – رضي الله عنه– قال : قال رسول الله – صلى الله عليه وسلم– : " المؤمن القوي خير و أحب إلى الله من المؤمن الضعيف، و في كل خير، احرص على ما ينفعك، و استعن بالله ولا تعجز، و إن أصابك شئ فلا تقل : لو أني فعلت كان كذا وكذا، و لكن قل : قدر الله و ما شاء فعل، فإن لو تفتح عمل الشيطان." رواه مسلم

Abū Hurayrah ﷺ related that the Messenger of God ﷺ said, "The faithful one who is strong is better and more beloved to God than the one who is weak, yet in both there is goodness. Be watchful over what is of use to you, and seek the aid of God, and do not lose your resolve! And if anything befalls you, do not say, 'If only I had done such-and-such it would have turned out so-and-so.' But rather say, 'God has determined and He has done what He wills.' For the words, 'If only…,' open the way for the work of Satan." (Muslim)

عن أبي ذر، عن النبي – صلى الله عليه وسلم – قال : " الزهادة في الدنيا ليست بتحريم الحلال، ولا إضاعة المال، و لكن الزهادة في الدنيا أن لا تكون بما في يديك أوثق بما في يد الله، و أن تكون في ثواب المصيبة إذا أنت أصبت بها، أرغب فيها لو أنها أبقيت لك." رواه الترمذي و ابن ماجه

The Prophet ﷺ said, "Abandonment of worldly desires does not consist in forbidding what is lawful or in squandering wealth, but it means that you do not place more reliance in what you possess than in what God possesses; and to prefer that the recompense of affliction befall you in this world than to have it stored for you in the next world." (Tirmidhī & Ibn Mājah)

عن ابن عباس – رضي الله عنه– قال : كنت خلف رسول الله – صلى الله عليه وسلم– يوما فقال:" يا غلام إني أعلمك كلمات ، احفظ الله يحفظك، احفظ الله تجده تجاهك، و إذا سألت فأسأل الله، و إذا استعنت فاستعن بالله، و اعلم أن الأمة لو اجتمعت على أن ينفعوك بشئ لم ينفعوك إلا بشئ قد كتبه الله لك، و لو اجتمعوا على أن يضروك بشئ لن يضروك إلا بشئ قد كتبه الله عليك، رُفِعَت الأقلام و جفت الصحف." رواه أحمد و الترمذي

Ibn ʿAbbās ﵄ was following behind the Messenger of God ﷺ one day when he turned and told him, "Young man, preserve God and He will preserve you, preserve God and you will find Him facing you. When you ask for anything, ask it of God, and if you seek help, seek help from God. Know that if the entire community were to unite to benefit you, they could benefit you only with what God has decreed for you. And if they were to unite to harm you, they could harm you only with what God has decreed for you. The Pens have been lifted and the pages have become dry!" (Aḥmad & Tirmidhī)

عن أنس – رضي الله عنه– أن النبي – صلى الله عليه وسلم – قال: " من كانت نيته الآخرة همه جعل الله غِناه في قلبه، و جمع له شمله، و أتته الدنيا و هي راغمة،و من كانت نيته الدنيا همه جعل الله الفقر بين عينيه، وفرق عليه شمله، ولم يأته من الدنيا إلا ما قُدر له." رواه الترمذي

Anas ﷺ related that the Prophet ﷺ said, "If one's intention is to seek the other world, God will make his wealth in his heart, and He will integrate his affairs, and the world will submit to him willingly. But if one's intention is to seek this world, God will make him see nothing but poverty, and He will disperse his affairs, and he will get nothing from this world except what has already been decreed for him." (Tirmidhī & Aḥmad)

عن أبي هريرة – رضي الله عنه– قال : قال رسول الله – صلى الله عليه وسلم– : " من خاف أدلج، و من أدلج بلغ المنزل، ألا إن سلعة الله غالية، ألا إن سلعة الله الجنة." رواه الترمذي

Abū Hurayrah said that the Messenger of God ﷺ said, "The one who fears (having the caravan set upon by robbers) journeys through the night, and the one who journeys through the night reaches the station. Oh, the merchandise of God is precious! Oh, the merchandise of God is Paradise!" (Tirmidhī)

عن عبد الله بن مسعود – رضي الله عنه– قال: قال رسول الله – صلى الله عليه وسلم – : " ما من عبد مؤمن يخرج من عينيه دموع، و إن كان مثل رأس الذباب من خشية الله، ثم يصيب شيئا من حر وجهه إلا حرمه الله على النار." رواه ابن ماجه

ᶜAbdullāh ibn Masᶜūd ﷺ related that the Messenger of God ﷺ said, "No sooner do the tears flow from the eyes of the person of faith in awe of God and touch his cheek, even if they were as little as a fly's head, than God will sanctify him from the Fire." (Ibn Mājah)

عن أبي ذر – رضي الله عنه– أن رسول الله – صلى الله عليه وسلم – قال :" إني لأعلم آية لو أخذ الناس بها لكفتهم (من يتق الله يجعل له مخرجا و يرزقه من حيث لا يحتسب)." رواه أحمد و ابن ماجه والدارمي

According to Abū Dharr ﷺ, the Messenger of God ﷺ said, "Verily, I know a verse that, if people were to live by it, it would suffice them: *Whoever is conscious of God, He will make for him a way, and He will provide for him from where he cannot fathom*" (*Sūrah aṭ-Ṭalāq* 65:2-3). (Aḥmad, Ibn Mājah)

عن عمرو بن العاص – رضـي الله عنـه– قـال : قـال رسـول الله – صـلى الله عليه وسلم– :" إن من قلب ابن آدم بكل واد شعبة، فمن أتبع قلبـه الشـعب كلهـا، لم يبال الله بأي واد أهلكه، و من توكل على الله كفاه الشعب." رواه ابن ماجه

The Messenger of God ﷺ said, "People's hearts are scattered in every valley; so whoever lets his heart disperse in every direction, God will not care in which valley He causes him to perish. As for the one who puts his trust in God, He will spare him all distractions." (Ibn Mājah)

عن أبي هريرة – رضي الله عنه– قال : قال رسول الله – صلى الله عليه وسلم– : " ستكون فتن، القاعد فيها خير من القائم، و القائم فيها خير من الماشي، و الماشي فيها خير من الساعي، من يشرف لها تستشرفه، ومن وجد ملجأ أو معاذا فليَعُذ به." رواه البخاري ومسلم

Abū Hurayrah ﷺ reported that the Messenger of God ﷺ said, "There will be periods of sedition and turmoil when the one who sits will be better than the one who stands, the one who stands better than the one who walks, and the one who walks better than the one who runs. He who contemplates them will be drawn by them, so whoever finds a refuge or shelter should go to it." (Bukhārī & Muslim)

عن أبي هريرة – رضي الله عنه– قال : قال رسول الله – صلى الله عليه وسلم– : " و الذي نفسي بيده لا تذهب الدنيا حتى يأتي على الناس يوم لا يدري القاتل فيم قتل ؟ و المقتول فيم قتل ؟." فقيل : كيف يكون ذلك ؟. قال : " الهَرجُ، القاتل والمقتول في النار." رواه مسلم

According to Abū Hurayrah ﷺ, the Messenger of God ﷺ said, "By the One who holds my soul in His hand, the world will not pass away until a day comes to mankind when the killer will not know why he killed, nor the one who is killed why he was killed." They asked him "How is this possible?" He replied, "It is the time of sedition in which both the killer and the killed are in the Fire." (Muslim)

تابع – عن معقل بن يسار – رضي الله عنه– قال : قال رسول الله – صلى الله عليه وسلم– : "العبادة في الهَرج، كهجرة إليَّ ." رواه مسلم

The Messenger of God ﷺ said, "To worship and serve God sincerely during times of sedition and tribulation is equivalent to emigrating (*hijrah*) to come to me." (Muslim)

عن أنس – رضي الله عنه– قال: قال رسول الله – صلى الله عليه وسلم– :" لا تقوم الساعة حتى يتقارب الزمان، فتكون السنة كأشهر، و الشهر كالجمعة، و تكون الجمعة كاليوم، و يكون اليوم كالساعة، و تكون الساعة كالضَّرمة بالنار." رواه الترمذي

Anas ﵁ related that the Messenger of God ﷺ said, "The Hour will not come before time contracts, a year being like a month, a month like a week, a week like a day, a day like an hour, and an hour like the spark from a fire." (Tirmidhī)

عن أبي هريرة – رضي الله عنه– قال: قال رسول الله – صلى الله عليه وسلم– : " إذا اتـُخِذ الفَيَئ دُوَلا، و الأمانة مغنما، و الزكاة مغرما، و تفقه في الدين لغير الله ، و أطاع الرجل امرأته، و عَقَّ أمه، و أقصى أباه، ولعن آخر هذه الأمة أولها ، و ساد القبيلة فاسقهم، و كان زعيم القوم أرذلهم، و أكرِمَ الرجل إتقاء شره فيومئذ يكون ذلك ويفزع الناس يومئذ إلى الشام تعصمهم من عدوهم قلت : وهل يفتح الشام ؟ قال : نعم وشيكاً ثم تقع الفتن بعد فتحها." المعجم الكبير للطبراني

According to Abū Hurayrah ﵁, the Messenger of God ﷺ said, "When gains are taken in turns among the wealthy, and when trusts are taken as spoils, and when *Zakāt* is taken as a fine, and when people seek knowledge for purposes other than religion, and when the husband obeys his wife and disobeys his mother, and when he seeks intimacy with his friends and deserts his father, and when the last of this community curses its first, when the worst of the people become the masters of their tribes, when the most vile of the people become their leaders, when a person is honored for fear of his evil, then when this happens people will flee to Syria where they will be protected from their enemy." I asked, "Will Syria be conquered?" He replied, "Yes, soon then seditions will come after its conquest." (Ṭabarānī)

عن أبي هريرة – رضي الله عنه– قال : قال رسول الله – صلى الله عليه وسلم– : " ألا أحدثكم حديثا عن الدجال، ما حدث به بني قومه ؟ إنه أعور، و إنه يجئ معه بمثل الجنة و النار، فالتي يقول : إنها الجنة، هي النار، و إني أنذركم كما أنذر به نوح قومه." رواه البخاري ومسلم

Abū Hurayrah ﷺ related that the Messenger of God ﷺ said, "Shall I tell you something about the Dajjal[3] and what he does with his people? He is one-eyed and he will bring with him what appears to be like Paradise and Hell. But what he calls Paradise, that itself is Hell. Truly I warn you in the same way that Noah warned his own people." (Bukhārī & Muslim)

عن حذيفة– رضي الله عنه– عن النبي – صلى الله عليه وسلم– قال : " إن الدجال يخرج، و إن معه ماء و نارا، فأما الذي يراه الناس ماء فنار تحرق، و أما الذي يراه الناس نارا فماء بارد عذب، فمن أدرك ذلك منكم، فليقع في الذي يراه نارا، فإنه ماء عذب طيب." رواه البخاري و مسلم

Ḥadhīfah ﷺ said that the Prophet ﷺ said, "The Dajjal will come forth having with him water and fire, and what mankind sees as water will be fire which burns, and what they see as fire will be cool sweet water. So whoever among you realizes this, let him fall into what he sees as fire for it is sweet, pure water." (Bukhārī & Muslim)

عن أبي سعيد الخدري – رضي الله عنه– قال: قال رسول الله – صلى الله عليه وسلم– : " كيف أنعم، و صاحب القرن قد إلتقم القرن ، وأستمع الأذن، متى يؤمر بالنفخ ؟." فكأن ذلك ثقل على أصحاب النبي صلى الله عليه وسلم فقال لهم : " قولوا حسبنا الله و نعم الوكيل توكلنا على الله ربنا وربما قال سفيان على الله توكلنا." رواه الترمذي

Abū Saʿīd al-Khudrī ﷺ said that the Messenger of God ﷺ said, "How can I be at ease when the one who blows the trumpet has put it to his mouth, and inclined his ear waiting to see when he will be ordered to

[3] Literally, "the Deceiver," a false messiah who will come sometime shortly before the return of Christ.

blow it?" His companions seemed burdened by these words, so he told them, "Say, 'God is sufficient for us and He is the best of trustees! We put our trust in God our Sustainer.'" (Tirmidhī)

عن أبي سعيد الخدري – رضي الله عنه– أن ناساً في زمن رسول الله صلى الله عليه وسلم قالوا: يا رسول الله، هل نرى ربنا يوم القيامة ؟. قال رسول الله صلى الله عليه وسلم نعم قال: "هل تضارون في رؤية الشمس بالظهيرة صحواً ليس معها سحاب ؟." قالوا: لا. قال: " وهل تضارون في رؤية القمر ليلة البدر صحواً ليس فيها سحاب ؟." قالوا: لا. قال : " ما تضارون في رؤية الله تبارك وتعالى يوم القيامة إلا كما تضارون في رؤية أحدهما." رواه مسلم

Abū Hurayrah ﷺ said that some people asked the Messenger of God whether they would see their Lord on the Day of Resurrection. He asked them, "Would you dispute about seeing the sun at noon on a clear day?"; to which they said "No." Then he asked them, "Would you dispute about seeing the moon on the night when it is full and there are no clouds?" to which they said "No." Then he proclaimed, "You will not dispute about seeing God, may He be blessed and exalted, any more than you would dispute about seeing these two!" (Muslim)

قال رسول الله – صلى الله عليه وسلم– :" إذا كان يوم القيامة، أذن مؤذن ليتبع كل أمة ما كانت تعبد " ... فيقول : هل بينكم و بينه آية فتعرفونه بها ؟. فيقولون : نعم. فيُكشف عن ساق، فلا يبقى من كان يسجد لله من تلقاء نفسه إلا أذن الله له بالسجود، ولا يبقى من كان يسجد اتقاء و رياء إلا جعل الله ظهره طبقة واحدة، كلما أراد أن يسجد خر على قفاه ... ، ثم يضرب الجسر على جهنم، و تحل الشفاعة، و يقولون: اللهم سلم سلم ... ، فيمر المؤمنون كطرف عين، و كالبرق، و كالريح، و كالطير، و كأجاويد الخيل، و الركاب، فناج مُسَلَّم، و مخدوش مُرسَل، و مكدوسٌ في نار جهنم، حتى إذا خلصَ المؤمنون من النار، فوالذي نفسي بيده ما من أحد منكم بأشد مناشدة لله في استقصاء الحق من المؤمنين لله يوم القيامة لإخوانهم الذين في النار، يقولون : ربنا كانوا يصومون معنا، و يصلون، و يحجون. فيقال لهم : أخرجوا من عرفتم، فتُحرَّم صورهم على النار، فيخرجون خلقا كثيرا، ثم يقولون: ربنا ما بَقِيَ فيها أحد ممن أمرتنا به، فيقول : ارجعوا فمن وجدتم في قلبه مثقال دينار من خير فأخرجوه، فيخرجون خلقا كثيرا، ... ثم يقول : ارجعوا فمن وجدتم في قلبه مثقال نصف دينار من خير

فأخرجوه، فيخرجون خلقا كثيرا، ... ثم يقول : ارجعوا فمن وجدتم في قلبه مثقال ذرة من خير فأخرجوه، فيخرجون خلقا كثيرا، ثم يقولون : ربنا لم نذر فيها خيرا ، ... فيقول الله : شفعت الملائكة، و شفع النبيون، و شفع المؤمنون، و لم يبق إلا أرحم الراحمين، فيقبض قبضة من النار فيخرج منها قوما لم يعملوا خيرا قط، قد عادوا حمما فيلقيهم في نهر في أفواه الجنة يقال له نهر الحياة، فيخرجون كما تخرج الحبة في حميل السيل،... فيخرجون كاللؤلؤ، في رقابهم الخواتم، يعرفهم أهل الجنة : هؤلاء ... عتقاء الله، الذين أدخلهم الله الجنة بغير عمل عملوه، ولا خير قدموه ثم يقول ادخلوا الجنة فما رأيتموه فهو لكم فيقولون ربنا اعطيتنا ما لم تعط احداً من العالمين فيقول لكم عندي أفضل من ذلك فيقولون يا ربنا أيُّ شيء أفضل من هذا فيقول رضاي فلا أسخط عليكم بعده أبداً " . أخرجه البخاري ومسلم

Abū Hurayrah ﷺ related that the Messenger of God ﷺ said, "On the Day of Resurrection, a caller will cry out, 'Let every people follow what they worshiped!' They will be asked, 'Is there a sign between you and Him that will let you know Him?' They will say, 'Yes!' So their legs will be uncovered and Allāh will give permission to all those who used to prostrate to Him by their own free will to prostrate. And Allāh will make those who used to prostrate only to be seen by others or to ward off criticism unable to prostrate. Their backs will be made as a stiff single part, so whenever they try to prostrate, they topple on their backsides. Then they will come upon the bridge over Hell and intercession will begin. They will murmur, 'O Allāh, bring them to safety! Bring them to safety!' And the faithful ones will pass over the bridge in a wink of an eye. Others will pass like lightning, others like the wind, others like birds, others like strong horses. Some will cross over whole and safe, others will be sent across bruised, while others will be flung into the fire of Gehenna. By the One who holds my soul in His hand, none of you will be more vehement in pleading for justice than the faithful ones will at that time for their brothers who are in the fire. They will say, 'Our Lord, they fasted with us! They prayed with us! They made pilgrimage with us!' He will say to them, 'Bring out of it all the ones that you know.' So their forms will be forbidden to the fire as they enter it and they will bring out many people, until they say, 'Our Sustainer none are left of those You have commanded us to extract.' Then He will say to them, 'Go back and bring out whoever you find that has a dinar's worth of goodness in them.' And they will bring out many people. And He will say to them, 'Go back and bring out whoever you find that has half a dinar's worth of goodness in them.' And they will bring out many people. Then He will say to them, 'Go back again and bring out whoever you find who has an atom's weight of goodness in them.' And they will bring out many people. And this will go on until they say to Him, 'Our Lord, we have left no one in it who has any trace of goodness in them.' Allāh will then declare, 'The angels have interceded, and the prophets have interceded, and the faithful have interceded. Only the Most Merciful of those who show mercy (*Arḥamur-Rāḥimīn*) is left to intercede!' And He will bring out with His grasp the people who have never done any good and He will throw them into a river at the mouth of Paradise called the River of Life and they will emerge from it like pearls. When the people of Paradise see them, they will know them, 'These are Emancipated of God. He has made them enter Paradise without any of their own actions, and without any goodness that they offered!' And God will say to them, 'Enter Paradise! What you have seen is yours.' They will say, 'Our Sustainer, You have given us what You have not given anyone of the worlds!' He will say, 'I have for you what is even better than this.' They will ask, 'O Our Sustainer, what could be better than this?' He will say, 'My contentment with you, for I shall not be displeased with you after this ever again.'" (Bukhārī & Muslim)

عن أبـي سـعيد – رضـي الله عنـه– قـال : قـال رسـول الله – صـلى الله عليـه وسلم– : " يخلص المؤمنون من النـار فيحبسـون علـى قنطـرة بـين الجنـة و النـار، فيُقَص لبعضـهم من بعض مظالم كانت بينـهم في الدنيا، حتى إذا هُذبوا و نُقوا، أذن لهم في دخول الجنة، فو الذي نفس محمد بيده، لأحدهم أهدى بمنزلـه فـي الجنـة منـه بمنزلـه كان له في الدنيا." رواه البخاري

Abū Saᶜīd ﷺ related that the Messenger of God ﷺ said, "When the faithful ones have been saved from the fire they will be held in a channel between Paradise and the Fire while the rights of each that have been violated in the world are settled, until they are cleansed and purified. And then they are granted permission to enter Paradise. By the One who holds the soul of Muḥammad in His hand, each will find his way more easily to his dwelling in paradise than he did to his dwelling which he had on earth." (Bukhārī)

عن أبـي سـعيد – رضـي الله عنـه– قـال : قـال رسـول الله – صـلى الله عليـه وسلم– : " إن الله تعالى يقول لأهل الجنـة: يـا أهل الجنـة. فيقولـون : لبيك ربنـا و سعديك و الخير كله في يديك، فيقول: هل رضيتم ؟. فيقولون : و ما لنـا لا نرضـى يا رب، و قد أعطيتنا ما لم تعط أحدا من خلقك ؟. فيقول : ألا أعطيكم أفضـل من ذلـك ؟. فيقولـون : يـا رب، و أي شـئ أفضـل مـن ذلـك؟. فيقـول : أحـل علـيكم رضواني فلا أسخط عليكم بعده أبدا." رواه البخاري ومسلم

Abū Saᶜīd ﷺ reported that the Messenger of God ﷺ said, "God Most High will call out, 'O people of Paradise!' And they will respond, 'Here we are, our Lord, at your command, and all goodness is in Your Hands.' He will ask them, 'Are you pleased?' They will reply, 'How can we not be pleased, O Lord, when You have given us what you have given to no other of Your creatures?' He will tell them, 'Shall I give you something more excellent than that?' They will reply, 'O Lord, what can be more excellent than this?' He will say, 'I shall make My good pleasure (*Riḍwān*) available to you, and I will never frown upon you.'" (Bukhārī & Muslim)

عن سليمان بن بريدة – رضي الله عنه– عن أبيه أن رجلاً سأل النبي صلى الله عليه وسلم فقال يا رسول الله : هل في الجنة من خيل قال : إن الله دخلك الجنة فلا تشاء أن تحمل فيها على فرس من ياقوته حمراء يطير بك في الجنة حيث شئت قال : وسأله رجل فقال : يا رسول الله، هل في الجنة من إبل ؟قال : فلم يقل له مثل ما قال لصاحبه قال: " إنْ يدخلك الله الجنة، يكن لك فيها ما اشتهت نفسك، و لذت عينك." رواه الترمذي

A man asked the Messenger of God ﷺ whether there were any horses in Paradise. He said to him, "Verily, God has brought you into Paradise, would you not like to be borne in it upon a steed from His red rubies that will fly you wherever you wish?" Another man asked him whether there were any camels in Paradise. He did not say to him what he said to the other man, he said, "If God brings you into Paradise, you will have what your soul desires and your eye takes pleasure in." (Tirmidhī)

عن علي – رضي الله عنه– قال: قال رسول الله – صلى الله عليه وسلم– : " إن في الجنة لسوقا، ما فيها شراء ولا بيع إلا الصور من الرجال و النساء، فإذا اشتهى الرجل صورة دخل فيها.". رواه الترمذي

ᶜAlī ﷺ related that the Messenger of God ﷺ said, "In Paradise there is a market in which there is no buying or selling, but only the forms of men and women; and when someone desires a form, he enters it." (Tirmidhī)

عن ابن عمر – رضي الله عنهما– قال : قال رسول الله – صلى الله عليه وسلم– : " إن أدنى أهل الجنة منزلة لمن ينظر إلى جنانه، و أزواجه، و نعيمه، و خدمه، و سرره مسيرة ألف سنة، و أكرمهم على الله من ينظر إلى وجهه غدوة، وعشية." ثم قرأ رسول الله صلى الله عليه وسلم : (وجوه يومئذ ناضرة إلى ربها ناظرة). رواه أحمد والترمذي

Ibn ʿUmar ﷺ related that the Messenger of God ﷺ said, "The lowest in station among the inhabitants of Paradise will be one who looks at his gardens, his wives, his bliss, his servants, and his couches stretching a thousand years' journey; and the one who will be most honored by God will be the one who looks at His face morning and evening." The Prophet then recited, "*On that day will faces be resplendent, looking upon their Lord*" (*Sūrah al-Qiyāmah* 75:22-23). (Aḥmad & Tirmidhī)

عن أبي ذر – رضي الله عنه– قال: سألت رسول الله – صلى الله عليه وسلم– : هل رأيت ربك ؟. قال : " نور أنّى أراه." رواه مسلم

Abū Dharr ﷺ asked the Messenger of God ﷺ whether he had seen his Lord, and he replied, "He is Light. Where shall I see Him?" (Muslim)

عن جابر بن عبد الله – رضي الله عنه– عن النبي – صلى الله عليه وسلم– : " بينما أهل الجنة في نعيمهم، إذ سطع لهم نور، فرفعوا رؤوسهم، فإذا الرب قد أشرف عليهم من فوقهم، فقال : السلام عليكم، يا أهل الجنة. قال: و ذلك قوله: (سلام قولا من رب رحيم). قال: فينظر إليهم و ينظرون إليه، فلا يلتفتون إلى شئ من النعيم ما داموا ينظرون إليه، حتى يحتجب عنهم و يبقى نوره، و بركته عليهم في ديارهم." رواه ابن ماجه

Jābir ﷺ related that the Prophet ﷺ said, "While the inhabitants of Paradise are in their bliss, a light shines upon them and, raising their heads, they will see their Lord has looked down upon them from above. He will then say, 'Peace be upon you, People of Paradise!' and this is His saying, *Peace, a word from a merciful Lord* (*Sūrah Yā Sīn* 36:58). He will then look upon them and they will look upon Him, and they will not turn aside to any of their bliss so long as they are looking upon Him, until He veils Himself from them. But His light and blessing remains upon them in their abodes." (Ibn Mājah)

عن أنس بن مالك– رضي الله عنه– قال : قال رسول الله – صلى الله عليه وسلم– : " يُؤتىَ بأنعم أهل الدنيا من أهل النار يوم القيامة، فيصبغ في النار صبغة، ثم يقال : يا ابن آدم، هل رأيت خيرا قط ؟ هل مر بك نعيم قط ؟. فيقول : لا، و الله يا رب. و يُؤتىَ بأشد الناس بؤسا في الدنيا من أهل الجنة، فيصبغ صبغةً في الجنة. فيقال له : يا ابن آدم، هل رأيت بؤسا قط ؟ و هل مر بك شدة قط ؟. فيقول: لا، و الله يا رب، ما مَرَّ بي بؤس قط، ولا رأيت شدة قط." رواه مسلم

According to Anas ﷺ, the Messenger of God ﷺ said, "The one among the inhabitants of Hell who had the most pleasant life in the world will be brought on the Day of Resurrection and dipped once in Hell. Then it will be said, 'Son of Adam, have you ever experienced any good? Has any pleasure come your way?' to which he will reply, 'No, my Lord, I swear by God!' Then the one among the inhabitants of Paradise who had the most miserable life in the world will be brought and dipped once in Paradise. Then it will be said, 'Son of Adam, have you ever experienced any misfortune? Has any distress come your way?' to which he will reply, 'No, my Lord, I swear by God, no misfortune has ever come my way and I have never experienced any distress.'" (Muslim)

عن أبي هريرة – رضي الله عنه– قال : سمعت رسول الله – صلى الله عليه وسلم – يقول: " إن الله تعالى كتب كتابا قبل أن يخلق الخلق : " إن رحمتي سبقت غضبي" فهو مكتوب عنده فوق العرش." رواه البخاري ومسلم

Abū Hurayrah ﷺ reported that the Messenger of God ﷺ said, "Before creating the world God inscribed the words, 'My mercy has preceded My wrath,' and that is written in His presence, above the Throne." (Bukhārī & Muslim)

عن أبي هريرة – رضي الله عنه– قال : قال رسول الله – صلى الله عليه وسلم– : " ليلة أسريَ بي لقيت موسى قال : فنعته – فإذا رجل حسبته قال مضطرب، رَجِل الرأس كأنه من رجال شنوءة، و لقيت عيسى فنعته النبي صلى الله عليه وسلم ربعة أحمر، كأنما خرج من ديماس – يعني الحمام– و رأيت إبراهيم و أنا أشبه ولده به." قال: " وأُتيت بإناءين : أحدهما لبن والآخر فيه خمر . فقيل لي . خذ أيهما شئت. فأخذت اللبن فشربته، فقيل لي : هُديت الفطرة، أو أصبت الفطرة أمَا إنك لو أخذت الخمر، غوَت أمتك." رواه البخاري ومسلم

According to Abū Hurayrah ﵁, the Messenger of God ﷺ said, "On the night when I was taken up into Heaven I met Moses and Jesus and Abraham, and I was, of all his offspring, the most like him. Then I was presented with two vessels: one containing milk, and the other wine. And I was told to take whichever of them I wished. I took the milk and drank it, and I was told, 'You have been guided to the innate nature (*fiṭrah*), for had you taken the wine your community would have gone astray.'" (Bukhārī & Muslim)

عن أبي هريرة – رضي الله عنه– قال : قال رسول الله – صلى الله عليه وسلم– : " أنا أولى الناس بعيسى بن مريم في الأولى و الآخرة، قالوا : كيف يا رسول الله قال : الأنبياء إخوة من علات، و أمهاتهم شتى، و دينهم واحد، و ليس بيننا نبي." رواه البخاري ومسلم

Abū Hurayrah ﵁ related that the Messenger of God ﷺ said, "I am the one closest to Jesus, son of Mary, in this world and the other one. The prophets are like brothers, sons of one father and various wives. Their mothers are different, but their religion is one. There is no other prophet between us." (Bukhārī & Muslim)

عن أبي هريرة – رضي الله عنه– قال رسول الله – صلى الله عليه وسلم– :
" كل بني آدم يطعن الشيطان في جنبيه بأصبعيه حين يولد غير عيسى بن مريم،
ذهب يطعن، فطعن في الحجاب." رواه البخاري

The Messenger of God ﷺ said, according to Abū Hurayrah ﵁, "At birth all the descendants of Adam have their sides pierced by the devil with two of his fingers, except for the son of Mary. When he tried to pierce him, he pierced the veil." (Bukhārī & Muslim)

عن أبي هريرة – رضي الله عنه– قال : قال رسول الله – صلى الله عليه
وسلم– : " مثلي و مثل الأنبياء من قبلي كمثل رجل بنى بيتاً فأحسنه وأجمله إلا
موضع لبنة من زاوية فجعل الناس يطوفون ويعجبون له ويقولون هلا وضعت
هذه اللبنة قال : فأنا اللبنة وأنا خاتم النبيين ." رواه البخاري ومسلم

Abū Hurayrah ﵁ said that the Messenger of God ﷺ said, "The relationship between me and the prophets who came before me is as the analogy of a man who built a beautiful house, but in which the space of one brick was left incomplete. The onlookers go around it, admiring the beauty of its construction, with the exception of the place of that brick. Now I have filled up the place of that brick: in me the building is completed, and in me the messengers are completed." (Bukhārī & Muslim)

عن عمرو بن قيس – رضي الله عنه– أن رسول الله – صلى الله عليه وسلم
– قال : " إن الله أدرك بي الاجل المرحوم واختصر لي اختصاراً فنحن
الآخرون، و نحن السابقون يوم القيامة، و إني قائل قولا غير فخر: إبراهيم خليل
الله، و موسى صفي الله، و أنا حبيب الله، و معي لواء الحمد يوم القيامة، و إن الله
عز وجل وعدني في أمتي، و أجارهم من ثلاث : لا يَعُمُّهم بسَنَة، ولا يستأصلهم
عَدُوٌّ، ولا يجمعهم على ضلالة." رواه الدارمي

The Messenger of God ﷺ said, "Verily God has realized in me the merciful time and has made for me the nearest of handholds. We are the last, but we shall be the leaders on the Day of Resurrection. Verily what I say is not from pride: Abraham is the intimate friend of God, Moses is the purified of God, and I am the beloved of God. With me is the banner of praise on the Day of Resurrection. God has given me a promise regarding my community, and He has protected them from three things: He will not blind them by tradition, He will not let an enemy uproot them, and He will not cause them all to unite in misguidance." (Dārimī)

عن جبير بن مطعم – رضي الله عنه– قال : سمعت النبي – صلى الله عليه
وسلم – يقول : " إن لي خمسة أسماء : أنا محمد، و أنا أحمد، و أنا الماحي الذي
يمحو الله بي الكفر، و أنا الحاشر الذي يحشر الناس على قدمي، و أنا العاقب."
رواه البخاري ومسلم

The Prophet ﷺ said, "Verily, I have five names. I am Muḥammad (Made for Praise); I am Aḥmad (Most Praised); I am al-Māḥī (The Effacer), by whom God effaces infidelity; I am al-Ḥāshir (The Collector), who will collect mankind at my feet; and I am al-ʿĀqib (The Successor)." (Bukhārī & Muslim)

عن أنس – رضي الله عنه– قال : كان رسول الله – صلى الله عليه وسلم–
أزهر اللون، كأن عرقه اللؤلؤ، إذا مشى تكفأ، و لا مسست ديباجة، ولا حريرة
ألين من كف رسول الله صلى الله عليه و سلم، ولا شممت مسكة، ولا عنبرة
أطيب من رائحة النبي." رواه البخاري ومسلم

Anas رضي الله عنه said, "The Messenger of God ﷺ had a clear complexion, his veins were like pearls, and when he walked he bent forward. I have not touched brocade or silk softer than the palm of God's Messenger's ﷺ hand, or smelled musk or ambergris sweeter than the Prophet's odor." (Bukhārī & Muslim)

عن عبيدة بن محمد بن عمار بن ياسر، قال: قلت للربيع بنت معوذ بن
عفراء – رضي الله عنها– : صفي لنا رسول الله – صلى الله عليه وسلم– قالت :
يا بني، لو رأيته رأيت الشمس طالعة . رواه الدارمي

Ar-Rubaiy^c^, the daughter of Ibn ^c^Afra^ɔ^, ﷺ was asked to describe God's Messenger ﷺ, and she replied, "If you had seen him, my son, you would have seen the sun rising!" (Dārimī)

عن أبي هريرة – رضي الله عنه– عن النبي – صلى الله عليه وسلم– أنه قال: "إنما أنا رحمة مهداة." رواه الدارمي والبيهقي

Abū Hurayrah ﷺ said that the Messenger of God ﷺ said, "I am nothing but a mercy given freely." (Dārimī & Bayhaqī)

عن أنس– رضي الله عنه– قال : خدمت النبي– صلى الله عليه وسلم – عشر سنين، فما قال لي : أف، ولا: لم صنعت ؟. ولا: ألا صنعت ؟ . رواه البخاري ومسلم

Anas ﷺ said, "I served God's Messenger ﷺ for ten years, and he never scolded me or complained to me, 'Why didn't you do such-and-such?'" (Bukhārī)

عن أبي هريرة – رضي الله عنه– قال : قيل: يا رسول الله، ادع لنا على المشركين. قال : " إني لم أبعث لعانا، و إنما بُعثت رحمة." رواه مسلم

Abū Hurayrah ﷺ related that the Messenger of God was once asked to curse the idolators, to which he replied, "I was not sent to curse; I was sent only as a mercy." (Muslim)

عن عائشة أم المؤمنين– رضي الله عنها– أنها قالت : أول ما بُدِئَ به رسول الله– صلى الله عليه وسلم– من الوحي الرؤيا الصالحة في النوم، فكان لا يرى رؤيا إلا جاءت مثل فلق الصبح، ثم حبب إليه الخلاء، و كان يخلو بغار حراء، فيتحنث فيه – و هو التعبد – الليالي ذوات العدد قبل أن ينزع إلى أهله، و يتزود لذلك، ثم يرجع إلى خديجة، فيتزود لمثلها، حتى جاءه الحق و هو في غار حراء،

فجاءه الملك فقال : اقرأ. قال :"ما أنا بقارئ." قال : " فأخذني فغطني حتى بلغ
مني الجهد، ثم أرسلني." فقال : اقرأ. قلت :"ما أنا بقارئ، فأخذني فغطني الثانية،
حتى بلغ مني الجهد، ثم أرسلني." فقال : اقرأ . فقلت : "ما أنا بقارئ، فأخذني
فغطني الثالثة ، ثم أرسلني." فقال : (اقرأ باسم ربك الذي خلق . خلق الانسان من
علق . اقرأ و ربك الأكرم). فرجع بها رسول الله – صلى الله عليه وسلم– يرجف
فؤاده، فدخل على خديجة بنت خويلد رضي الله عنها ، فقال : " زملوني،
زملوني." فزملوه حتى ذهب عنه الروع، فقال لخديجة و أخبرها الخبر: " لقد
خشيت على نفسي " فقالت خديجة : كلا ، و الله ما يخزيك الله أبدا، إنك لتصل
الرحم ، وتحمل الكل، و تكسب المعدوم، و تقري الضيف، و تعين على نوائب
الحق، فانطلقت به خديجة حتى أتت به ورقة بن نوفل بن أسد بن عبد العزى ، إبن
عم خديجة ، وكان إمرأ قد تنصر في الجاهلية وكان يكتب الكتاب العبراني فيكتب
من الانحيل بالعبرانية ما شاء الله أن يكتب وكان شيخاً كبيراً قد عمي . فقالت له
خديجة : يا ابن عم، اسمع من ابن أخيك، فقال له ورقة : يا ابن أخي ماذا ترى ؟.
فأخبره رسول الله – صلى الله عليه وسلم– خبر ما رأى. فقال له ورقة : هذا
الناموس الذي نزّل الله على موسى، يا ليتني فيها جذعا، ليتني أكون حيا إذ
يخرجك قومك، فقال رسول الله – صلى الله عليه وسلم– : " أو مخرجي هم ؟!"
قال : نعم، لم يأت رجل قط بمثل ما جئت به إلا عودي، و إن يدركني يومك
أنصرك نصرا مؤزرا، ثم لم ينشب ورقة أن توفي، و فتر الوحي . رواه البخاري
ومسلم

ʿĀʾishah ؓ related that, "Just before revelation descended upon him, the Prophet ﷺ started to see true visions in his sleep. Whatever vision came to him, it would happen as clearly as the daybreak.

"Then he was made to yearn for seclusion, so he used to go to the cave of Ḥirāʾ where he would spend several long nights purifying himself in worship before returning home to Khadījah. He would then take more provisions and return to the cave until Truth came to him while he was in the cave.

"The angel came and said to him, '*Recite!*' The Prophet ﷺ replied, 'I am not a reciter.' So he took hold of him to the point where he was struggling to breathe, then the angel let him go and said, '*Recite!*' and he said, 'I am not a reciter.' So he took hold of him a second time to the point where he struggled to breathe then he let him go and said, '*Recite! By the name of your Sustainer who created. The One who created mankind from a clinging substance. Recite, for your Sustainer is the most generous! The One who taught by the pen, taught mankind what it knew not!*' (*Sūrah al-ʿAlaq* 96:1-5).

"So the Messenger of God ﷺ returned home with this and he was trembling at the core of his heart. When he saw Khadījah he pleaded,

'Cover me! Cover me!' so she covered him until his shock receded. He told Khadījah what happened and said, 'I am afraid for myself.' To which she responded, 'No! By God, He shall never shame you. You maintain the bonds of relationships, you are truthful in speech, you bear the burden of the weak, you help the deprived, you comfort the guest, and you support the bearers of truth.'

"Then she took him to her paternal cousin, Waraqa ibn Nawfal, who was a Christian who knew Hebrew and wrote from the Bible in Hebrew. He was an old, blind man. She implored him, 'O cousin, listen to your nephew!' So Waraqa asked him, 'What did you see?' and when the Prophet told him he said, 'This is the angel who descended upon Moses! O how I wish I was a youth, how I wish I could be alive to witness it when your own folk will drive you out!' The Messenger of God ﷺ asked him, 'Are they really going to drive me out?' Waraqa replied, 'Yes! No one has ever come with what you have been given except that he is opposed. How I wish I could see your day so I could support you completely!'

"But Waraqa died soon afterwards and the revelation stopped for a while." (Bukhārī & Muslim)

و عن جابر – رضي الله عنه– أنه سمع رسول الله – صلى الله عليه وسلم – يحدث عن فترة الوحي، قال : " فبينا أنا أمشي سمعت صوتا من السماء، فرفعت بصري، فإذا الملك الذي جاءني بحراء قاعد على كرسي بين السماء والأرض، فجَئِثتُ منه رعبا حتى هويت إلى الأرض، فجئت أهلي، فقلت : زملوني زملوني، فزملوني، فأنزل الله تعالى : (يا أيها المدثر . قم فأنذر و ربك فكبر . و ثيابك فطهر و الرجز فاهجر) قال ابو سلمة والرجز الأوثان ثم حَمي الوحي و تتابع."
رواه البخاري ومسلم

Jābir ﵁ related that the Messenger of God ﷺ spoke about the period of the interruption of revelation saying, "Until one time while I was walking I heard a voice from Heaven and when I looked up there was the same angel who came to me at Ḥirā' and he was seated on a footstool between heaven and earth. I fled from him in fear, falling to the ground until I reached home pleading to them, 'Cover me! Cover me!' And when they covered me, God revealed, *O concealed one! Rise and let it be known, and your Sustainer extol, and your garments purify, and agitation abandon* (Sūrah al-

Muddaththir 74:1-5). After this, revelation intensified and became frequent." (Bukhārī & Muslim)

و عن عائشة – رضي الله عنها– أن الحارث بن هشام سأل رسول الله صلى الله عليه وسلم– فقال : يا رسول الله، كيف يأتيك الوحي ؟ فقال رسول الله – صلى الله عليه وسلم – : " أحيانا يأتيني مثل صلصلة الجرس، و هو أشده علي، فيفصم عني و قد وعيت عنه ما قال، و أحيانا يتمثل لي الملك رجلا فيكلمني، فأعي ما يقول." قالت عائشة : و لقد رأيته ينزل عليه الوحي في اليوم الشديد البرد، فيفصم عنه و إن جبينه ليتفصَّد عرقا . رواه البخاري ومسلم

ʿĀʾishah ﷺ said that the Messenger of God ﷺ was asked, "How does revelation come to you?" and he replied, "At times it comes to me like the ringing of a bell, which is the hardest for me; when it leaves me I am aware of what he said. At other times the angel appears to me as a man who speaks to me and I understand what he says." And ʿĀʾishah said, "I saw him on bitterly cold days when revelation descended upon him; and when it leaves him, his brow would be dripping with sweat." (Bukhārī & Muslim)

و عن عبادة بن الصامت – رضي الله عنه– قال: كان النبي – صلى الله عليه وسلم– إذا نزل عليه الوحي كرب لذلك، و تربَّد وجهه. و في رواية : نكس رأسه، و نكس أصحابه رؤوسهم فلما أتلي عنه رفع رأسه. رواه مسلم

It is related that when revelation descended upon the Prophet ﷺ he became distressed, and his face became ashen, and he bowed his head, and so did his companions, until he recited what he received; and then he would raise his head up. (Muslim)

The Mi^crāj (Night Journey)

عن قتادة، عن أنس بن مالك عن مالك بن صعصعة – رضي الله عنهما – أن نبي الله – صلى الله عليه وسلم– حدثهم عن ليلة أسري به :"بينما أنا في الحطيم – و ربما قال في الحجر – مضطجعا إذ أتاني آت، فقد قال وسمعته يقول : فشَقَّ ما بين هذه إلى هذه – فقلت للجارود وهو إلى جنبي ما يعني به قال : من ثغرة نحره إلى شعرته وسمعته يقول من قصِّه إلى شعرته – فاستخرج قلبي، ثم أتيت بطست من ذهب مملوءة إيمانا، فغسل قلبي، ثم حُشي، ثم أعيد." و في رواية : " ثم غسل البطن بماء زمزم، ثم ملئ إيمانا، و حكمة ، ثم أتيت بدابة دون البغل و فوق الحمار، أبيض فقال له الجارود هو البراق يا أبا حمزة قال أنس نعم يضع خَطوَهُ عند أقصى طرفه، فحُمِلت عليه، فانطلق بي جبريل حتى أتى السماء الدنيا، فاستفتح. فقيل : من هذا ؟. قال : جبريل . قيل : و من معك ؟. قال : محمد . قيل : و قد أرسل إليه . قال : نعم . قيل : مرحبا به، فنعم المجئ جاء، ففتح فلما خلصت، فإذا فيها آدم، فقال : هذا أبوك آدم، فسلم عليه، فسلمت عليه، فرد السلام، ثم قال : مرحبا بالابن الصالح، و النبي الصالح، ثم صعد بي حتى أتى السماء الثانية، فاستفتح. قيل : من هذا ؟ قال : جبريل، قيل : و من معك ؟ قال محمد . قيل : و قد أرسل إليه ؟ قال : نعم . قيل : مرحبا به، فنعم المجئ جاء، ففتح . فلما خلصت إذا يحيى و عيسى و هما ابنا الخالة قال : هذا يحيى و عيسى فسلم عليهما، فسلمت فردا، ثم قالا : مرحبا بالأخ الصالح و النبي الصالح، ثم صعد بي إلى السماء الثالثة، فاستفتح . قيل : من هذا ؟ قال : جبريل. قيل : و من معك ؟. قال : محمد . قيل : و قد أرسل له ؟ قال : نعم . قيل : مرحبا به فنعم المجئ جاء، ففتح، فلما خلصت إذا يوسف، قال : هذا يوسف، فسلم عليه، فسلمت عليه، فرد . ثم قال : مرحبا بالأخ الصالح و النبي الصالح، ثم صعد بي حتى أتى السماء الرابعة، فاستفتح. قيل : من هذا ؟. قال : جبريل . قيل : و من معك ؟ قال : محمد . قيل : و قد أرسل إليه ؟ . قال : نعم . قيل : مرحباً به فنعم المجئ جاء، ففتح فلما خلصت فاذا إدريس، قال : هذا إدريس، فسلم عليه، فسلمت عليه، فرد، ثم قال : مرحبا بالأخ الصالح و النبي الصالح، ثم صعد بي حتى أتى السماء الخامسة، فاستفتح، قيل : من هذا ؟. قال : جبريل . قيل : من معك ؟ قال : محمد . قيل : و قد أرسل اليه؟ قال : نعم . قيل : مرحبا به فنعم المجئ جاء، فلما خلصت، فاذا هارون . قال : هذا هارون فسلم عليه، فسلمت عليه، فرد، ثم قال : مرحبا بالأخ الصالح و النبي الصالح، ثم صعد بي حتى أتى السماء السادسة فاستفتح . قيل : من هذا ؟. قال : جبريل . قيل : من معك ؟ قال محمد . قيل : و قد أرسل اليه ؟ قال : نعم . قال : مرحبا به، فنعم المجئ جاء، فلما خلصت فإذا موسى، قال : هذا

موسى فسلم عليه، فسلمت عليه، فرد، ثم قال : مرحبا بالأخ الصالح و النبي الصالح، فلما تجاوزت بكى، قيل له : ما يبكيك ؟ . قال : أبكي لأن غلاما بعث بعدي، يدخل الجنة من أمته أكثر ممن يدخلها من أمتي، ثم صعد بي إلى السماء السابعة، فاستفتح جبريل، قيل : من هذا ؟ قال : جبريل، قيل : و من معك ؟ قال : محمد . قيل : و قد بعث إليه ؟ قال : نعم . قال : مرحبا به، فنعم المجئ جاء، فلما خلصت، فإذا إبراهيم، قال : هذا أبوك ، فسلم عليه، قال فسلمت عليه، فرد السلام ، قال : مرحبا بالابن الصالح و النبي الصالح، ثم رفعت إليَّ سدرة المنتهى، فإذا نبقها مثل قِلالِ هَجَرَ، و إذا ورقها مثل آذان الفيلة، قال : هذه سدرة المنتهى، وإذا أربعة أنهار: نهران باطنان و نهران ظاهران. فقلت : ما هذان يا جبريل ؟ . قال : أما الباطنان فنهران في الجنة، و أما الظاهران فالنيل و الفرات، ثم رفع لي البيت المعمور، ثم أتيت بإناء من خمر، و إناء من لبن، و إناء من عسل، فأخذت اللبن، فقال : هي الفطرة التي أنت عليها و أمتك، ثم فرضت علي الصلوات خمسين صلاة كل يوم، فرجعت فمررت على موسى، فقال : بما أمرت ؟ قال : أمرت بخمسين صلاة كل يوم . قال : إن أمتك لا تستطيع خمسين صلاة كل يوم، و إني و الله قد جربت الناس قبلك، و عالجت بني إسرائيل أشد المعالجة، فارجع إلى ربك، فأساله التخفيف لأمتك، فرجعت فوضع عني عشرا، فرجعت إلى موسى فقال مثله ، فرجعت فوضع عني عشرا، فرجعت إلى موسى فقال مثله، فرجعت فوضع عني عشرا، فأمرت بعشر صلوات كل يوم، فرجعت إلى موسى فقال مثله، فرجعت فأمرت بخمس صلوات كل يوم، فرجعت إلى موسى فقال بما أمرت ؟ قلت : أمرت بخمس صلوات كل يوم، قال : إن أمتك لا تستطيع خمس صلوات كل يوم، و إني قد جربت الناس قبلك، و عالجت بني إسرائيل أشد المعالجة، فارجع إلى ربك، فأساله التخفيف لأمتك، قال : سألت ربي حتى استحييت، و لكني أرضى و أسلم . قال : فلما جاوزت، نادى مناد : أمضيت فريضتي وخففت عن عبادي" . رواه البخاري ومسلم

The Prophet ﷺ spoke to the Companions about the night he was transported on the night journey (*Mi*ʿ*rāj*). "While I was sleeping someone came to me and split me open from my groin to my head and extracted my heart. And a golden bowl filled with faith was brought and he cleansed my heart in it and placed it back inside of me.

"Then an animal was brought to me, its form between a mule and a donkey with a wide stride, named Buraq. I was placed upon it and Gabriel took me until he reached the lower heaven, where he announced us to its inhabitants who asked who it was. 'It is Gabriel,' he said. 'And who is with you?' he was asked. 'Muḥammad,' he replied. 'Was he sent for?' he was asked. 'Yes,' he said. 'Welcome to him, the best of visitors.' And the way was opened and we entered and found Adam. Gabriel told me, 'This is your father, Adam.' And we both greeted him, and he returned our greeting and told me, 'Welcome, my righteous son and prophet.'

"Then he took me and ascended to the second heaven, where he announced us to its inhabitants who asked who it was. 'It is Gabriel,' he said. 'And who is with you?' he was asked. 'Muḥammad,' he replied. 'Was he sent for?' he was asked. 'Yes,' he said. 'Welcome to him, the best of visitors.' And the way was opened and we entered and found both John and Jesus, the two maternal cousins. I greeted them and they returned the greeting, saying, 'Welcome, our righteous brother and prophet.'

"Then he took me up to the third heaven, where he announced us to its inhabitants, who asked who it was. 'It is Gabriel,' he said. 'And who is with you?' he was asked. 'Muḥammad,' he replied. 'Was he sent for?' he was asked. 'Yes,' he said. 'Welcome to him, the best of visitors.' And the way was opened and we entered and found Joseph. I greeted him and he returned the greeting and said, 'Welcome, my righteous brother and prophet.'

"Then he took me up to the fourth heaven, where he announced us to its inhabitants who asked who it was. 'It is Gabriel,' he said. 'And who is with you?' he was asked. 'Muḥammad,' he replied. 'Was he sent for?' he was asked. 'Yes,' he said. 'Welcome to him, the best of visitors.' And the way was opened and we entered and found Idris. I greeted him and he returned the greeting and said, 'Welcome, my righteous brother and prophet.'

"Then he took me up to the fifth heaven, where he announced us to its inhabitants, who asked who it was. 'It is Gabriel,' he said. 'And who is with you?' he was asked. 'Muḥammad,' he replied. 'Was he sent for?' he was asked. 'Yes,' he said. 'Welcome to him, the best of visitors.' And the way was opened and we entered and found Aaron. I greeted him and he returned the greeting and said, 'Welcome, my righteous brother and prophet.'

"Then he took me up to the sixth heaven, where he announced us to its inhabitants, who asked who it was. 'It is Gabriel,' he said. 'And who is with you?' he was asked. 'Muḥammad,' he replied. 'Was he sent for?' he was asked. 'Yes,' he said. 'Welcome to him, the best of visitors.' And the way was opened and we entered and found Moses. I greeted him and he returned the greeting and said, 'Welcome, my righteous brother and prophet.' And as I passed him, he wept and I asked him why, and he replied, 'Because one who was sent after me will have more of his community enter Paradise than from my own community.'

"Then he took me up to the seventh heaven, where he announced us to its inhabitants who asked who it was. 'It is Gabriel,' he said. 'And who is with you?' he was asked. 'Muḥammad,' he replied. 'Was he sent for?' he was asked. 'Yes,' he said. 'Welcome to him, the best of visitors.' And the way was opened and we entered and found Abraham, and he told me, 'This is your father, Abraham.' And we both greeted him and he returned our greeting and told me, 'Welcome, my righteous son and prophet.'

"Then I was raised to the lote tree of the outer limit whose fruit was as big as water jugs and whose leaves were as large as elephant ears. And there were four rivers, two apparent and two hidden. I asked Gabriel about them and he said, 'The two hidden rivers are rivers of Paradise and the two visible rivers are the Nile and Euphrates.' Then the Flourishing House was raised up for me. Then I was presented with a jug of wine, a jug of milk, and a jug of honey and I took the one with milk and he told me, 'This is the innate nature (*fiṭrah*) of you and your community.'

"Then prayer (*salāt*) was prescribed fifty times a day. On my return I came by Moses who asked me what I was commanded and I told him I was commanded to uphold fifty prayers a day. He told me, 'Your community cannot uphold fifty prayers a day. By God, I have experienced people and labored with the Children of Israel in every way, so go back to your Lord and ask Him to lighten the burden on your community.' So I went back and asked, and He reduced it by ten. But Moses told me to go back again and ask for less. And He reduced it by another ten. But Moses told me to go back again, until the prayers were reduced to ten a day. But Moses sent me back again to ask for less and it was reduced to five prayers a day. Moses told me to go back again because my community would not bear five prayers a day, but I told him, 'I've gone back so many times to my Lord to ask for less that I am embarrassed to go back again. I will be content and submit to this.' And as I departed, a voice called out, 'It has been accepted and I have lightened its burden upon My servants.'" (Bukhārī & Muslim)

عن عائشة – رضي الله عنها– قالت : إن من نعم الله علي، أن رسول الله – صلى الله عليه وسلم – توفي في بيتي، و في يومي و بين سحري ونحري، و أن الله جمع بين ريقي و ريقه عند موته، دخل علي عبد الرحمن بيده السواك و أنا مسندة رسول الله – صلى الله عليه وسلم– فرأيته ينظر إليه، و عرفت أنه يحب السواك، فقلت : آخذه لك؟. فأشار برأسه أن: نعم. فتناولته، فاشتد عليه، و قلت : أليِّنه لك؟. فأشار برأسه أن: نعم. فليَّنته، فأمره و بين يديه ركوة أو علبة يشك عمر فيها ماء، فجعل يدخل يديه في الماء فيمسح بهما وجهه، يقول : " لا إله الا الله، إن للموت سكرات." ثم نصب يده، فجعل يقول : " في الرفيق الأعلى." حتى قبض و مالت يده." رواه البخاري

و عنها قالت : كنت أسمع أن رسول الله – صلى الله عليه وسلم – "لا يموت حتى يخيّر بين الدنيا والأخرة فأخذته بحة من مرضه الذي مات فيه) يقول : ما من نبي يمرض إلا خير بين الدنيا والآخرة فسمعته وهو يقول :"مع الذين أنعمت عليهم من النبيين والصديقين والشهداء والصالحين وحسن أولئك رفيقاً." فظننت أنه خُيِّرَ. سنن النسائي . عن أنس – رضي الله عنه– قال: لما ثقل النبي صلى الله عليه وسلم – جعل يتغشاه. فقالت فاطمة عليها السلام : وا كرب أباه . فقال لها : " ليس على أبيك كرب بعد اليوم." فلما مات. قالت : يا أبتاه، أجاب ربا دعاه، يا أبتاه، من جنة الفردوس مأواه، يا أبتاه، إلى جبريل ننعاه. فلما دفن قالت فاطمة عليها السلام : يا أنس، أطابت أنفسكم أن تحثوا على رسول الله – صلى الله عليه وسلم– التراب . رواه البخاري وفي رواية للترمذي قال : لما كان اليوم الذي دخل فيه رسول الله – صلى الله عليه وسلم– المدينة أضاء منها كل شئ، فلما كان اليوم الذي مات فيه أظلم منها كل شئ، و لما نفضنا عن رسول الله صلى الله عليه وسلم الأيدي و إنا لفي دفنه، حتى أنكرنا قلوبنا. وعن عائشة – رضي الله عنها– قالت : لما قبض رسول الله – صلى الله عليه وسلم– اختلفوا في دفنه. فقال أبوبكر : سمعت من رسول الله – صلى الله عليه وسلم – شيئا ما نسيته ، قال : "ما قبض الله نبيا إلا في الموضع الذي يحب أن يدفن فيه." ادفنوه في موضع فراشه. رواه الترمذي عن عائشة – رضي الله عنها– قالت : كان رسول الله – صلى الله عليه وسلم– يقول و هو صحيح : " إنه لم يقبض نبي حتى يرى مقعده من الجنة ثم يخير." فلما نزل به، و رأسه على فَخذي غشي عليه، ثم أفاق، فأشخص بصره إلى سقف البيت ثم قال :" اللهم الرفيق الأعلى." فقلت : إذن، لا يختارنا . وعرفت أنه الحديث الذي كان يحدثنا و هو صحيح قالت: فكانت آخر كلمة تكلم بها " اللهم الرفيق الأعلى." رواه البخاري ومسلم عن ابن عباس – رضي الله عنهما– قال : لما حُضِر رسول الله – صلى الله عليه وسلم– و في البيت رجال، فيهم عمر بن الخطاب، قال النبي – صلى الله عليه وسلم– : " هلم أكتب لكم كتابا لا تضلوا بعده." فقال عمر إن النبي صلى الله عليه وسلم : قد غلب عليه الوجع، وعندكم

القرآن، حسبنا كتاب الله، فاختلف أهل البيت فاختصموا، منهم من يقول : قربوا، يكتب لكم النبي – صلى الله عليه وسلم – كتاباً لن تضلوا بعده و منهم من يقول ما قال عمر: فلما أكثروا اللغو والاختلاف، عند النبي صلى الله عليه وسلم لن تضلوا بعده : " قوموا قال عبيد الله : فكان ابن عباس يقول : إن الرزية كل الرزية ما حال بين رسول الله – صلى الله عليه وسلم– و بين أن يكتب لهم ذلك الكتاب من اختلافهم و لغطهم " رواة البخاري ومسلم .

و عن أنس – رضي الله عنه– قال : قال أبو بكر– رضي الله عنه– بعد وفاة رسول – صلى الله عليه وسلم لعمر – : انطلق بنا إلى أم أيمن نزورها، كما كان رسول الله – صلى الله عليه وسلم – يزورها، فلما انتهينا، إليها بكت . فقالا لها : ما يبكيك ؟ ما عند الله خير لرسوله – صلى الله عليه وسلم– ؟ . فقالت : ما أبكي أن لا اكون أعلم ما عند الله خير لرسوله – صلى الله عليه وسلم– ، و لكن أبكي أن الوحي قد انقطع من السماء، فهيجتهما على البكاء، فجعلا يبكيان معها رواه مسلم و عن أبي سعيد الخدري – رضي الله عنه– ، قال : خرج علينا رسول الله – صلى الله عليه وسلم– في مرضه الذي مات فيه، ونحن في المسجد، عاصبا رأسه بخرقة، حتى أهوى المنبر ، فاستوى عليه و أتبعناه، قال : " و الذي نفسي بيده إني لأنظر إلى الحوض من مقامي هذا." ثم قال : " إن عبدا عرضت عليه الدنيا و زينتها، فاختار الآخرة." قال : فلم يفطن لها أحد غير أبي بكر، فذرفت عيناه، فبكى، ثم قال : بل نفديك بآبائنا، و أمهاتنا، و أنفسنا، و أموالنا يا رسول الله . قال : ثم هبط فما قام عليه حتى الساعة . رواه الدارمي و عن ابن عباس– رضي الله عنهما– قال : لما نزلت : (إذا جاء النصر الله و الفتح) دعا رسول الله– صلى الله عليه وسلم– فاطمة قال: " نعيت إلى نفسي." فبكيت، قال " لا تبكي فإنك أول أهلي لاحق بي." فضحكت، فرآها بعض أزواج النبي – صلى الله عليه وسلم– فقلن : رأيناك بكيت ثم ضحكت . قالت : إنه أخبرني أنه قد نعيت إليه نفسه، فبكيت، فقال لي : " لا تبكي فأنك أول أهلي لاحق بي." فضحكت. رواه الدارمي و عن عائشة – رضي الله عنها– أنها قالت : وا رأساه، فقال رسول الله – صلى الله عليه وسلم– :" ذاك لو كان و أنا حي فأستغفر لك، و أدعو لك." فقالت عائشة : وا ثكلياه، و الله إني لأظنك تحب موتي، ولا كان ذلك لظللت آخر يومك مُعَرِّسا ببعض أزواجك، فقال النبي– صلى الله عليه وسلم– : " بل أنا وا رأساه، لقد هممت – أو أردت – أن أرسل إلى أبي بكر و ابنه و أعهد، أن يقول القائلون، أو يتمنى المتمنون." ثم قلت : يأبى الله و يدفع المؤمنون، أو يدفع الله و يأبى المؤمنون. رواه البخاري و عنها قالت : رجع إلي رسول الله – صلى الله عليه وسلم – ذات يوم من جنازة من البقيع، فوجدني وأنا أجد صداعا، و أنا أقول: وا رأساه قال : " بل أنا يا عائشة وا رأساه، قال : " و ما ضرك لو مت قبلي، فغسلتك، و كفنتك، و صليت عليك، و دفنتك ؟." قلت : لكأني بك و الله لو فعلت ذلك لرجعت إلى بيتي فعرست فيه ببعض نسائك، فتبسم رسول الله – صلى الله عليه وسلم – ثم بدئ في وجعه الذي مات فيه . رواه الدارمي

و عن جعفر بن محمد، عن أبيه – رضي الله عنه– أن رجلا من قريش دخل على أبيه – علي بن الحسين– فقال: ألا أحدثك عن رسول الله – صلى الله عليه وسلم– ؟. قال : بلى، حدثنا عن أبي القاسم – صلى الله عليه وسلم– قال : لما مرض رسول الله – صلى الله عليه وسلم– أتاه جبريل، فقال : يا محمد، إن الله أرسلني إليك تكريما لك، و تشريفا لك، خاصة لك، أسألك عما هو أعلم به منك، يقول : كيف تجدك ؟. قال :" أجدني يا جبريل مغموما، و أجدني يا جبريل مكروبا." ثم جاءه اليوم الثاني، فقال له ذلك، فرد عليه النبي – صلى الله عليه وسلم – كما رد أول يوم، ثم جاءه اليوم الثالث فقال له كما قال أول يوم، و رد عليه كما رد عليه، و جاء معه ملك يقال له : إسماعيل على مائة ألف ملك، كل ملك على مائة ألف ملك، فاستأذن عليه، فسأله عنه . ثم قال جبريل: هذا ملك الموت يستأذن عليك، ما استأذن على آدمي قبلك، ولا يستأذن على آدمي بعدك. فقال : "ائذن له." فأذن له، فسلم عليه، ثم قال: يا محمد، إن الله أرسلني إليك، فإن أمرتني أن أقبض روحك قبضته، و إن أمرتني أن أتركه تركته. فقال :" أو تفعل يا ملك الموت ؟." قال : نعم، بذلك أمرت و أمرت أن أطيعك، قال : فنظر النبي – صلى الله عليه وسلم– إلى جبريل عليه السلام، فقال جبريل : يا محمد، إن الله قد اشتاق إلى لقائك، فقال النبي – صلى الله عليه وسلم– لملك الموت : " امض لما أمرت به." فقبض روحه، فلما توفي رسول الله – صلى الله عليه وسلم– ، و جاءت التعزية سمعوا صوتا من ناحية البيت: السلام عليكم أهل البيت و رحمة الله و بركاته، إن في الله عزاء من كل مصيبة، و خلفا من كل هالك، و دركا من كل فائت، فبالله فاتقوا، و إياه فارجوا، فإنما المصاب من حرم الثواب . فقال علي : أتدرون من هذا ؟ هو الخضر عليه السلام . رواه البيهقي

ʿĀʾishah ﵂ related, "Verily, one of Allāh's favors upon me is that the Messenger of God ﷺ passed away in my house and in my embrace, and that God united my saliva and his at the time of his death. My brother, ʿAbdur-Raḥmān, entered with a tooth-stick (*siwāk*) while I was holding the Prophet ﷺ in my lap, and I saw him eye it. I knew how much he liked to clean his teeth with it, so I asked him, 'Do you want me to bring it to you?' He nodded, so I gave it to him, but it was too hard for him. So I asked him, 'Would you like me to soften it for you?' He nodded, so I chewed it to make it softer, and gave it to him. There was also a bowl filled with water before him, which he used to wipe his face to cool his fever. He kept saying, 'There is no god but God, truly death has its intoxications.' Then he raised his hands and said, 'In the highest of companionships!' Until his soul was seized and his hands dropped."

She said, "I heard the Prophet ﷺ say, 'Whenever a prophet falls seriously ill he is given a choice between this world and the other world.' During his final illness he was suffering from a strong fever and I heard him saying, '...with those You have favored of the prophets, the truthful ones, the martyrs, and righteous ones.' And I knew then he was given his choice."

When the heaviness of death approached he was overcome with grief and Fāṭimah seeing him said, "My father is grief-stricken!" but he replied, "Today there is no grief upon your father." And when he died she said, "O father! The Lord answered your prayer. O father! The garden of Paradise is your abode. O father! To Gabriel is his epitaph!" Then when he was buried she lamented, "O Anas, how were you able to bear covering the Messenger of God with dust?"

In a narration by Tirmidhī, he said, "The day when the Messenger of God ﷺ entered Medina, the light shone from all of it; and on the day he died, darkness fell over all of it. And even before we had shaken the dust off our hands after burying him, we felt dejection in our hearts."

ʿĀʾishah ؓ said, "When the Messenger of God was taken the people disagreed over his place of burial, Abū Bakr said, 'I heard the Messenger of God say something that I cannot forget: God does not seize the soul of a prophet except in the place where he likes to be buried. So bury him on the spot of his bed.'

"I heard the Messenger of God ﷺ say, while he was in good health, 'No prophet will be taken by death before he sees his place in the Garden and is given the choice.' Then when he was dying and his head was in my lap and he fainted, then revived, he fixed his sight upon the ceiling and said, 'O my God, the most exalted Companion!' so I said, 'He will not choose us,' for I recalled what he said about being given the choice. And so his last words were, 'O my God, the most exalted Companion!'"

When the Messenger of God ﷺ was in the throes of death, there were men in the house, among them ʿUmar ibn al-Khaṭṭāb. The Prophet ﷺ said, "Come let me write you a message following which you will not be misguided." ʿUmar said, "The pain has overcome him. You already have the Qurʾān; the Book of God is sufficient for you." So the people differed and became adversaries over this issue. And when the argument and tension increased, the Prophet ﷺ said, "Leave me!" Later Ibn ʿAbbās would say, "Verily, the affliction, all the affliction, was caused by the dissention and clamor that prevented the Messenger of God ﷺ from writing for them that message."

After the death of the Messenger of God ﷺ, Abū Bakr told ʿUmar to accompany him to visit Umm Ayman. When they saw her, she started to weep; and they said to her, "What makes you weep? Don't you know that what is with God is better for the Messenger of God ﷺ?" She told them, "I know this. What makes me weep is that revelation has come to an end." This provoked their own tears, and they wept together.

During his final illness, the Prophet ﷺ entered his mosque with his head wrapped in a cloth and he ascended the pulpit and said, "By the One who holds my soul in his hand, I surely can see the Fountain from my station! A servant has been offered the world and its ornaments and he chose the other world." No one grasped what he had said except Abū Bakr, whose eyes overflowed with tears and he cried out, "We would sacrifice our fathers and mothers, ourselves and our wealth for you, O Messenger of God!" The Prophet ﷺ then descended from the pulpit and he did not last an hour longer.

When the revelation, *When Allāh's succor and opening comes* (*Sūrah an-Naṣr* 110:1) came, the Prophet ﷺ called his daughter, Fāṭimah, to him and said to her, "I have received my epitaph." At this she wept, but he told her, "Do not weep, for you are the first of my family to join me!" When she heard this, she laughed.

ʿĀʾishah رضي الله عنها said, "One time the Messenger of God ﷺ returned from the Baqīʿ (the graveyard) and I was suffering from a bad headache and I was crying out, 'O my head!' To which he said, 'It's my head that hurts, ʿĀʾishah!' Then he told me, 'What harm would it be for you if you died before me, and I would wash you, wrap you in your shroud, and pray for you?' So I told him, 'By God, if it happened, you would then return to my house and celebrate with another one of your wives!' The Messenger of God ﷺ smiled at this, and then his fatal ailment began."

Jaʿfar ibn Muḥammad (Imām Jaʿfar Ṣadiq) said that a man came to ʿAlī ibn Husayn and said to him, "Shall I tell you about the Messenger of God ﷺ?" ʿAlī replied, "Of course, tell us about him." So the man said, "When he fell ill, Gabriel came to him and said to him, 'O Muḥammad, God sends me in honor and respect of you, especially to ask you about what He already knows better than you. He asks, 'How are you?' He replied, 'O Gabriel, I am distressed and depressed.' On the next day,

Gabriel returned and asked him the same question and he gave him the same answer. And on the third day, the same thing happened but that time another angel was with him who was at the head of a hundred thousand angels, each of which was at the head of another hundred thousand angels. This angel asked permission to enter, and the Prophet ﷺ asked Gabriel about him, who said, 'This is the Angel of Death asking your permission. He has never asked the permission of any other human being before you, nor will he ask anyone's permission after you.' The Prophet ﷺ said, 'Give him permission.' The angel entered and said, 'Peace upon you. O Muḥammad, God has sent me to you. If you command me to take your soul I will and if you command me to leave it I will.' The Prophet ﷺ asked, 'You would do this, Angel of Death?' The angel replied, 'Yes, this I was commanded and I was ordered to obey you!' The Prophet ﷺ looked over to Gabriel who said to him, 'O Muḥammad, God longs for your meeting!' So the Prophet ﷺ said to the Angel of Death, 'Proceed with what you have been commanded!' So he took his soul and after he died and people were attending his funeral they heard a voice from the direction of the house saying, 'Peace upon you, people of the house, and God's mercy and blessings. In God is comfort from every calamity, and He is what remains after everything that perishes, and He is what is reached after all that is missed, so be conscious of God, and wish for Him. For truly the one who is in calamity is the one who is deprived of forgiveness.' ʿAlī asked the people, "Do you know who this is? It is Khiḍr, peace upon him." (Bayhaqī)

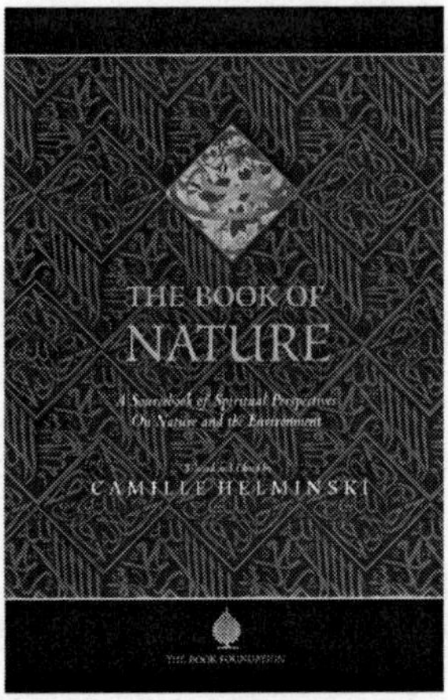

The Book of Nature

A Sourcebook of Spiritual Perspectives on Nature and the Environment

Camille Helminski (Author)

This anthology of spiritual treatments of nature and the environment presents an uplifting and universal approach to appreciating the natural order from a Muslim perspective. Each chapter is introduced with a passage from the Qur'an and followed by pieces that highlight the human role in maintaining balance in the world. Selections range from poems to short essays and cover topics such as unity, interdependence, communication, the four elements, diversity, and wonder. Including contributions from Muhammad Asad, Alain de Botton, Thomas Berry, Guy Eaton, Seyyid Hossein Nasr, and Vandana Shiva, these reminders of the power of the Divine Order allow for a deeper appreciation of the interdependence of life and nature.

Camille Helminski is the author of *Women of Sufism, The Book of Character, The Light of Dawn*, and numerous translations. She is the first woman to translate and publish a significant portion of the Qur'an.

Price: $32.95
Pages: 500
Book Type: Paper
Size: 6 x 9
ISBN: 1904510159

The Book of Language:

Exploring the Spiritual Vocabulary of Islam
Kabir Helminski,
with an Essay, "Truth and Knowledge,"
by Prince Ghazi Bin Muhammad

This book clarifies 200 key spiritual, philosophical, and metaphysical terms in Arabic and English, from *ahl, Allah*, and *amanah* to will, worship and witnessing. Its task is not only to elucidate Islamic concepts within a comprehensive model of the human soul and its spiritual faculties, but to develop a spiritual vocabulary in English, as well. Included is an essay by Prince Ghazi Bin Muhammad, entitled "Truth and Knowledge," which explores Islamic epistemology, or "what we know and how we know it."

Kabir Helminski, the author and translator of numerous works on Islamic spirituality, brings to this work more than thirty years experience in the translation of Islamic concepts.
Prince Ghazi Bin Muhammad is the author of *The Sacred Origin of Sports and Culture*. He teaches Islamic philosophy in Jordan and is Chairman of the Board Royal Aal al-Bayt Institute for Islamic Thought, Jordan.

$17.95 £10.95
2006 Paperback ISBN 1904510167 (9781904510161)
150 pages 152mm x 241mm (6 x 9 inches)

The Book Foundation *has embarked on an important effort to develop books and teaching tools that are approachable and relevant to Muslims and non-Muslims.* ~**Shabbir Mansuri**, *Founding Director, Council on Islamic Education (CIE)*

The Book of Essential Islam

The Spiritual Training System of Islam

Ali Rafea,
with Aisha and Aliaa Rafea

$21 £10.95 6 x 9" 276 pp

1-904510-13-2

This book examines the main teachings and practices of Islam with lucidity and depth. It is a corrective to the distortions and misconceptions of Islam that abound. It can serve equally well to introduce non-Muslims to Islam, as well as to enhance Muslims understanding of their own faith. This book presents Islam as a spiritual training system that supports us in harmonizing ourselves with the Divine Order and thus with each other and our environment. It reveals the intent and inner significance of practices like ablution, ritual prayer, fasting, and pilgrimage.

The Fragrance of Faith

The Enlightened Heart of Islam

Jamal Rahman

$15.95 £9.95 6 x 9" 176pp

1-904510-08-6

The Fragrance of Faith reveals the inner Islam that has been passed down through the generations. Jamal is a link in this chain, passing along the message, just as he received it from his grandfather, a village wiseman in Bangladesh. We need reminders of this "enlightened heart of Islam" in our lives, our homes, and our schools. In Jamal Rahman's book Islam is alive and well. ~**Imam Feisal Abdul Rauf**, Author *Islam: A Sacred Law* and *What's Right With Islam.*

This heartfelt book is perfect for the classroom, whether in a Muslim context, or outside of it. It conveys a tradition of compassion and humor passed through one family that represents the best Islam has to offer. And Mr. Rahman is highly entertaining. ~**Michael Wolfe**, *The Hadj: An American's Pilgrimage to Mecca,* Producer of the PBS Documentary: *Muhammad: The Legacy of a Prophet.*

CPSIA information can be obtained at www.ICGtesting.com
Printed in the USA
LVOW051907180812
294901LV00002B/31/P